day trips®

shifra stein's

day trips® from houston

twelfth edition

getaway ideas for the local traveler

carol barrington

revised and updated by
rogayle franklin

travel

Guilford, Connecticut

**The prices and rates listed in this guidebook
were confirmed at press time. We recommend,
however, that you call establishments before
traveling to obtain current information.**

To buy books in quantity for corporate use
or incentives, call **(800) 962-0973**
or e-mail **premiums@GlobePequot.com.**

Text design by Linda R. Loiewski
Maps by XNR Productions, Inc. © Morris Book Publishing, LLC
Spot photography throughout © Richard Stockton/Index Open

ISSN 1535-8097
ISBN 978-0-7627-4542-5

Manufactured in the United States of America
10 9 8 7 6 5 4 3 2 1

contents

day trips from houston

about the author

CAROL BARRINGTON

Odds are good that in any given month a Carol Barrington photograph or story graces the travel pages of America's magazines and newspapers. Although she specializes in Texana—she considers the entire Houston-Galveston region her "backyard"—her general story/photo beat has covered the world. During her more-than-twenty-five-year, prizewinning career as a travel journalist, her work has appeared in more than fifty publications. Her professional memberships include the Society of Media Photographers, American Society of Journalists and Authors, and the Society of American Travel Writers, of which she is a past president. She now specializes in travel photography via her storefront Web site, www.destination photography.com

about the editor

ROGAYLE FRANKLIN

The mystery of what's in the next city or country has kept journalist Rogayle Franklin traveling. In magazines and newspapers she has shared her adventures on the canals of France, the Great Wall of China, and the glaciers of Alaska—but, according to Franklin, it's her native Texas that defines friendliness and makes it a pure pleasure to explore Houston's neighboring regions.

>> **preface**

For a tank of gas, plus lunch money, the countryside around the fourth-largest city in the United States offers a fantastic change. The terrain in all directions varies, and the friendly folks of smaller towns populate it.

An hour's drive away, usually less, there's plenty of open land and sky. Off the interstate highways the local folks have time to ask, "How are you?" And wait for your answer. It's such a change in total habitat for most of us; it's difficult to imagine a fast-lane metropolis nearby.

Some day-trip devotees say for maximum pleasure, they simply choose an area of the book and don't fix on a destination. As they wander and unwind they have the freedom to spend time on what attracts them. But a gorgeous sunset is ruined if it's growing dark and you're lost without signage or a gas station. Take an up-to-date Texas map. It will also help with the "Wandering the Back Roads" sections of this book and move you seamlessly to other day trip sections.

If there's a specific place you must see or dine, it's better to call before going. The hours they open or close—and sometimes even the days they are open—vary. Most museums have faithful volunteers, or they could not open. So telephone ahead and you'll be rewarded with a valuable insiders' view, and—if you ask—they'll share more about their hometown than could be put in this book.

Travel writer extraordinaire Carol Barrington spent eighteen years collecting and organizing these historic and appealing areas into a comprehensive treasure of day trips for you. As the caretaker for this twelfth edition, I have tried to renew and add new gems to these pages. Enjoy and update us on your discoveries.

—Rogayle Franklin

using this book

Hours of operation: In most cases hours of operation are omitted because they are subject to change frequently. Instead, telephone numbers and Web sites (when available) are listed so that you can call for specifics. Also be aware that many of the restaurants and activity options are closed on major holidays, although that may not be noted in the text.

Restaurants: Restaurant prices are designated as $$$ (expensive, $17 or more), $$ (moderate, $7–$17), or $ (inexpensive, less than $7) per person.

Organization: Listings in the "What to Do" and "Where to Eat" sections generally are in alphabetical order.

Credit cards: Most of the restaurants in this book accept credit cards, unless noted otherwise.

NOTE: No payment of any kind is either solicited or accepted to gain mention in this book.

additional resources

For a **Texas map** and travel guide, contact the **Texas Department of Transportation, Travel and Information Division,** P.O. Box 5064, Austin, TX 78714-9248; (800) 452-9292. The travel counselors at that number can also advise on events, lodging, attractions, and trip routings throughout the state. You'll find a great deal of this advice online at www.traveltex.com, as well as links for requesting more information.

For information on state parks, wildlife, or fisheries, contact the **Texas Parks and Wildlife Department,** 4200 Smith School Road, Austin, TX 78744; (800) 792-1112; www.tpwd.state.tx.us. You can check availability and reserve campsites, group facilities, and cabins in state parks online or by calling (512) 389-8900. To cancel a reservation, call (512) 389-8900.

The **Great Texas Coastal Birding Trail** maps are available from either of the two state resources noted above; the upper Texas coast version is relevant to the areas covered in this book.

The **East Texas Tourism Association** puts out a free fun map. Contact the association at 421 North Center, Longview, TX 75601; (903) 757-4444; www.easttexasguide.com.

For information on the **Sam Houston National Forest,** contact the Sam Houston Ranger District, 394 FM 1375 West, New Waverly, TX 77358; (936) 344-6205. For information on the **Davy Crockett National Forest,** contact the Davy Crockett Ranger District, Route 1, Box 55FS, Kennard, TX 75847; (936) 655-2299. You'll find online information for both parks at www.southernregion.fs.fed.us/texas.

The **Texas Forestry Association** puts out a booklet on woodland hiking trails: P.O. Box 1488, Lufkin, TX 75902; (936) 632-8733; www.texasforestry.org.

For lists of Christmas tree farms, wineries, farmers' markets, and pick-your-own fruit farms statewide, contact the **Texas Department of Agriculture,** P.O. Box 12847, Austin, TX 78711; (512) 463-7624; www.agr.state.tx.us. Information is also available at the Texas Agricultural Extension Service, 2 Abercrombie Drive, Houston, TX 77084; (281) 855-5600; http://harris-tx.tamu.edu/.

The **Houston Audubon Society** maintains a "Texas Rare Bird Alert" hotline: (281) 992-2757. Find more information online at www.houstonaudubon.org.

northwest

day trip 01

northwest

the lake effect:
tomball, montgomery, conroe,
the woodlands, spring

tomball

One of the most scenic drives from Houston into the Brazos Valley or to the Lake Conroe area begins by following Highway 249 (Tomball Parkway) north through rural woodlands. Although none of the towns included in this day trip is of major interest in and of itself, together they have enough interesting stops to make a great drive.

First up is the farming community of Tomball, named for early-twentieth-century congressman Thomas H. Ball. Turn east on Main Street at the Highway 249/FM 2920 intersection to find numerous antiques stores in the heart of town. For advance information and an excellent map of the Tomball/North Harris County region, contact the Tomball Area Chamber of Commerce, P.O. Box 516, Tomball, TX 77377-0516; (281) 351-7222; www .tomballchamber.org. If you're traveling on a weekday, you'll find that office at 14011 Park Drive, Suite 111.

what to do

The Arbor Gate. 15635 FM 2920; (281) 351-8851; www.arborgate.com. So much more than a nursery, the Arbor Gate is an education center, a home store, and the place to go for gardening inspiration. Within the large complex, you'll find stunning plants (and a knowledgeable staff to tell you how to make them thrive), one-of-a-kind gifts, gourmet food products, handcrafted jewelry, and whimsical home accessories. Open daily.

northwest day trip 01

Burroughs Park. 9738 Hufsmith Road, 1.3 miles east of FM 2978. This beautiful, 320-acre park offers a large lake with floating piers for catch-and-release fishing (largemouth bass and catfish), 8 miles of nature trails, a playground accessible to handicapped children, an elevated boardwalk, baseball and soccer fields, and extensive picnic facilities. For pavilion rentals call (281) 353-4196 or log on to www.cp4.hctx.net/parks/burroughs/. Developed at a cost of more than $3.2 million, this rural park preserves classic Big Thicket growth, including blackjack oak, bogs and water-elm ponds, canebreaks along creeks, short-leaf pines, stands of hickory, and holly and farkleberry bushes. Open daily, dawn to dark.

Camelot Horse Center. 18010 Burkhardt Road (1 block south of FM 2920 and 7 miles north of U.S. Highway 290 via Cypress-Rosehill Road); (281) 351-8368. This full-service horse training facility is devoted to classic English riding, including dressage. The public is welcome to visit, observe, and attend horse shows and demonstrations; no rental horses or trail rides are available. Appointments required; closed Monday.

Christmas tree farms. Although tree cutting officially begins Thanksgiving weekend, many tree farms offer great family activities such as pumpkin patches, educational tours, hayrides, hot dog roasts, and so on during other times of the year. Call the following for information and directions: Merry Christmas Tree Farm, (281) 351-0818, www.merrychristmastree.com; Old Time Christmas Tree Farm, (281) 370-9141; or Spring Creek Growers, (281) 259-8114, www.springcreekgrowers.com.

Flying High at David Wayne Hooks Airport. 20803 Stuebner Airline, Spring (at FM 2920); (281) 376-5436; www.hooksairport.com. The largest privately owned airport in Texas, this sprawling place offers numerous ways to get a bird's-eye view of Houston. Looking for an unusual birthday or anniversary present? Helicopter Services (look for sign on large hangar; 281-370-4354) offers demonstration rides in a Robinson R-22 (introductory flights $125 for thirty minutes), or a panoramic exploration of Houston, including the Ship Channel and River Oaks (fee varies based on aircraft). This is a federally licensed facility; all aircraft are maintained to federal standards.

Hooks is home to numerous flight schools that offer sightseeing tours as well as discovery flights, during which you actually put hands on the controls. For specifics call Mercury Flight Services, (281) 376-9141; Hi-Tech Aviation, (281) 370-5235; or United Flight Systems, (281) 376-0357.

The Griffin Memorial House is next door. Built in 1860 by one of Houston's earliest pioneers, Eugene Pillot, it stood at the intersection of Willow Creek and an early stage route known as the Atascosita Trail. Sam Houston frequently spent the night in this house, waiting for the morning stage, and it also was a local gathering place. The antique furnishings are of the later Victorian period and in themselves constitute the Magdalene Charlton Memorial Museum. The complex's other transplanted buildings include the pioneer country doctor's office where Dr. William Ehrhardt practiced for more than fifty years; a museum containing early farm machinery, tools, and a hundred-year-old gin moved from nearby Spring; a log house and corncrib built in 1857 in Serbin; the Henry Theis House, built locally prior to 1866; a 1940s four-room oil-camp house with furnishings; and a 1920s one-room schoolhouse with period furnishings, brought in from Bellville. Free, but donations are greatly appreciated. Open Thursday midday and on Sunday afternoon; hours vary. Tours also by appointment.

Kleb Nature Preserve. 20605 FM 2920 (Waller-Tomball Road), on south side, 7 miles west of Tomball. In addition to picnic tables, a pavilion, and toilet facilities, there's a mile-long trail through dense, second-growth forest, ideal for birding or a walk in the woods. This mini–Big Thicket is what much of north Harris County looked like before the subdivision era. Open daily, dawn to dusk.

The Matt Family Orchard. 21110 Bauer Hockley Road; (281) 351-7676 or (281) 467-9758; www.mattfamilyorchard.com. This 145-acre farm has 33 acres under cultivation. You are welcome to pick blackberries mid-May–mid-July, jujubes and Asian pears July–August, figs July–September, Asian persimmons September–November, and citrus November–January. Charges are by the pound. They also host group tours year-round, offer bow hunting for white-tailed deer and feral pig by advance arrangement (fee), and put on an extended Harvest Festival in October (reservations required). The festival usually includes hayrides and activities for kids, including pumpkins, dressing scarecrows, jumping in a haystack, assorted games, and face painting; picnickers are welcome. Open by appointment only; call for a reservation and directions.

Silverado Farms. 30337 Dobbin Huffsmith Road; (281) 259-9378; www.outbackww.com. Hidden deep in the woods northeast of Tomball and best accessed via FM 2920 East, FM 2978 North, and Hardin Store Road, this unusual, eight-acre facility includes the Outback Western Wear store, a country wedding chapel and event hall, and a horse arena where there are often rodeo-style competitions and other events. They also have dance lessons (fee). Free. Open Monday–Saturday.

Spring Creek Park. Brown Road; (281) 353-4196; www.cp4.hctx.net/parks. One mile north of Tomball via Highway 249; watch for sign. On weekdays this oak-shaded park is a delightful place for a picnic. There's a large children's play area, and a rough, asphalt-banked ramp for skateboarders. The park also provides space for RV hookups and tent camping. Unfortunately, this park often is spoiled on weekends by rowdy crowds.

Tomball Community Museum Center. 510 North Pine Street; (281) 255-2148. Clustered on this cul-de-sac are some bits of the past collected by the Spring Creek County Historical Association. The Trinity Evangelical Lutheran Church was a volunteer construction project of local German families in 1905, and all furnishings and appointments today are original to this well. Locals particularly love the house salad and the outstanding desserts. Baked apple dumpling a la mode, maple sweet potato custard, walnut fudge pie, and apricot bread pudding are standard on the menu, but ask about the day's specials as well. Open for lunch and afternoon tea or wine and cheese Monday–Saturday and for champagne brunch on Saturday; traditional high teas by advance reservation. $–$$.

Walden Yacht Club. 13105 Melville Drive; (936) 582-4222; www.waldenonlakeconroe.com. (From Highway 105 take Walden Road north approximately 5 miles. Turn left on Emerson and left again on Melville.) One of the best but least-known restaurants in the entire Lake Conroe area, this handsome, romantic place gives off the aura of being a private club. Not true. The public is most welcome here, although reservations are strongly advised. A few additional caveats: no coat or tie is required for men (golf clothes are okay), but you won't be welcomed if you arrive in extremely casual attire such as shorts, tank tops, or bathing suits. Also be aware that while well-behaved children are welcome, there's no kiddie menu. That said, let's focus on the magnificent lake view, the fine table settings, the excellent formal service, and the classic American menu with prices far lower than comparable restaurants in downtown Houston. The kitchen is at its best with fish and prime rib, but everything is good, and the menu changes almost nightly. Live music turns ordinary evenings into special events, plus a stroll on the terrace in nice weather is a memory-maker. Open for dinner Wednesday–Saturday and brunch on Sunday. $$–$$$.

Other restaurant choices in the Highway 105/Lake Conroe area, a short drive east of Montgomery, are listed in the Conroe section.

wandering the back roads

To continue this day trip from Montgomery to Conroe and Spring, travel east on Highway 105. A turn west on Highway 105 will connect you with Northwest Day Trips 3 through 6.

Or you can continue north on FM 149 through Montgomery to Anderson (see Northwest Day Trip 5). From Anderson you can return to Houston via Navasota and Hempstead on Highway 90 and Highway 6.

How about heading east to New Waverly and Huntsville (see Northwest Day Trip 2)? From FM 149 on the northern outskirts of Montgomery, turn northeast on FM 1097; this enjoyable road arcs east to Willis, crossing Lake Conroe in the process.

conroe

In 1880 the Central and Montgomery Railroad had a line running from Navasota to Montgomery. With the extension of the track in 1885 to a small sawmill run by Isaac Conroe some 15 miles to the east, the town of Conroe came into being. Within five years Conroe was thriving with 300 citizens and aced Montgomery out of the county seat honor by some sixty-two votes. Always the center of a prosperous lumber industry, it hit the financial big time with George Strake's discovery of oil southeast of town in 1931.

Conroe today needs no introduction to Houstonians, as it is a prosperous business and bedroom satellite 39 miles north on Interstate 45. Although little history has been preserved here, it's fun to visit the circa-1930 Crighton Theater (936-441-7469; www.crightonplayers .org) near the courthouse on North Main. Restored in vaudevillian style, it again hosts the performing arts upon occasion. To day-trippers, however, Conroe is attractive primarily as the gateway to an extensive forest and water playground and as a locale for great factory discount shopping, courtesy of the fifty-six-store Conroe Outlet Center (www.conroeoutlet center.com) north of town on I-45. For those who want to stay over to play another day, Heather's Glen Bed & Breakfast (936-441-6611; www.heathersglen.com) offers Victorian- style lodgings in the former Wahrenberger Mansion in downtown Conroe.

For more information on the Conroe area, including Montgomery, contact the Greater Conroe/Lake Conroe Chamber of Commerce, P.O. Box 2347, Conroe, TX 77305; (936) 538-7112; www.lakeconroecvb.org. For on-site information weekdays, stop at 505 West Davis.

what to do

Bridgewood Farms. 11680 Rose Road; (936) 856-6460; www.bridgewoodfarms.org. Day programs at this facility benefit more than 160 mentally challenged teens and adults, and the public is welcome to picnic on the grounds, shop in Nichol's Niche gift shop, explore the small greenhouse, and walk the nature trails on this seventeen-acre rural property. Ask about their unique handmade rugs, so beautiful that one graces the corporate headquar- ters of Mitchell Energy. There's also a possibility of hayrides if they know you are coming, plus you can cut a live Christmas tree here during the holidays. Open weekdays, but call for directions and to make sure this not-for-profit campus will be open when you plan to visit.

Heritage Museum of Montgomery County. 1506 North I-45; (936) 539-6873; www .heritagemuseum.us. Take the Highway 105 exit from I-45 North and stay on the frontage road to Candy Cane Park. The Grogan and Cochran families jointly owned and operated twenty-five sawmills in Montgomery County, the first of which was on the 55,000 acres later developed as the Woodlands. This makes their 1924 frame home a fitting matrix for local history. One gallery features "Glimpses of Montgomery County," including Dr. Charles Stewart's original drawings of the Lone Star flag and state seal of the Texas Republic (still in use). A second gallery focuses on people and events that influenced the area. Free, but donations gratefully accepted. Open Wednesday–Saturday.

Lake Conroe. Numerous points of access from I-45, Highway 105, and FM 149. The dam, a small county park on the lakefront, several of the larger marinas, and the entrances to three major resorts lie 10 to 12 miles west of I-45 in Conroe via Highway 105. The upper west side of the lake can be reached from Montgomery via FM 149 and FM 1097; the east side can be accessed by both FM 1097 and FM 1375 from I-45 north of Conroe.

One of the most beautiful lakes in the state, Lake Conroe is 15 miles long and covers 22,000 acres. A complete list of marinas, campgrounds, and public services is available from the Conroe/Lake Conroe Chamber of Commerce.

Want an affordable weekend escape? Several resorts on Lake Conroe welcome guests with advance reservations. Inquire about accommodations and available activities at the following: April Sound in Montgomery, (800) 417-6667, www.aprilsoundrentals.com; and Landing at Seven Coves in Willis, (936) 856-5501, www.sevencoves.com.

Located 7 miles west of I-45 via Highway 105, Lake Conroe Park & Pavilion (936-788-8302) offers swimming, two fishing piers, a playground, and picnic facilities, but no boat ramp. Admission ($2 for those ages five and older) is charged from March through Labor Day; thereafter the park is free.

The *Southern Empress* (7039 Kingston Cove Lane, Willis, TX 77318; 936-588-3000 or 936-856-5162; www.southernempress.com), a replica of an old-time paddle wheeler docked at Sunset Harbor Resort at Seven Coves, offers brunch, lunch, and dinner cruises, as well as a variety of specialty cruises. Call for reservations.

The Montgomery County Bulls. Are you ready for some football? The Bulls play in the North American Football League, a semiprofessional league that plays its schedule July through September. The team plays at Bulls Field in Charles Taylor Memorial Park in Conroe. Fee. For a schedule or the team's latest appearance schedule, you can log on to www .montgomerycountybulls.com.

Moorhead's Blueberry Farm. 19531 Moorhead Road; (281) 572-1265; www.moorheads blueberryfarm.com. Who says you can't grow plump, luscious blueberries in Texas? Sid Moorhead has fifteen acres planted with thirty-five different varieties that ripen from early June through late July. The best picking times are in the early morning and late afternoon. Mr. Moorhead also grows the nonastringent Fuju persimmons, known as the apple of the Orient, which ripen in November. What do you do with persimmons? He has great recipes— and this fruit is good to eat out of hand or use in pies. Other pickin' crops include figs in late August through mid-September and blackberries in early summer. His farm is deep in the woods between Conroe and Porter. From U.S. Highway 59 North take the Porter exit, go west on FM 1314 for 10 miles, turn left into Bennette Estates, and then follow signs. From I-45 take exit 83, go east on Crighton Road 2.5 miles, turn right on FM 1314 for 7.4 miles, and turn right into Bennette Estates. Open daily, dawn to dusk.

7 Acre Wood Family Park and Petting Zoo. 4401 North Frazier; (936) 856-1700; www .7acrewood.org. This shady and pleasant place is a child's dream—plenty of small animals to experience as well as extensive play zones. Kids love to burn energy at the hippity-hop corral, Big Wheel track, and western town. Open to the public on weekends when weather permits; reservations otherwise required. It's best to always call ahead to make sure they'll be open. Fee.

where to eat

Burger Fresh. 804 Gladstell; (936) 756-4414. When an obscure strip-mall eatery like this one sports a major clientele, it's worth searching out. The draws are juicy burgers made from lean Angus beef, crisp onion rings, malts so thick you eat them with a spoon, and classic sandwiches made to order. If you're fed up with trite fast food, a meal in this red-checked, Coca-Cola atmosphere will make you feel like you're back in the 1950s. Open for lunch and early dinner Monday–Saturday. $.

Coronelli's Villa Italia. 213 Simonton; (936) 539-5599. This "Italian Ristorante" serves outstanding rack of lamb, Dover sole, chateaubriand, and assorted veal entrees, along with California and French wines. The menu also offers pastas, seafood, chicken, and steak. Open for lunch and dinner Monday–Saturday (closed 2:30–4:30 p.m.). $–$$$.

Giovanni's Continental Cuisine. 10104 Highway 105 West; (936) 588-4666. Considered by many people to be the best fine-dining restaurant on the Highway 105 strip, this pleasant place offers exceedingly good (and often unusual) beef, veal, fish, pasta, and chicken entrees at prices substantially less than the Houston area's going rates. Chef Giovanni grows fresh herbs out back, and they make all the difference. In addition to the day's special offerings, top choices include chicken artichoke, mussels garlic, and grilled quail. Service is excellent, and the wines by the glass are affordable. Open for dinner daily. $–$$$.

McKenzie's Barbeque. 1501 North Frazier; (936) 539-4300; www.mckenziesbarbeque .com. When you want smoky barbecue or sandwiches, this is a reliable bet. Open for lunch and dinner Monday–Saturday. $–$$.

Moonstruck Cafe. 330 North Main Street; (936) 756-5282. If deli sandwiches, quiche, salads, soups, cheesecakes, homemade chili, and gumbo sound good, hunt up this small place across from the Montgomery County Courthouse in downtown Conroe. You'll also find smoothies and an incredible variety of coffees and lattes. Open for breakfast and lunch until 4:00 p.m. Monday–Friday and until 8:00 p.m. on Saturday. $.

Papa's on the Lake. 14632 Highway 105 West, Montgomery; (936) 447-2500; www .papasonthelake.com (7 miles west of I-45). One of the hot spots on Lake Conroe, this bar and grill serves pizzas, salads, sandwiches (including muffulettas), and a variety of snacks as well as beer and wine. There's a large deck overlooking the lake and live music on summer weekends. Open daily for lunch and dinner. $–$$.

Taverna Restaurant and Winery. 12820 Highway 105 West; (936) 588-6464; www.taverna winery.com. It's easy to miss this hidden gem midway between Conroe and Montgomery, so be alert for their sign on the north side of the highway and turn immediately. Local food and wine lovers now have a destination/special-occasion restaurant to call their own, and the setting amid tall trees and a rolling green lawn is a winner as well. There's a nice terrace for outside dining when weather permits, and wine sampling is inexpensive and highly recommended to get you started. The extensive menu is best viewed online; suffice to say it shows off award-winning chef Richard Knight's many talents with primarily local products. There's also a children's menu, but be aware that best manners would be in order; this isn't a pizza joint or fast-food spot. Open for dinner daily, tapas every late afternoon and weekends, lunch on Saturday, and champagne brunch on Sunday. $$–$$$$.

Vernon's Kuntry Barbecue. 5000 West Davis (Highway 105); (409) 539-3000 (on the north side of Highway 105, 3.5 miles west of I-45). This beer garden serves good brisket, ribs, links, hamburgers, and chicken. Open daily for lunch and dinner. $–$$.

Vernon's Kuntry Katfish. 5901 West Davis (Highway 105); (409) 760-3386 (6.5 miles west of I-45). Even if you don't like catfish, come here. Tasty choices run from frog legs to chicken-fried steak and burgers, and the homemade desserts and breads are terrific. Even *Gourmet* magazine has taken favorable notice of this eatery; you'll find the framed write-up near the cashier's desk. Open for lunch and dinner daily. $–$$.

continuing on

To continue this day trip to the Woodlands, travel south from Conroe on I-45 to exits 78–76.

the woodlands

North of downtown Houston some 27 miles via I-45, the lakes and neighborhood parks of this extensive master-planned development are for residents only. Several other recreations, however, are open to the general public. More than 50 miles of trails thread beautiful woods, just right for hiking, jogging, in-line skating, or biking. Bring your own wheels and park by the visitor center. Nonmember golfers (for a fee, of course) are welcome on the Woodlands Country Club's Tournament Players Course (281-364-6368; www.thewoodlandscc.com), former home of the Shell Houston Open.

what to do

Cynthia Woods Mitchell Pavilion. 2005 Lake Robbins Drive; (281) 363-3300; www .woodlandscenter.org. April-to-October playbill offerings at the Woodlands' beautiful outdoor performing-arts center range from bluegrass to ballet and Broadway shows, rock to Rachmaninoff, Gershwin to Willie Nelson; the setting recalls Tanglewood and Interlochen. In all, there are 5,000 seats available by reservation. Get advance tickets from Ticketmaster outlets or by calling (713) 629-3700 or logging on to www.ticketmaster.com. Tickets are also available at the Pavilion's box office Monday–Saturday and on event days through intermission. Except for specific classical arts "picnics," no food, coolers, or beverages are allowed. There is space for an additional 12,000 people on the grassy hill flanking the seating area; blankets are permitted, but lawn chairs must be rented at the Pavilion ($5, but $1 is rebated when you return the chair). Recorders, cameras, umbrellas, and pagers are also verboten. Parking is free.

The Great Western Trading Company. 30822 Nichols Sawmill Road, Magnolia; (281) 356-2165. This bit of old Texas welcomes everyone to their Saturday-night horse and tack auctions. The action starts around 7:00 p.m. There's a small concession stand on the premises (hamburgers, hot dogs, and so on) in case you get hungry.

Main Event. 19441 I-45, Shenandoah; (281) 355-5511; www.maineventusa.net. This high-tech, high-energy, 60,000-square-foot entertainment complex offers black-light bowling, laser tag, billiards, big-screen televisions, and a full-service bar and grill. Don't miss the chance to design your own roller coaster and then ride it. Open daily, but hours change seasonally. Fee.

Montgomery County Preserve. 1122 Pruitt Road (behind the recycling facility); (281) 367-7283. Created by the not-for-profit Legacy Land Trust, this seventy-one-acre, wooded nature preserve is a magnet for birding enthusiasts as well as fans of butterflies. More than seventy species of birds make the preserve a regular stop, and seventeen varieties of butterflies have been reported. Among the earth-bound creatures that call the preserve home: feral hog, fox, bobcat, beaver, rabbit, and white-tailed deer. Open dawn to dusk daily. Free.

SouthWest PaddleSports. 26322 I-45 North, the Woodlands; (281) 292-5600; www.paddle sports.com. This firm operates quiet-water kayaking and canoe trips on Lake Woodlands, the San Jacinto River, and numerous other waters in the greater Houston area. They also teach basic canoeing and kayaking skills and organize group trips. Want to go birding by kayak in Christmas Bay (near Freeport) or make an easy loop trip on Lake Stubblefield? How about kayaking Spring Creek from Jesse Jones Park to Forest Cove Marina or paddling under a full moon? These are the folks to call.

W. Goodrich Jones State Forest. Five miles northwest via I-45 and FM 1488 West; (936) 273-2261. Logged in 1892 and burned in 1923, these 1,725 acres again are a verdant wildlife refuge, now under the watchful eye of the Texas Forest Service and part of the Texas A&M system. The Sweet Leaf Nature Trail is self-guided, and a small lake offers picnicking as well as fishing for catfish and bass. A prime birding spot, this park now provides excellent habitat for the red-cockaded woodpecker. Horseback riding is allowed if you bring your own steed. Open year-round during daylight hours. Guided tours available for groups by appointment.

The Woodlands Resort & Conference Center. 2301 North Millbend Drive, the Wood-lands; (281) 367-1100 or (800) 433-2624; www.woodlandsresort.com. Make a weekend of it. Check out the tennis, golf, and pampering packages. This swank resort boasts five restaurants and a family-friendly Forest Oasis Waterscape. The Waterscape features a 30-foot racing slide, underwater murals, children's "sprayground," and, for adults, a relaxation pool and super-size spa.

Woodlands Town Center. Tucked into the community's pride-worthy pines, Town Center is so well designed that most motorists zipping past on I-45 can't really get a feel for the enormity of this mall/leisure complex, which comprises more than 400 shops, restaurants, hotels, and entertainment venues. Town Center, the Woodlands Pavilion, and the Woodlands' downtown are linked by a 1.5-mile "river" complete with water taxis. For infor-mation contact the Woodlands Town Center Improvement District, 1450 Lake Robbins Drive, Suite 410, the Woodlands, TX 77380; (281) 363-2447; www.town-center.com.

where to eat

Although numerous franchises offer good eats along I-45 in the vicinity of Woodlands Mall, the following are worth searching out.

Amerigo's Grille. 25050 Grogans Park Drive; (281) 362-0808; www.amerigos.com. When it's time to eat Italian, come here. The atmosphere equals the high quality of the food. Try the lobster risotto or the veal scaloppini, and save room for the tiramisu. On weekends, there's live entertainment in the swanky piano lounge. Open for lunch and dinner weekdays; dinner only on Saturday and Sunday. $$–$$$.

The Glass Menagerie. 2301 North Millbend Drive; (281) 364-6326; www.woodlands resort.com. A longtime favorite of Woodlands residents, this beautiful and dressy restaurant seems only to improve with age. The dinner menu ranges through some continental standards—lobster, red snapper, filet mignon, chicken Wellington, grilled Muscovy duck, rib eye of lamb—and the Sunday champagne brunch truly earns the title of "lavish spread." Do what the locals do: Come hungry and make it your meal of the day. Open Tuesday–Saturday for dinner, Sunday for brunch; reservations strongly suggested. $$–$$$+.

Pallotta's Italian Grill. 27606 I-45 North, Spring (in the Woodridge Shopping Center across the interstate from the Woodlands Mall); (281) 364-9555. If the luscious refrigerated desserts displayed in the entry don't spark your appetite, the daily specials will. Menu choices range from pastas to rib eyes, with pizzas and sandwiches as alternate choices. Open daily for lunch and dinner. $–$$.

Tavola's Bistro. 32623 FM 2978. (See details under Magnolia in Northwest Day Trip 4.)

continuing on

From the Woodlands, Day Trip 1 swings south on I-45 to the Spring-Cypress Road exit. Turn left (east) under the freeway and follow Spring-Cypress to the railroad tracks.

spring

Back in the 1870s, a community called Spring sprang up to serve the International and Great Northern Railroad as a switching station north of Houston. As the railroads prospered through the turn of the twentieth century, so did the town, and in 1902 the Wunche Brothers' Saloon was built within a toot of the roundhouse. It had eight rooms upstairs to house railroad personnel.

But we all know what happened to the railroads of America and to the many small towns that depended on them. By the 1920s the roundhouse had relocated to Houston, and the Texas Rangers had enforced Prohibition laws by shooting every bottle in the saloon. Then came the Depression of the 1930s, and when I-45 bypassed Spring in the 1960s, it was the final blow. The old town area lapsed into civic limbo as businesses began to thrive around the new freeway interchange a mile west.

So much for yesterday. Today Old Town Spring is in its second bloom and is a great day-trip destination. More than 150 specialty shops, eateries, antiques stores, and art galleries are right at home in the quaint old houses. In general, the shops are open Tuesday–Saturday and on Sunday afternoon. If you are coming north from Houston, take the 70A exit from I-45 and swing east (right) at the signal on Spring-Cypress Road. When you see the OLD TOWN SPRING sign, you're there. For more information call (281) 288-2355 or log on to www.shopspringtexas.com.

If you'd like to spend the night, McLachlan Farm (281-350-2400; www.macfarm.com), a 1911 home on thirty-five acres 1 mile south of Old Town Spring, welcomes overnight guests.

what to do

Carter's Country. 6231 Treaschwig Road, Spring; (281) 443-8393. From I-45 take the FM 1960 exit east; then turn north onto Aldine-Westfield Road to Treaschwig. Tucked away in the woods, this well-designed place offers pistol, rifle, trap, skeet, and country clay shooting at a variety of distances. Children can shoot BB guns here if they have adult supervision. Open daily. Fee.

Cypress Trails Stable. 21415 Cypresswood Drive, Humble; (281) 446-7232; www .horseridingfun.com. Actually located midway between Spring and Humble, this is one of the very few places in the region that offers public horseback riding. You'll be in good hands:

Owner Darolyn Butler has won the National Champion Endurance Rider championship three times. Now in addition to riding lessons, horse leasing and sales, training, and horsemanship clinics, she offers a nice string of spirited Arabian horses for adventure trail rides through the woods along Cypress Creek. Small children can be hand-led on ponies. Cost is $35 for the first hour, $55 for two hours, and $70 for three hours; discounts are available for groups of three or more. Butler also organizes parties focused on horseback riding for groups.

Mercer Arboretum and Botanic Gardens. 22306 Aldine-Westfield Road, Humble; (281) 443-8731; www.cp4.hctx.net/mercer/. This 214-acre county park is a sleeper, often overlooked by day-trippers. What they miss is an outstanding collection of native Texas plants, a series of self-guided nature trails, a bird sanctuary, special gardens (ferns, ginger, water lilies, azaleas), picnic areas, and educational programs, all along a wooded stretch of Cypress Creek. There's also a canoe launch site here. Free and open daily.

Meyer Park. 7700 Cypresswood Drive, Spring; (281) 353-4196; www.hep4.net/Parks/meyer. There's hardly a dull minute at this 286-acre county-run park. Among its amenities are sixteen soccer fields, two softball fields, and a barbecue pavilion. Take a walk on its nature trails or test your angling abilities on its pretty fishing lake. Barbecue grills and picnic tables make this a terrific place to tailgate.

Splashtown USA. 21300 I-45 North (exit 70A), Spring; (281) 355-3300; www.splashtownpark.com. When summer's heat hits, there's no better cooler than the thrill rides in this forty-six-acre water park. It has a Wild Wave pool, screaming Hydra Thrill slides, Zoom Flooms, the breathtaking Texas Free Fall and other shriek and holler white-knuckle rides. You're not allowed to bring your own food and beverages inside the gates, but you are welcome to bring lunches and coolers for a family picnic on the outside grounds. Food also can be purchased inside the park. Open daily from late May to mid-August; weekends only in May and from mid-August to mid-September. Live entertainment and special events often highlight those off-season weekends. Fee.

Spring Historical Museum. 403 Main Street (at western entrance to Old Town Spring); (281) 651-0055. The human stories of the members of this small community from its German homesteading days in the 1840s to our times are well illustrated here. Open daily Thursday–Saturday and on Sunday afternoon. Donations appreciated.

Winery. You don't have to be "sideways" in California to taste fine wines. The Wimberley Valley Winery Tasting Room, 206 Main, Spring (281-350-8801; www.wimberleyvalleywinery.com), features award-winning Texas wines and some California vintages. Hours vary.

where to eat

NOTE: All the following eateries are in Old Town Spring.

Bluebonnet Cafe. 123 Midway; (281) 288-4882. This is a good spot to rest while munching on soups, salads, sandwiches, and lunch specials. Open for morning coffee and lunch Tuesday–Saturday. $.

British Trading Post. 26303 Hardy Road; (281) 350-5854. Have a hankering for meat pies, mushy peas, or a shandy? This is the place. Owner-chef Maureen Corless-Vlcek also serves delicious fresh scones as well as several memorable signature entrees such as Crab Diane casserole and Shrimp Sarah. Everything is served on bone china, and nothing is fried. Her meat pies also can be ordered in advance for takeout. Open for lunch only Tuesday–Sunday. $–$$.

Hyde's Cafe. 26608 Keith; (281) 350-8530. Formerly the Spring Cafe, this local institution still brags that it has the best food and slowest service anywhere. The old Spring Cafe was widely known for its marvelous hamburgers, and the tradition continues, including the time-honored thirty- to sixty-minute wait. If that's too long, try the fried veggie tray, buzzards' chili, barbecue, or sausage-on-a-stick. Open for lunch and dinner Tuesday–Sunday. $.

Puffabellys Old Depot Restaurant. 100 Main; (281) 350-3376; www.puffbellys.com. Burgers, spuds, salads, and sandwiches served amid peanut-shells-on-the-floor decor in a 1902 train depot. Kids eat free on Thursday night, longnecks are cheap on Friday night, and catfish is all-you-can-eat on Saturday night. Save room for the outstanding desserts, and don't forget to blow the train whistle when you leave. *Fun to know:* This old depot, a near duplicate of Spring's original depot, which burned some years back, was built in 1902 in Lovelady to serve the International and Great Northern Railroad; it was moved onto this site in 1985 and rebuilt in 2000 after a fire. Open for lunch Tuesday, Wednesday, and Sunday; lunch and dinner Thursday, Friday, and Saturday. $–$$.

Wunsche Brothers' Cafe and Saloon. 103 Midway; (281) 350-1902; www.wunsche broscafe.com. This historic landmark, circa 1902, offers some nifty live music (everything from progressive country to rock 'n' roll) Tuesday–Saturday evenings, along with loads of down-home food. Lunch ranges from burgers to sandwiches and salads, and the sideboard holds free samples of Texas-grown jellies (fig, dewberry, mayhaw, tomato, muscadine, and elderberry). Save room for dessert—the chocolate whiskey cake is a house specialty. Open for lunch on Monday; lunch and dinner Tuesday–Saturday. $–$$.

day trip 02

northwest

>>> sam's place:
willis, new waverly,
huntsville, crockett

willis

Begin this day trip by driving north from Houston on Interstate 45 for approximately 70 miles and taking exit 94 to Willis. Willis was founded in 1870 as a timber town. Among its historical treasures are two churches, including one that predates the town. The Thomas Chapel Methodist Episcopal Church, South, was organized in 1867. Members worshipped in log buildings and brush arbors until its Gothic Revival–style sanctuary with bell tower was completed in 1899. The other spiritual landmark is Willis Methodist Church, completed about 1878.

Perhaps most interesting is the town's history, albeit short-lived, as a tobacco titan. After the Civil War, farmers began experimenting with tobacco, and by the early 1890s enormous fields of extremely high-quality crops were supporting more than a half dozen cigar factories. Unfortunately, the smoke cleared—and the industry evaporated—shortly after the turn of the century, when the United States lifted tariffs off Cuban tobacco.

what to do

Jungle Eyes Refuge. 10134 Calvary Road; (936) 856-2848; www.jungledomain.org. Where do domesticated lions, tigers, panthers, cougars, and leopards go when their original homes disappear? A dozen exotic cats now have permanent sanctuary on a shaded, thirteen-acre spread in north Montgomery County. The nonprofit rehabilitation center also

northwest day trip 02

cares for wolves, prairie dogs, snakes, and other wildlife that have nowhere else to go. In fact, Jungle Eyes cares for more than 200 creatures, native and exotic. Humans with advance reservations and appointments are welcome to tour the facility March through October. The center also can schedule field trips, birthday parties, and other events. Fee.

North Lake Conroe Paddling Company. 13988 Calvary, Stow-A-Way Marina; (936) 203-2697; www.northlakeconroepaddlingco.com. Explore 22,000-acre Lake Conroe from the comfort of a kayak. In addition to renting kayaks, this friendly little outfit will show you how it's done and provide you with tips to make your day more fun. Two-hour rentals start at about $30, depending on the type of kayak.

where to eat

Peppermill Grille. 11525 FM 1097; (936) 890-5866. This airy sports bar hits one out of the park with its ambitious menu, which includes twenty-two-ounce porterhouse steaks, St. Louis–style ribs, pecan-smoked brisket, and grilled salmon rubbed with Mediterranean spices. Oh, and for those who are less picky, there are burgers and fries. Dozens of televisions and clever seating arrangements mean that sports fans won't miss a moment of the action. Open for lunch and dinner daily. $–$$.

The Upper Deck Restaurant and Lounge. 12947 Lake Conroe Hills, Northshore Marina; (936) 890-9998. When the weather is perfect, and all you want in life is to sit in the sun and enjoy Lake Conroe, come here. Light food is available (appetizers, sandwiches, burgers, and so on), and drinks are generous and well priced. Specials such as $2 margaritas all day on Monday and $2 hamburgers on Tuesday draw a loyal clientele. Open daily for lunch and dinner. $.

new waverly

Take Interstate 45 approximately 10 miles north to New Waverly. Settled in the 1850s, the community of Waverly thrived for a time on pioneer cotton and cattle businesses. Fearing damage to their cattle and the town's economy, residents turned down the International and Great Northern Railroad Company's request in 1870 for a right-of-way through town, a fatal mistake. The tracks were laid 6 miles west, people began relocating around the station of "New" Waverly, and the original Waverly was doomed. Visitors to the latter now find only an old cemetery with interesting headstones and the visually charming Waverly Presbyterian Church, built around 1904 and still filled every Sunday. "Old" Waverly is 6.8 miles east of I-45 on Highway 150.

New Waverly had a heavy Polish immigration from 1870 to 1902. After working in the fields to pay back the area's landowners who had advanced their passage money, the Poles began their own businesses and left a strong ethnic stamp on this community. Stately,

Gothic-style St. Joseph's Catholic Church in the heart of town is one of their legacies. Built between 1905 and 1908, it is well worth a visit.

what to do

The Sam Houston National Forest. Although not fully developed, this extensive woodland offers fishing, hunting, camping, hiking, photo opportunities, berry picking, bird-watching, picnicking, and boating access to Lake Conroe. For additional information on locations listed, contact the U.S. Department of Agriculture, Forest Service, Sam Houston Ranger District, 394 FM 1375 West, New Waverly, TX 77358; (936) 344-6205; www.southernregion.fs.fd.us/texas. *NOTE:* The ranger station, 3 miles west of New Waverly on FM 1375, is open on weekdays. Unless otherwise noted, all the following are free-use facilities.

Cagle Recreation Area. From I-45 at New Waverly, take FM 1375 west 4.2 miles, then turn southwest on FSR 205 for 3 miles. Big upgrades in this newly developed recreation area offers campers a choice of two loops with forty-seven camping and RV sites, all with full-service hookups (sewer, drinking water, and electricity). The tent pads have lantern posts and fire rings. Fee.

Kelly's Pond Campground. From I-45 at New Waverly, take FM 1375 west 11 miles, turn south 1 mile on FSR 204, and then drive west 1 mile on FSR 271. This scenic spot offers limited primitive tent camping (fire grates and picnic tables but no restroom facilities or water) and fishing in three small ponds. Nice for a picnic, but no boating or swimming.

Little Lake Creek Wilderness Area. From I-45 at New Waverly, take FM 1375 west 14 miles; turn south on FM 149 for 4 miles. Good for hiking.

Off-road vehicle (ORV) trails. Two ORV loops total 56 miles of trail. No vehicles more than 40 inches in width are allowed, however; check ORV regulations posted at the Sam Houston Ranger Station. East trailhead access: From New Waverly take FM 1375 approximately 4 miles west to FSR 233; turn north and follow signs approximately 3 miles. West trailhead access: From New Waverly take FM 1375 approximately 11 miles west to FSR 215; go north (right) for 1 mile and bear left on FSR 208; trailhead is on immediate left. *NOTE:* Hikers may be happier on the quieter Lone Star Hiking Trail, accessed from Stubblefield Recreation Area (see below).

Scott's Ridge. From Willis exit of I-45, take FM 1097 West 8 miles, then FSR 212 North for 1 mile. No facilities aside from boat ramp accessing Lake Conroe. Parking fee.

Stubblefield Lake Recreation Area and Campground. From I-45 at New Waverly, take FM 1375 West 11 miles to FSR 215; turn north and follow pavement to signs. That latter road passes a seventy-acre woodpecker cluster with numerous cavity trees, a National Forest Service effort to save the endangered red-cockaded woodpecker. The birds are active primarily at sunrise and sunset. Situated on the wide and shallow west fork of the San Jacinto River, this park offers twenty-eight campsites for either tents or RVs (up to 20 feet in length). Fee. You'll find tables, fire rings, and hot showers. Swimming not recommended (broken glass, possible alligator problem), but shallow-draft boating, canoeing, and bass fishing are pleasures in these beautiful backwaters of Lake Conroe. The park also accesses the Lone Star Hiking Trail. Interested in joining the Lone Star Hiking Trail Club, Inc.? Call the National Forest Service at (936) 344-6205 or log on to www.lshtclub.com.

where to eat

Waverly House. 9337 U.S. Highway 75 South (at the intersection of FM 1375 and US Highway 75 on the western edge of New Waverly); (936) 344-6552. When a Houston newspaper asked its readers to vote for the Best Country Cafes in Texas in 1989, this friendly place was in the top ten, and nothing's changed. Known for its homemade cream pies, it also dishes out freshly baked cobbler almost year-round. Order the chicken-fried steak only if you're starving or sharing; it laps over both sides of the plate. If you are in New Waverly on a weekday, don't pass up the workingman's steam-table lunch. Open for breakfast and lunch until 2:00 p.m. daily, for dinner on Friday and Saturday. $–$$. No credit cards.

continuing on

From New Waverly continue this day trip by driving north on I-45 to Huntsville.

huntsville

In the early 1830s an adventurous frontiersman named Pleasant Gray thought this rolling, wooded wilderness looked like his former home in Huntsville, Alabama. Because there were good springs nearby, he settled in and established an Indian trading post. By 1836 the tiny settlement of Huntsville was thriving, and in 1848 Sam Houston built his family home and plantation, Woodland, at the southern edge of town.

Sam's home now is right downtown, across from the Sam Houston State University campus, and those old Indian trails long since have been formalized into highways. Today's visitors can "stand with Sam," however: A somewhat startling 67-foot-high statue of this Texas legend borders I-45, the centerpiece of a visitor center and park. This is the world's tallest statue of an American hero. Open daily, the Sam Houston Statue Visitor Center also distributes Texas state maps and official travel information, the only such resource in the north-from-Houston region. Access is exit 109 from I-45 North, exit 112 from I-45 South. For more information call (800) 289-0389.

To reach downtown Huntsville from either direction on I-45, take the Highway 30 exit and head east. You'll soon find a main square retrogressing visually to the 1860s, courtesy of an ongoing trompe l'oeil program designed to bring back the style and architecture of the city's past.

Driving-tour booklets are available weekdays from the Sam Houston Statue Visitor Information Center or the Huntsville Chamber of Commerce, 1327 Eleventh Street, P.O. Box 538, Huntsville, TX 77342-0538; (936) 295-8113 or (800) 289-0389; www.huntsvilletexas

.com. Weekend explorers will find area information available outside that office. Expect numerous antiques stores around the square as well as an interesting museum and an old-fashioned soda fountain.

Want to overnight? Bed-and-breakfast is available at the Whistler (936-295-2834 or 800-432-1288; www.thewhistlerbnb.com), an 1859 Victorian that has been in the same family for six generations.

what to do

The Blue Lagoon. North of Huntsville on Pinedale Road, off FM 247; (936) 291-6111; www.bluelagoonscuba.com. Also known as Cozumel in the Pines, this old rock quarry offers some exciting scuba territory to certified divers. There are two large lakes, both with 40-foot underwater visibility and sunken shipwrecks to explore. You must have your C-card with you to be admitted, and no children under fourteen, pets, or glass containers are allowed. Open seasonally; call for directions and more information. Fee.

Christmas tree farms. This is prime tree-cutting territory. Call either of the following for directions: A-C Christmas Tree Farm (936-295-9523) or Mill Hollow Christmas Tree Farm (409-377-4044; www.millhollowtexas.com).

Gibb Bros. Building. 1118½ Eleventh Street, on the corner of Eleventh Street and Sam Houston Avenue, across from the courthouse. Started in 1841 as a store, this business evolved into the town's first bank because Thomas and Sanford Gibbs owned the only safe. The third structure on this site, the current building dates from 1890 has been restored to its early appearance after being disguised for decades by a modern brick front. The Gibb Brothers banking offices continue on the second floor, making this the oldest business in Texas still on its original site and under the same family ownership.

The Gibbs-Powell Home. 1228 Eleventh Street (Eleventh Street and Avenue M). This excellent example of Greek Revival architecture was built in 1862 and can be toured on weekend afternoons and by appointment. Donation. For group tour information call the Huntsville Chamber of Commerce at (936) 295-2914 or (800) 289-0389, or log on to www.huntsvilletexas.com.

H.E.A.R.T.S. Veterans Memorial Museum. 1600 Financial Plaza; (936) 295-5959; www.heartsmuseum.com. Located inside the West Hill Mall (exit 116 from I-45, and turn west). The initials stand for Helping Every American Remember Through Serving, and the exhibits include firsthand accounts of what specific wars and battles were actually like, recorded by soldiers who were there. Open Tuesday–Saturday. Donations appreciated.

Huntsville State Park. Eight miles south of Huntsville via I-45, then west on Park Road 40; (936) 295-5644 or (800) 792-1112; www.tpwd.state.tx.us. These 2,000-plus acres center on Lake Raven and offer swimming, canoeing, and limited sailing and motorboating. Hiking and birding are excellent, and Lake Raven Stables (936-295-1985) offers trail horseback riding year-round. The forest is dominated by loblolly and shortleaf pine, dogwood, sweet gum, sassafras, and assorted oaks. Good camping and picnicking. Fee. Open daily.

Oakwood Cemetery. Two blocks north of Eleventh Street on Avenue I. (Those 2 blocks of Avenue I are Highway 1, the shortest official highway in the state.) Sam Houston sleeps with good company in this historic cemetery. Deeded as a free burial place in 1847 by Huntsville's founder, Pleasant Gray, Oakwood has several tombstones carrying burial dates as early as 1842. Self-guided tour information is available at the Sam Houston Statue Visitor Center.

Sam Houston Memorial Park and Museum. 1836 Sam Houston Avenue (between Seventeenth and Nineteenth Streets); (936) 294-1832; www.samhouston.org. During a turbulent life that saw him the governor of Tennessee, a general in the Texas Army, the victor at the battle of San Jacinto, and the first president of the Republic of Texas, Sam Houston had many homes. None was as lovely or as beloved by him as Woodland Home, built on this site in 1847. Restored in 1981, this square log house with its white clapboard siding is just one of the pleasures in this shady park/museum complex.

Start at the museum, touring the right wing first to keep the chronology straight, and then visit Woodland, its separate kitchen, Houston's law office, and a blacksmith shop. Close by are the War and Peace House and the unusual Steamboat House, where Houston died in 1863. The docents in both homes speak of Sam and his wife, Margaret, as if they might return at any moment. The park's small lake was a fresh, bubbling spring during Houston's residency here; today it is reshaped to resemble the state of Texas and is a pleasant spot for a picnic lunch. Spring visits get a bonus of flowering dogwood and azaleas. Sam Houston's grave also is interesting, across town in Oakwood Cemetery. Part of the Sam Houston State University complex, the park and museum are open Tuesday–Sunday. Free.

Sam Houston State University. Five blocks south of the town square on Sam Houston Avenue (Highway 75). Founded in 1879 as a normal (teacher-training) institute, SHSU's campus landmark is Austin Hall (1853), the oldest educational facility in the Southwest.

Guided walking tours of this picturesque campus are offered weekdays by appointment (call 936-294-1844). Many cultural, sports, and special events are open to the public. Call the public relations office at (936) 294-1833 to find out what's going on when you're planning to be in town.

The on-campus planetarium hosts public "Star Parties," and the SHSU Observatory north of Huntsville offers sky viewing through a 24-inch telescope; call (936) 294-1601 for schedules. You also can arrange tours of the school's agricultural operations, including the plant science greenhouse, as well as animal facilities focused on beef cattle, horses, and goats. For more information call (936) 294-1215.

Texas Prison Museum. 491 Highway 75 North, P.O. Box 1271, Huntsville, TX 77342-1271; (936) 295-2155; www.txprisonmuseum.org. Want to keep your kids on the straight and narrow? Bring them here for a look at a 9-by-6-foot cell. Candid signage explains the Texas prison system, including current execution policies, recent prison breaks, and gang life. Exhibits include rifles belonging to the romanticized killers Clyde Barrow and Bonnie Parks; "Old Sparkie," the electric chair used through 1964; rare balls and chains; and assorted contraband confiscated within the nearby prison units. This interesting museum can special-order any type of prisoner-made leather goods, from "Bubba" belts to snuffcan holders, dolls to artwork. Prices are reasonable and the craftsmanship excellent. Open daily. Admission is $4, $2 for children.

The Walls. Three short blocks east of the town square. This is the original main unit of the Huntsville State Prison. *Of interest:* The "prisoner count" whistle that blows daily at 7:00 a.m. and again in the late afternoon assures Huntsville residents that all's well—every felon is accounted for. Self-guided tour information for the prison is available at the Sam Houston Statue Visitor Center.

where to eat

Bob Luby's Seafood Grill. 139 I-45 North (on the west side of I-45, north of the U.S. Highway 190 intersection); (936) 435-0944. Fish, shrimp, and crawfish are featured, as well as catfish, salmon, tilapia, and many other seafood selections. Open for lunch and dinner daily. $–$$.

The Cafe Texan. 1120 Sam Houston (at the corner of Twelfth Street on courthouse square); (936) 295-2381. Chicken-fried steak and pepper steak are "home-cooked" here. Open for breakfast, lunch, and dinner daily (specials at lunch). $–$$.

The Catfish Place. 3400 Highway 19; (936) 295-8685. Between the freshly roasted peanuts on the table and the numerous catfish/shrimp/oyster selections, you won't go hungry here. Open for lunch and dinner Wednesday–Sunday. $–$$.

The Homestead on 19th. 1215 Nineteenth Street (across from Sam Houston Memorial Park and Museum); (936) 291-7366; http://homesteadon19th.com. No contest, this is the best fine dining in Huntsville, a destination in itself. Owner-chef John Eschenfelder serves innovative American cuisine within an interesting historic matrix: conjoined log cabins circa 1834–50 that were moved to this site in 1980. The courtyard between the cabins now serves as a shady setting for special events. In a hurry? How about a Black Angus tenderloin done in whiskey butter or stuffed with garlic and fresh mozzarella cheese? With a phone call, these and other tasty entrees are available as takeout. Open for dinner Tuesday–Saturday. $$–$$$.

The Junction Restaurant. 2641 Eleventh Street; (936) 291-2183; www.shophuntsville .com/thejunction. Just look for an 1849 plantation house with an old-fashioned buggy on the front porch. Inside, the house specialties are catfish, fresh seafood, steaks, and chicken. Open for lunch and dinner; closed Wednesday and major holidays. $–$$.

King's Candies and Such. 1112 Eleventh Street (on the square); (936) 291-6988; www .kingscandiesandsuch.com. First cousin to King's Confectionery on the Strand in Galveston, this old-fashioned sweet shop makes traditional shakes, malts, and banana splits at its soda fountain, squeezes lemons for the lemonade, makes its own candy, and serves Blue Bell ice cream. It's also a good place for a lunch sandwich or salad. Open Monday–Saturday. $.

McKenzie's Barbeque. 1700 Eleventh Street; (936) 291-7347; www.mckenzies barbeque.com. These folks smoke their tasty meats in three pits out back. Dine in or take out. Open daily for lunch and dinner. $–$$.

The New Zion Missionary Baptist Church. 2601 Montgomery Road (FM 1374), 2 miles east of I-45; (936) 295-3445. A few years back a Houston housepainter named D. C. Ward volunteered to paint this country church, and when his wife, Annie Mae, began fixing some barbecue ribs for his workday lunch, the wonderful aroma stopped traffic. The congregation took the hint and began selling the Wards' barbecue on weekends from a shady spot near the church.

Next came a "real" kitchen and dining room, serving up some of the best barbecue in east Texas, the profits from which built a new brick church with stained-glass windows. In a hurry? Just ask for the $11.50 family-style special—four meats, beans, potato salad, and iced tea—that arrives as fast as the staff can dish it up. Open 11:00 a.m. to 6:00 p.m. Wednesday–Saturday. $–$$.

wandering the back roads

The OSR turnoff, 40 miles north of Huntsville on I-45, is a meandering country drive with more than a touch of history. The initials stand for Old San Antonio Road, but it also is known as El Camino Real because it was created by the order of the king of Spain in 1691. The Spaniards, through their control of Mexico, claimed Texas from 1519 to 1821, but the French also coveted this rich, wild land, sending explorers into Texas in the late 1600s. To reinforce its claim, Spain created a series of missions in East Texas and blazed this road to bolster and serve those primitive outposts. Today Highway 21 follows, after a fashion, that historic route from San Marcos northeast to the Louisiana border, one portion linking the Madisonville area to Crockett. If you love vistas of rolling fields edged by ancient oaks, don't miss this drive.

Turning west on OSR from I-45 takes you through pretty countryside en route to Bryan–College Station (see Northwest Day Trip 3).

If you're hungry and out roaming, take I-45 23 miles north from Huntsville to Madison-ville for a tasty meal at the vintage Woodbine Hotel (936-348-3333; www.woodbinehotel texas.com). Now owned by noted chef Reinhard Warmuth and his wife, Susan, this bed-and-breakfast hotel's dining room serves soups, salads, and sandwiches for lunch Tuesday–Friday and outstanding dinners Tuesday–Saturday. The evening menus usually include chicken and steak, grilled salmon topped with one of several flavorful sauces, and prime rib (Friday and Saturday). $–$$$.

Fun to know: The Woodbine is a survivor, built in 1904 by joining two kit houses (one in Eastlake style, the other Queen Anne) possibly ordered from Sears Roebuck. Its saloon, now called Brimberry House (circa 1870) and relocated to this site in 1920, is the oldest building in the county. Now on the National Register of Historic Places and a Texas Historic Landmark, the hotel sported Madisonville's only telephone back in 1904; that original phone booth is still there.

continuing on

From Huntsville, two routes take you to Crockett, the final stop on this day trip. A longer but very scenic alternative travels 30 miles north to Madisonville via either US 75 or I-45, then swings northeast 36 miles to Crockett via Highway 21, part of the previously mentioned Old San Antonio Road.

A shorter route to Crockett follows Highway 19 northeast from Huntsville for 49 miles, passing through the communities of Trinity and Lovelace en route.

crockett

Davy Crockett and two companions had to do some fast talking here. Local folks found Crockett's campsite near this area in 1836 (the trio were en route to their destinies at the Alamo) and nearly hanged them as horse thieves. The fifth-oldest town in Texas and loaded with vintage buildings, Crockett has a history that is easy to trace.

Visitors should start at the traditional square in the heart of town—good gift-shopping territory—and then go exploring. For advance information contact the Houston County Chamber of Commerce, 1100 Edmiston Drive, P.O. Box 307, Crockett, TX 75835; (936) 544-2359; www.crockettareachamber.org. More than 210 historic markers and sites in Houston County reflect its heritage as the first county of the Republic of Texas (1837). For a list contact the Houston County Historical Commission, Second Floor, Houston County Courthouse, Crockett, TX 75835; (936) 544-3255, ext. 238.

Consider turning this day trip into an overnight with accommodations at Warfield House (936-544-4037; www.warfieldhouse.net), built in the 1890s and now elegantly restored as a bed-and-breakfast lodging in the heart of town.

what to do

Camp Street Cafe. 215 South Third Street; (936) 544-8656; www.campstreetcafe.com. Owned by the same family since its stagecoach days, this restored but rustic, western-styled property is a lively country-style entertainment venue. In addition to assorted bluegrass, blues, and folk music, there's often cowboy-style entertainment on Saturday evening, courtesy of Guy and Pipp Gillette. Professional performers who were named the best duo by the 1998 Academy of Western Artists, the Gillettes specialize in cowboy poetry mixed with country music, and they play to standing-room crowds when on tour. Crockett residents, they now have a prime performance setup close to home. Inquire about food service.

Davy Crockett Spring. West Goliad at the railroad underpass, west of the town square. Though not much to see, the spring still flows and serves as a public drinking fountain at what is thought to be Crockett's campsite. The area has been improved recently and is now part of the newly developed Brewer Park and Davy Crockett Springs, which includes the century-old Strode-Pritchett log home.

Downes-Aldrich Historical Home. 207 North Seventh Street; (936) 544-4804. Listed on the National Register of Historic Places, this Victorian survivor now is the historical and cultural activities center for the town. Open Wednesday, Saturday, and Sunday afternoons. Fee.

Houston County Visitors Center–Museum. 629 North Fourth Street; (936) 544-2359. This 1909 railroad depot with a retired fire engine is near the Davy Crockett Spring and Old Town at Camp Street. The museum depicts the history of Houston County, which became the first county of the Republic of Texas on June 12, 1837. Displays include early farm implements, an old newspaper press, and railroad memorabilia dating from 1872. Call first for open times and hours. Donation.

Monroe-Crook Home. 709 East Houston Avenue; (936) 544-5820. Built in 1854 and listed on the National Register of Historic Places, this Greek Revival home is open for public tours on Wednesday morning and weekend afternoons, March–December. Fee.

Salmon Lake Park. P.O. Box 483, Grapeland, TX 75844-0483; (936) 687-2594; www.salmonlakepark.com. Twelve miles north of Crockett, this old-fashioned swimming hole and RV park is open to day-trippers and overnighters. The privately owned park is the site of several festivals each year, including an August bluegrass festival that's been held for three decades. Fifteen cabins are available for rental.

where to eat

Betty Boop's Sandwich & Soup Shop. 509 East Houston Avenue; (936) 544-4297. If you're looking for a quick bite while strolling Crockett's courthouse square, drop in here. Open weekdays for lunch. $. No credit cards.

Brass Lantern. 1117 East Loop 304; (936) 544-4091. Standard menu here, plus a good buffet and lunch specials. Open for lunch and dinner Tuesday–Saturday. $–$$.

Cowboy Bean Café. 1409 East Loop 304; (936) 546-2326. You can feed your truck-driving spirit here. The kitchen isn't Mom's, but the helpings are huge. The menu's heavy with home cooking, and the ambience is country and friendly. Open daily except Sunday. $–$$.

Fowler's Restaurant & Sports Bar. Highway 7 East and Loop 304; (936) 544-9690. Check out the daily specials at lunch and dinner at this long-established local favorite. Open Tuesday–Sunday. $–$$.

Stockman's Steakhouse. Highway 21 West, 3 miles west from Loop 304, inside the Houston County Livestock Auction Barn; (936) 544-3545. Nothing like going to the source for great steaks. The seafood entrees are good bets as well. Open Thursday for lunch and dinner, Friday and Saturday for dinner only. $–$$.

wandering the back roads

There are numerous possibilities if you feel like extending your drive well beyond the two-hour limit of this book. First option is to continue north on OSR (Highway 21) from Crockett through the Davy Crockett National Forest to the Mission Tejas State Historical Park (936-687-2394; www.tpwd.state.tx.us). The Rice family log home is special here, built between 1828 and 1838 and used as a stage stop. Nearby is a commemorative log structure similar to the old Spanish mission established here in 1690 to serve the Tejas Indians. That mission was the first of its kind in Texas.

Continuing northeast another 7 miles on OSR brings you to Caddoan Mounds State Historic Site (936-858-3218), 6 miles southwest of Alto. In addition to two large ceremonial mounds, archaeological digs have led to a full-size replica of a Caddoan house built with Stone Age–type tools. A visitor center explains all. Open Thursday–Monday. Fee.

A second option from Crockett follows Highway 7 approximately 18 miles east to the Ratcliff Lake Recreation Area (936-655-2299) in the Davy Crockett National Forest. A picturesque forty-five-acre swimming and fishing lake surrounded by extensive picnic areas and campgrounds, this facility also sports canoe rentals and countless deer amid a hardwood forest that's particularly beautiful in spring and fall. Fee. The 20-mile-long Four C Hiking Trail begins here and continues northeast to the Neches Bluff Overlook on the Neches River, just south of Highway 21 northeast of Weches. For more trail information contact the Texas Forestry Association, P.O. Box 1488, Lufkin, TX 75902; (936) 632-8733.

A third long-drive alternative is FM 229 northwest from Crockett to Houston County Lake. Locally, this is considered the best bass fishing in the state.

Following U.S. Highway 287 southeast from Crockett takes you through the Kickapoo Recreation Area near Groveton and hits the northern limit of the Livingston-Woodville day trip (see Northeast Day Trip 2).

And finally, there's Lufkin, which was founded in 1872. About 43 miles east of Crockett, this town was built on the railway and lumber industries. Today it attracts nearly a million visitors annually. Among its attractions are the Texas Forestry Museum, the Museum of East Texas, and the surprisingly good Ellen Trout Zoo. Only the latter charges admission, but its diverse collection is worth the small fee. For zoo information call (936) 633-0399 or log on to www.ellentroutzoo.com.

For general information, including special events and lodging options, call the Lufkin Convention & Visitors Bureau at (800) 409-5659 or log on to www.visitlufkin.com.

day trip 03

hello, mr. president:
bryan–college station and the
brazos river valley

bryan–college station

From Houston follow Highway 6 and U.S. Highway 290 north to Hempstead and continue north on Highway 6 through Navasota into Bryan and College Station.

These joint communities tend to have a single connotation to Houstonians—Texas A&M University. While visitors to that sprawling campus will find much of interest, there are several other things to do near Aggieland.

Bryan and College Station today flow into a combined metropolitan area that ranked first in growth in the state and sixth in the entire country in the 1980 census. Not bad for a slow starter. This rich sliver of agricultural land, bounded by the Brazos River on the west and the Navasota River on the east, was sparsely settled until the advent of the Houston & Texas Central Railroad in 1866. The Reconstruction years after the Civil War were rough on the young town of Bryan, and it wasn't until the formal opening of Texas A&M College in 1876 that the area settled down to some semblance of respectability.

Some footnotes on Bryan's past are interesting. The original street grid inadvertently provided for present-day traffic by making Main Street wide enough to turn a five-yoke oxen team, and the college was deliberately sited on the open prairie 5 miles south of town so as to be well removed from the influence of demon rum, which flowed freely in Bryan's saloons.

An information-loaded historic guide and map covers Bryan's old commercial and residential districts, as well as the remains of several small pre–Civil War settlements outside

northwest day trip 03

town. This and other area guides are found at the Bryan–College Station Chamber of Commerce Convention & Visitor Bureau, 715 University Drive East, College Station, TX 77840; (979) 260-9898 or (800) 777-8292; www.bryan-collegestation.org. Open Monday–Friday only; contact in advance for maps and brochures if you intend to explore on a weekend.

Leaving Texas A&M to its own section following, here are some suggestions of what to see in Bryan and College Station.

what to do

Birding. The Brazos Valley hosts an enormous variety of birdlife. A self-guided tour covering five areas and a list of birds common to the Brazos County Arboretum are available from the convention and visitor bureau.

Brazos Center. 3232 Briarcrest, Bryan; (979) 776-8338 (center); (979) 776-2195 (museum); www.thebrazoscenter.com. Take the Briarcrest exit east from the Highway 6 bypass. This is the special-events place for the area, hosting giant weekend antiques shows periodically. Year-round visitors can enjoy the Brazos Valley Museum of Natural History, and there is a park adjacent to the center with a covered picnic pavilion, barbecue area, nature trail, and restrooms. Museum open daily. Fee.

Canoeing on the Brazos River. First, so you'll sound like a native, it's pronounced *Braa-zas,* not *Bray-zos,* as you might expect from the spelling. Although its water is muddy with sediment, the Brazos generally is quiet and otherwise scenic, a good one- or two-day float if you have your own canoe. As of this writing there are no canoe rentals available in the Bryan–College Station area. You'll find float information in several river books available at major bookstores.

The Children's Museum of the Brazos Valley. 202 South Bryan Street, Bryan; (979) 779-5437; www.mymuseum.com. Make-believe and creativity thrive in this hands-on learning environment. Children can pretend to grocery-shop or drive an ambulance, dress up and strut their stuff on a small stage, play a piano, or actually paint a Volkswagen "Bug." Open Tuesday–Saturday. Fee.

Lake Bryan. From Highway 6 north of Bryan, take the FM 2818 exit south for approximately 5 miles. At Sandy Point Road (blinking yellow light), turn right and go 3.4 miles; lake is on the right. Operated by the City of Bryan Parks and Recreation Department, this 886-acre lake is surrounded by 1,700 acres of oak-shaded land, of which 150 acres are developed for both primitive and RV camping, picnicking, and other recreational uses. There's lots of water access, including a sand beach and a special restricted area for Jet Ski operation. Other popular activities here include sailing (no waterskiing), walking and nature trails, and mountain biking along 20 miles of challenging terrain, much of it in view of the lake. Although the park is open year-round, lake hours are seasonal; inquire. Primitive camping is $8 per night; RV sites with water and electricity are $15. Admission is $5 per car. For information or to reserve an RV site, call (979) 361-0861 or (979) 209-5207.

Messina Hof Wine Cellar and Vineyard. 4545 Old Reliance Road, Bryan; (979) 778-9463 or (800) 736-9463; www.messinahof.com. Exit Highway 6 at Boonville Road; stay on access road going north; turn right on Old Reliance Road; winery is 3 miles east. Follow signs. Paul and Merrill Bonarrigo began planting grapes in 1977; their successful vineyard now covers forty-six acres and produces about 250,000 gallons (780,000 bottles) annually. Using the classic European grape Vinifera grafted onto Texas root stock, they bottle sixteen varieties of wine, including chardonnay, cabernet, port, red and white zinfandels, and champagne. Harvest time is July and August, and you can pick and stomp grapes yourself by signing up in advance for their Pickers' Club (free). The early-twentieth-century Howell manor house has been restored as the winery's retail sales and tasting room. It is open daily, and there are winery tours at specific times. The Bonarrigos also invite the public for Springfest in April and a premiere party for new wines and vintages in November. Other special events occur monthly throughout the year (get on their mailing list). If a luxurious weekend retreat sounds good, inquire about overnighting at the Villa at Messina Hof (ten nonsmoking rooms furnished with European antiques). Visitors also rave about the food at the winery's Vintage House restaurant (see "Where to Eat").

P. David Romei Arts Center. 2275 Dartmouth Street, College Station; (979) 696-2787; www.acbv.org. Exhibits, juried shows featuring regional artists, and outstanding handcrafts make this a place to stop and shop. The center is operated by the Arts Council of Brazos Valley, which also is responsible for much of the public artwork seen in Bryan and College Station. Open Monday–Friday. Free.

exploring texas a&m university

Even if you haven't a prospective student in tow, this handsome 5,250-acre campus has much to offer. Located in the heart of College Station and hard to miss on the west side of Highway 6, Texas A&M was the first public institution of higher education in the state. Originally an all-male military college, it now has a coed enrollment of approximately 44,000 and is in the top ten schools nationally in expenditures for research.

Aggie traditions are stories in themselves. Ask about the Elephant Walk, the Twelfth Man, and Silver Taps at the Visitor Information Center in Rudder Tower for an insight into what makes Aggies so loyal to their alma mater.

Footsteps, a book of suggested walking tours on campus, can be bought in the student bookstore (979-845-8681), in the Memorial Student Center, or in advance from the Texas A&M University Press (979-845-1436). First-time visitors should begin at the visitor center in the lobby of Rudder Tower (979-845-5851). Hour-long tours start on the hour

10:00 a.m.–4:00 p.m. weekdays, except for holidays. For visitor information write Aggieland Visitor Center, Texas A&M University, MS 1372, College Station, TX 77843-1372, or log on to www.tamu.edu.

what to do

NOTE: All the following are on or near the Texas A&M Campus.

Bonfire Memorial. Located near the polo fields, this somber but moving memorial pays tribute to the twelve young people who, on November 18, 1999, were killed as they were constructing the Aggie bonfire, a nearly one-hundred-year-old tradition at A&M. Open dawn until dusk.

The Clayton W. Williams Jr. Alumni Center. Corner of George Bush Drive and Houston Street; (979) 845-7514. Displays include an Aggie ring collection.

The George Bush Presidential Library Center. Take the University Drive exit from Highway 6 in College Station, turn west, and follow signs; (979) 691-4000; http://bush library.tamu.edu. This $42-million project dedicated to the first Bush presidency sits amid ninety acres of oaks and greenbelt on the western edge of the A&M campus. As the nation's tenth (and most computerized) presidential library, it houses all George Bush's vice-presidential and presidential records as well as memorabilia and personal documents from his public service career as congressman, ambassador to the United Nations, chairman of the Republican National Committee, liaison to China, and director of the Central Intelligence Agency.

Experience the George Bush Presidential Library and Museum and discover his fascinating story, filled with adventure, courage, dedication, and service. The museum exhibits reveal the unique influences and challenges that shaped George Bush's life and presidency. The George Bush Presidential Library and Museum immerses the visitor in an interactive walk through the history textbooks, as the exhibits explore the most important events of the twentieth century from WWII through the Gulf War.

Original artifacts, film, photographs, documents, music, sound effects, interactive video and computerization surround the visitor, creating a museum experience that is both educational and entertaining. Some notable artifacts showcased include an actual World War II Avenger Torpedo Bomber, a 1947 Studebaker, and a section of the Berlin Wall. As a result of the $8.3-million renovation, guests can actually sit at the seat of power in a replica of President Bush's Oval Office, stroll through President Bush's office at Camp David, and even face tough decisions as part of the National Security Staff in the White House Situation Room. These exhibits provide a look into George Bush's exceptional leadership during times of crisis—the reunification of Germany, the collapse of the Soviet Union, and the Gulf War. Visitors also have an opportunity to discover the character of President Bush as a loving husband, father, and grandfather. Highlighted within the museum's walls is the importance of faith, family, and friends, and most importantly, the nobility of public service as exemplified by the lives of George and Barbara Bush. Hours are Monday–Saturday, 9:30 a.m.–5:00 p.m., Sunday noon–5:00 p.m. Fee.

Horticultural Gardens and Field Laboratory. On Hensel Drive, between Texas Avenue and South College Drive (watch for signs); (979) 845-3658. Several beautiful test gardens are open for walking here seven days a week. Come on a weekday, however, and you can pick up a guide brochure that tells you what you're seeing. All gardens are maintained by students and funded by grants for testing and research. Want to know what's wrong with your flowers or vegetables? Call the Department of Horticultural Sciences (weekdays only) at the number listed above.

Horticulture/Forest Sciences Building. On the west campus; (979) 845-5341. Don't miss the Benz Gallery of Floral Art, open during weekday business hours. Exhibits include paintings, sculptures, primitive art, ceramics, and gold orchids.

Kleberg Animal and Food Sciences Center (Kleberg Center). From George Bush Drive go right on Wellborn, left at the second stoplight (Old Main Drive), and left on Olsen Boulevard; Kleberg Center will be in front of you, on the left. The walls of the northeast stairwell contain 254 panels burned with the major brands of every county in Texas. Open weekdays.

Memorial Student Center (MSC). Part of the University Center complex. Ask at the visitor center in Rudder Tower as to the current locations of the Buck Schiwetz paintings and the Texan Campaign Staffordshire China (circa 1850). Also of interest are the Centennial Wood Carvings in the corridor between the student lounge and the cafeteria (six walnut panels that trace the history of the school from 1876). The MSC Forsyth Center Galleries is home to the more than 1,000 pieces of American and English glass that make up the Bill and Irma Runyon Art Collections. The collections also include more than sixty paintings by American artists, including Frederic Remington, Charles M. Russell, and Mary Cassatt. For a current schedule of what's showing and where, call (979) 845-8501. Don't miss shopping in the student bookstore.

Memorial Student Center Opera and Performing Arts Society. This campus group presents a full professional program every year, ranging from jazz bands to ballet. For current production information call (979) 845-1234.

Nuclear Science Center. Off campus, near the Easterwood Airport; (979) 845-7553, (979) 845-7551, or (979) 845-7552. This multimillion-dollar facility houses the largest nuclear reactor on any campus in the Southwest and produces radioactive isotopes for scientific research. Tours Monday–Friday (but call ahead). Free.

Rudder Tower. At University Center on Joe Routt Boulevard; (979) 845-5851. The visitor center in the lobby introduces you to the university with maps, an excellent movie and booklet about the school, and campus guides. Visitor parking (fee) is adjacent to the building. Tour reservations must be made at least two weeks in advance. Open Monday–Friday and on football weekends. Call for hours.

Sam Houston Sanders Corps of Cadets Center. Built with private funds in 1992 and dedicated to the past, present, and future of the university's famous corps, this outstanding facility exhibits several one-of-a-kind artworks, as well as the Metzger-Sanders Gun Collection (antique and historic firearms). Open Monday–Saturday and on football weekends. For information call (979) 862-2862.

Texas A&M Sports Museum. Located at Kyle Field. This interactive museum is devoted to the university's storied athletes and sports traditions, including the Twelfth Man and the Aggie bonfire.

Tours also can be arranged of the **Cyclotron Institute** (979-845-1411), the **Computing Services Center** (979-845-4211), and the **Veterinary Medicine College** (979-845-5051).

where to eat on the a&m campus

The Creamery. In the Meat Science and Technology Center, adjacent to the Kleberg Building; (979) 845-5652. The best chocolate ice cream in the world is sold here, along with milk, butter, cheese, eggs, and meats produced on the university's farms. Open weekdays. $. No credit cards.

Memorial Student Center. Two choices here: the cafeteria (979-845-1118) and Hullabaloo, a food court on the lower level (979-847-9464). $. No credit cards.

where to eat in the area

Cafe Eccell. 101 Church Avenue, College Station; (979) 846-7908; www.cafeeccell.com. Housed in what was the old city hall, this classy bistro features California-style food so fresh even the fish have never been frozen. Barbecued chicken pizza is a best-seller, along with award-winning desserts such as the fresh strawberry tart. In addition to daily specials, the basic menu changes seasonally, and the wine list is considered one of the best in town. Open for lunch and dinner Monday–Saturday, brunch on Sunday. $–$$.

Chicken Oil Company. 3600 South College, Bryan; (979) 846-3306. This giant wooden building is filled with antiques and memorabilia, and its hamburgers have been voted the best in town in local polls. Open for lunch and dinner daily. $. No credit cards.

Czech-Tex Barbeque Steakhouse and Bakery. In Snook, 10 miles west of College Station via FM 60; (979) 272-8501; www.czech-tex.com. No address is necessary for this popular eatery; just look for the biggest building in Snook. An assortment of Czech food on the menu echoes the area's strong ethnic heritage, but the big draws are the generous, handcut steaks. Open Tuesday–Saturday for lunch and dinner. $–$$$.

Dixie Chicken. 307 University Drive, College Station; (979) 846-2322; www.dixiechicken .com. Among this venerable watering hole's claims to fame is the title of "best college bar," bestowed by *Playboy* magazine in 2002. Several generations of Aggies have crowded this eatery for brews, burgers, and chicken finger baskets. Wanna fit in? Order a Shiner Bock and Frito Pie. Mmmmmm, good. $.

Madden's Casual Gourmet. 202 South Bryan Avenue, Bryan; (979) 770-2558; www .pmaddens.com. Chef Peter Madden apprenticed at the renowned Crescent Court Hotel in Dallas, so his menus are inspiring. Lunch sandwich fare at Madden's ratchets chicken sandwiches up to chile-rubbed blackened chicken. At dinner, seared sea scallops are paired with lobster tomato risotto. Open for breakfast, lunch, and dinner Monday–Saturday. $–$$$.

T Garden. North Avenue East, Bryan; (979) 268-4171; www.tgardencafe.com. Located in Bryan's Garden District, this cafe has earned a loyal following with its gourmet sandwiches presented by owner/chef Jennifer Lilleker, a graduate of New York's Culinary Institute. Quiches, salads, and freshly made soups are all winners. Open for lunch Monday–Saturday. On Wednesday afternoons, a traditional English tea with scones and tea sandwiches is offered. $–$$.

Vintage House at Messina Hof. 4545 Old Reliance Road, Bryan; (979) 778-9463, ext. 31, or (800) 736-9463; www.messinahof.com. If this well-designed restaurant were closer to Houston it would be mobbed every night. As it is, unless you go early, it's best to reserve to ensure a table. Lunches, served until late afternoon, offer unusual quiches, lasagna, salads, and sandwiches, all with appropriate vino tie-ins, of course. Dinners include such classics as beef Wellington, lamb chops, fish, and chicken, each designed with a fine wine touch. Both the horseradish-crusted salmon and the Gorgonzola pinwheel breast of chicken are local favorites. Whenever and whatever you eat here, save room for the house special: the memorable Port 'n' Cream Sundae. Open daily for lunch (closes at 3:00 p.m. on Sunday), Thursday–Saturday evenings for dinner. $$–$$$.

wandering the back roads

From College Station turn west on FM 60 at the University Drive signal and follow the local folks some 15 miles to Snook. The big attractions include fresh sausage from Slovacek's (979-272-8625) and a chance to chow down at Czech-Tex Barbeque Steakhouse and Bakery (see "Where to Eat" listings for Bryan–College Station).

As an alternative to returning home from Snook through College Station, backtrack only as far as FM 50 and swing south to Independence and Brenham (see Northwest Day Trip 6). Those fine fields you pass north of Independence are part of the Texas A&M Experimental Farms.

If wanderlust really takes over and you want to stretch the two-hour driving limit of this book, continue north on Highway 6 from Bryan some 45 miles to Calvert. Established in 1868, this nice old town is the unofficial antiques center of Texas, and you can see some outstanding vintage homes during the Annual Homes Tour in May and the Christmas celebration in early December. Calvert's Main Street is a 4-block collection of old brick and iron-front buildings, most of which now house antiques shops. For information on bed-and-breakfast accommodations in the area, call (800) 290-1213. For information on Calvert call the chamber of commerce at (979) 364-2559 or log on to www.rtis.com/calvert.

You can return to Houston from Bryan–College Station one of three ways. The first is the simplest—just reverse the route you followed coming up.

The second is more scenic. Follow Highway 6 South to Navasota and swing east on Highway 105 toward Conroe. Turn south on FM 1774 for a forest drive through Plantersville and Magnolia before connecting with Highway 249 South at Pinehurst. *NOTE:* This route is to be avoided on weekends from October 1 to November 15 because of Renaissance Festival traffic. Highway 249 South from Pinehurst ultimately intersects Interstate 45 North inside the Houston city limits.

If you feel like exploring farther, go east on Highway 30 to Huntsville (see Northwest Day Trip 2), and then scoot south on I-45 to home.

day trip 04

northwest

back at the ranch:
hockley and prairie view,
hempstead, magnolia

hockley and prairie view

The primary path from Houston into this northwest sector is U.S. Highway 290, rambling its way through Cypress and a lot of interesting country en route to Austin and points west. Hockley is pure country—ranches, a small business district, and a great fishing hole. Prairie View at present is home to Prairie View State University, but a little more than a century ago it was the site of the Kirby Plantation, known as Alta Vista. Deeded to the state in 1876 for use as a college for black youths, the old mansion was the school's first educational building. It is gone now, along with de facto segregation, but look for St. Francis Episcopal Church, a small frame building (1870) moved to the campus from Hempstead in 1958. The first Episcopal church north of Houston, it still has the original pews, hand made by its first congregation.

what to do

Bird-watching at Warren Ranch Lake. In Hockley turn west at the tallest rice dryer and follow Warren Ranch Road 3.4 miles. The lake will be on the left. It is private and a protected refuge, but the viewing (with binoculars) is excellent from the shoulder of the road. The largest winter concentration of ducks and geese in North America is found in the rice fields of this area, and the fifty wild acres of this lake have been known to host as many as 20,000 ducks and geese at one time. With luck you may spot a bald eagle, America's national bird

northwest day trip 04

and, happily, now removed from the endangered species list. For information call the Houston Audubon Society at (713) 932-1639 or log on to www.houstonaudubon.org.

Chmielewski Blueberry Farm. 23810 Bauer-Hockley Road, Hockley; (281) 304-0554; www.chmielewski-blueberry.com. Open seasonally for pick-your-own blueberries. Call ahead for hours.

MVP (Most Valuable Pilot) Aero Academy. 21904 US 290, Cypress (Weiser Air Park, between Huffmeister and Telge Roads); (281) 469-3009; www.mvpaeroacademy.com. Want to see Houston from the air or nurture a budding interest in flying lessons? This firm offers "flightseeing" or discovery flights in a Cessna 172 ($49 for thirty minutes).

Oil Ranch. P.O. Box 429, Hockley, TX 77447-0429; (281) 859-1616; www.oilranch.com. Go 20 miles northwest of Houston via US 290, then turn right on Hegar Road and right on Magnolia Road. Families are welcome to play "cowboy for a day" at this pleasant spread. Activities include pony rides in the corral, milking a cow, hayrides through the pastures, and exploring a large maze. There are also an Indian village, petting zoo, swimming pools, and miniature golf course, and kids can hand-feed the cattle and learn about the cattle industry. Special events include barn dances and free pumpkins in October. Reservations required; groups welcome. Fee. Open all year. Call for a free brochure and/or reservations.

Skydive Houston. 15355 Penick Road, Waller; (936) 931-1600 or (800) 586-7688; www.skydivehouston.com. From US 290 turn left on FM 362 (3 miles south of Waller) and follow signs. Care to float above the countryside? When weather permits, this company welcomes both neophyte and experienced skydivers. First-timers can choose between a tandem dive or accelerated free fall; more advanced lessons are available. Cost ranges from $179 to $295, depending on style of jump. Open daily.

Steam trains at Zube Park. From the intersection of US 290 and the Sam Houston Tollway, go north on US 290 for 17 miles, then north on Roberts Road for 1.2 miles; watch for a large gazebo and park on the right. Thanks to a $1 per year annual lease between Harris County and the Houston Area Live Steamers Inc. club, ridable model steam trains now chug along 4,000 feet of 7.5-gauge track at this county park. Want to ride? The public is welcome aboard (free) on the third Saturday of the month, weather permitting, March through November. Each of the coal- or oil-fired steam engines pulls three to five cars capable of holding up to three adults. All are scale models of past or existing trains. Club members also operate model steamboats on the park's pond. For information on the steamers club or to confirm that the trains will be operating, log on to www.hals.org. On the site you can sign up for an e-mail reminder that will alert you when the next date the public can ride is approaching.

Yogi Bear's Jellystone Park Lonestar Campground. 34843 Betka Road, Waller; (713) 876-2237; www.lonestarcamping.com. For a summer fling, this recently renovated resort has a big new water park—with a large swimming pool, big water dump, slides, and a water blaster. The old pool is now an adults-only pool. Good family values is the theme here: Yogi raises the flag each morning and says the Pledge of Allegiance. There are animals to pet, hayrides, and fishing in the campground's lake (no license required). Tennis and basketball compete with putt-putt golf for favorite sport. Contact for reservations. Fee.

where to eat

Stockman's Restaurant. 2014 US 290, Waller; (936) 372-2060. Where else can you get all-you-can-eat charbroiled steak, this place's Tuesday-night special? In addition to a full menu, Thursday's special is charbroiled or deep-fried quail, and Friday's is all the catfish and popcorn shrimp you can handle. There's also a hot-plate lunch daily. Open Monday–Saturday for breakfast, lunch, and dinner; Sunday for breakfast and lunch. $–$$.

hempstead

Resist the opportunity to zip past Hempstead via the US 290 bypass. You'll find a lot of history, some discount shopping, and good eating in this quiet town.

Given its somewhat sleepy air today, it's hard to believe that Hempstead once was known as Six-Shooter Junction, and that for several decades after the Civil War, it was a wild and woolly place. The rolling land south of town was settled as early as 1821, although only scattered historical markers tell the stories now.

The town was platted in 1856–57 as the terminus for the Houston and Texas Central Railroad, an early line that tooted over much of Waller County before expanding north to Bryan–College Station. During the Civil War the railroad made Hempstead a major supply and troop depot for Confederate forces, and when the war ended, the defeated men began their long walks home from here.

Hempstead was the turning point in Texas's battle for independence from Mexico. Sam Houston and his retreating forces camped and regrouped here from March 31 to April 14, 1836, and then began an aggressive march to San Jacinto, site of their ultimate victory over Santa Anna and his Mexican Army. A brief jaunt down FM 1887 now finds a historical marker about the Texian Army camp.

Hempstead slowly is reawakening to its heritage, but at present all vintage structures remain in private hands and are not open to the public. A windshield tour of the quiet residential streets on either side of US 290 offers such rewards as Coburn Cottage, 327 Twelfth Street; the Ahrenbeck-Urban Home, 1203 Bellville Highway; and the Houx House, on the corner of US 290/Highway 6 and New Orleans Street.

Another good reason to stop in Hempstead is Dilorio's thriving produce market on US 290 at the southeastern edge of town.

what to do

Bluebonnet Herb Farms. 2015 Thirteenth Street; (979) 826-4290; www.bluebonnetherb farms.com. For some day-trippers the herb farm is a destination, for others it's the tearoom. You can browse garden herbs—culinary and medicinal—as well as pick up new landscaping ideas, perennials, small unique gifts, and collectibles. Known for its squash soup, the Secret Garden Tea Room may make the state's best chicken salad. The secret? Soak the chicken in balsamic vinegar, go light on the mayo, and put in purple onion, tarragon, and Craisins. Open Monday–Saturday; farm from 9:00 a.m. to 5:00 p.m.; Secret Garden from 11:00 a.m. to 3:00 p.m. $–$$.

Bomber Field. FM 1887, Monaville, between Hempstead and Brookshire; (281) 471-6762; www.bomberfieldusa.com. Annually in September on B-17 Weekend, a three-day event, more than 150 pilots fly their large-scale (largest wing span is 20 feet) radio-control replicas of World War II bombers at Bomber Field. Last year more than 3,000 spectators watched the bombers go through their maneuvers. The field hosts smaller groups of War-Bird Fly-Ins on summer Saturdays. Fee.

E & B Orchards. 28268 Clarke Bottom; (979) 826-6303; www.eandborchards.com. In season, these orchards have peaches, white nectarines, and blackberries. Call for information.

Frazier's Ornamental and Architectural Concrete. 48639 US 290; (979) 826-6760; www.fraziersconcrete.com. Escape the concrete jungle of Houston's freeway system with a visit to this two-acre retail center. You'll discover a wonderland of concrete products, ranging from garden statuary to tabletop creations, as well as aluminum garden decor and furniture and the fixings for backyard fountains and waterfalls. Open daily except Wednesday.

Liendo Plantation. From US 290 in Hempstead, turn northeast at the FM 1488 signal and then right on Wyatt Chapel Road. The plantation's gate will be 1 mile down on the right. Originally a Spanish land grant of 67,000 acres, Liendo was one of the earliest cotton plantations in Texas, and its large Greek Revival–style home was built by slave labor in 1853. During the Civil War Liendo served as a Union camp for Confederate prisoners directed by George A. Custer, and from 1873 to 1911 it was the home of sculptress Elisabet Ney and her husband, Dr. Edmond Montgomery. Both are buried on the grounds. Now privately owned, this gracious old home has been restored and furnished much as it would have been during its cotton-growing days. Liendo is a Texas Historic Landmark and is on the National Register of Historic Places. Docents give guided tours at specific times on the first Saturday of almost every month; groups with reservations are welcome at any time. A wonderful public event, the Old South Festival at Liendo shows off this handsome and historic home every spring. "Civil War Weekend"—reenactments of what older Southerners often term the "Late Unpleasantness"—draws visitors the weekend before Thanksgiving. At other times this is a private residence; please do not wander the grounds without an advance appointment. Fee. Call (979) 826-3126 or log on to www.liendo.org for details.

Peckerwood Garden. Just south of FM 359 and the Business 290 intersection, near Hempstead; (979) 826-4580; www.peckerwoodgarden.com. This seven-acre, private experimental garden emphasizes Mexican trees, shrubs, and perennials and their counterparts from Texas, the southeast United States, and Asia. Dry-land gardens dramatically contrast with lush woodlands and formal topiary. Tours are available by appointment ($60 per hour for one to six persons, $80 per hour for seven to ten persons; two-week advance notice required). The gardens also are open to the public on the third weekend of each month (afternoons only), March–October. For tour information call (979) 826-3232. The Yucca Do Nursery is open Thursday–Saturday, February–October. For a plant catalog write them at P.O. Box 907, Hempstead, TX 77445-0907.

where to eat

Feed Store Restaurant. 52130 US 290 West (2 miles past Highway 6); (979) 921-9119. This is as rural as it gets: In a recent previous life this eatery was a feed and tack store. Now a tearoom with longhorn-skull lighting and vintage farm equipment displays, it's not all country—the Italian dishes compete with the meat loaf. Open daily for lunch and dinner. $–$$.

Julio's Mexican Restaurant. 425 FM 1488; (979) 826-3435. You'll find several departures from standard Tex-Mex here, starting with the shrimp enchiladas and special steak plates. Open daily for lunch and dinner. $–$$.

Lucy's. 936 New Orleans Street; (979) 826-4400. Dining here feels a little like stepping back in time to the 1800s. Built in 1882, this home has belonged to eleven different owners over the years. In the restaurant, Southern-fried specialties include Gulf coast seafood and steaks. Open for lunch and dinner; call for days and hours. $–$$.

continuing on

From Hempstead this day trip now swings east on FM 1488 en route to Magnolia, passing through rolling, oak-studded terrain that rates with the prettiest countryside in the state. If you've already explored the FM 1488/Magnolia area, however, Hempstead offers several other travel choices.

The easiest is to continue on US 290 West to Chappell Hill and do all or part of Northwest Day Trip 5. Or you can swing southwest 16 miles on Highway 159 to Bellville and pick up West Day Trip 4.

If you elect to continue this day trip to Magnolia via FM 1488, you'll pass through the barely-there community of Fields Store. This crossroads area got its name back in the late

1800s because there used to be a store here owned by the Fields family. Beginning more than a century ago, neighbors would gather here on the Fourth of July to clean the local cemetery and have a picnic.

magnolia

This semi-rural crossroads town draws day-trippers to its area antiques stores (ten at last count). In-season visitors enjoy the pick-your-own fruits and flowers available.

what to do

The Great Western Trading Company. 30822 Nichols Sawmill Road; (281) 356-2165. (For details see "The Woodlands," in Northwest Day Trip 1.)

The King's Orchard. Route 2, Box 653, Plantersville (7 miles north of Magnolia on FM 1774); (936) 894-2766; www.kingsorchard.com. At various times during summer, you can pick your pleasure of strawberries, blueberries, blackberries, apples, peaches, figs, and Asian pears at this forty-five-acre farm. Open Tuesday–Sunday from the third Saturday in March to early September. Call for fruit availability. There's also a large picnic area as well as a small store selling drinks, jams and jellies, hats, and assorted small sundries.

Texas Opry House. 32243 Old Hempstead Road; (281) 356-6779. Country music in a country setting, this tidy, family-run operation has put on a lively two-hour music show featuring local entertainers every Saturday night, year-round, since 1986. Expect singers, dancers, actors, and comedians at this mini–Grand Ole Opry, all backed by the house band. Have you always had a hankering to be in showbiz? Give them a call; they hold tryouts on a regular schedule. No alcohol is served or allowed, but the concession stand does a land-office business in homemade cakes and brownies. Bring the kids. Fee.

The Texas Renaissance Festival. Six miles north of Magnolia on FM 1774, 6 miles south of Highway 105 in Plantersville; (281) 356-2178, (936) 894-2516, or (800) 458-3435; www.texrenfest.com. For seven weekends starting around October 1, the sights and sounds of Merrie Olde England brighten up this fifty-acre woodland park. Visitors are encouraged to dress to the sixteenth-century theme and cavort with the jugglers, sword swallowers, harpists, belly dancers, and jesters to their hearts' content. Swordsmen fence, Shakespeare enlivens the Globe Theatre stage, and King Henry and his royal court parade around the grounds at high noon. Grand fun for the entire family, with full-contact jousts, assorted craftspeople, stout food, and more. Fee, but ask in advance about sources for discount tickets. Children four and under are free. Also, plan some alternate routes home; the departing traffic south via FM 1774 and Highway 249 is always bumper-to-bumper from 3:00 p.m. on.

where to eat

Hickory Hollow Restaurant. 18537 FM 1488 (in the Renaissance Center); (281) 356-7885. Barbecue in all its forms, plus steaks, chicken, and catfish highlight the extensive menu at this popular family spot. There's often live country music in the back room on Friday night. Open for lunch and dinner daily. $–$$$.

Rancho Grande Mexican Restaurant. 18914 FM 1488; (281) 356-1700. Spirits perk up as you come through the door of this lively, well-decorated spot, and appetites follow as soon as you've checked the menu. Signature dishes include Atomic Tacos (flour tortillas filled with shrimp jalapeños) and a rib-eye steak cooked with fresh jalapeños, tomatoes, and onions. Eight additional shrimp entrees as well as eleven steak/chicken offerings are also on the menu, and all are a far cry from standard Tex-Mex. Combination lunch specials run from $4.25 to $5.75, and happy hour ('ritas and domestic beers, $2.50) runs 2:00–6:00 p.m. weekdays. Open daily for lunch and dinner. $–$$.

Relay Station Restaurant. 15680 Highway 105, Plantersville; (936) 894-3111. This combination icehouse and saloon is pure country, from the wood bar stools carved like horses' rear ends to the corral out back. Come on a Wednesday or Friday night and you may catch the local cowboys doing some team penning practice. No surprises on the menu, unless you take up their challenge: The eighty-five-ounce steak with trimmings is free if you eat it all in seventy-five minutes. Open 10:00 a.m.–10:00 p.m. on weekdays, until 11:00 p.m. on weekends. $–$$$.

Tavola's Bistro. 32623 FM 2978; (281) 252-8700; www.tavolaonline.com. Off the beaten path midway between Magnolia and the Woodlands, this delightful eatery is worth the search. Basically an outstanding catering operation, it offers both take-home selections via its "Gourmet to Go" and table service featuring inventive salads, sandwiches, soups, pastas, hot entrees, and desserts. The tasty house salad (fresh greens, sun-dried cranberries, chèvre, and candied pecans in a piquant dressing) becomes a meal with the addition of grilled chicken, and the Texas Turkey Panini includes oven-roasted turkey topped with Jack cheese and barbecue sauce. Feel free to BYOB; there's no corkage charge. Phone in your order, and it will be waiting for you to pick up. Open for lunch Monday–Friday. $–$$.

day trip 05

northwest

river roads:
chappell hill, washington-on-
the-brazos, navasota, anderson

chappell hill

From Houston this day trip follows U.S. Highway 290 northwest approximately 60 miles through Hempstead to the intersection of FM 1155. A short jog north then takes you to the first stop, Chappell Hill.

This charming village just north of US 290 may seem like the Brigadoon of Texas, so true is it to its time. Settled in 1847 and named for early Texas hunter Robert W. Chappell, Chappell Hill thrived as a stage stop on the Houston-to-Austin/Waco run and became the cultural center of Washington County, the home of two four-year universities. But the fickle tides of progress soon flowed on, and visitors today often feel they have stumbled on a quiet place left over from the 1880s.

The universities have long closed, their charters transferred to become the seeds of Southwestern University in Georgetown, Southern Methodist University in Dallas, and the University of Texas Medical Branch in Galveston. But the old Stagecoach Inn is still here, a private home restored to its antique glory, and the local bank, circa 1900, has its original brass teller's cage. *Fun to know:* This was the last bank in the region to register its customers by name instead of magnetic codes and computers.

More than twenty-five historical medallions are scattered throughout this four-street settlement. Two treasured homes currently offer bed-and-breakfast accommodations:

northwest day trip 05

Stagecoach Inn (979-830-8861; www.thestagecoachinn.com) and Southern Rose Ranch (979-251-7871; www.southernroseranch.com).

Make your first stop the town's visitor center, which is located on Main Street in the former parsonage of Providence Baptist Church. The dog trot–style home was built in 1855 and recently restored by the Chappell Hill Historical Society. The center is open Tuesday–Saturday. Other portions of Main Street and seven additional local sites are on the National Register of Historic Places, and several of them now house antiques shops.

This community hosts a number of family-friendly events throughout the year, including fall's fabulous Scarecrow Festival. Call the chamber of commerce at (979) 337-9910 or log on to www.chappellhilltx.com.

what to do

Browning Plantation. 9050 Browning Street (1 mile south of US 290, off FM 1371); (979) 836-6144; www.browningplantation.com/. Listed on the National Register of Historic Places, this three-story wood home was built as the heart of a 2,000-acre plantation in 1856 by Col. W. W. Browning, a loyal Confederate supporter and one of Chappell Hill's leading citizens. By the early 1980s, however, the house was a teetering ruin surrounded by 170 acres of wild country. Completely restored in 1985, this 6,000-square-foot house is once again an elegant charmer and filled with antiques. Tours are given by appointment, and five bedrooms are available for classy bed-and-breakfast, as well as a private pool house with two bedrooms, two full baths, and a full kitchen. Don't miss the "before" photos in the downstairs parlor. Fee.

Chappell Hill Historical Museum and Methodist Church. On Church Street, 1 long block east of Main; (979) 836-6033; www.chappellhillmuseum.org. The museum is in the old school and is staffed Wednesday–Saturday and on Sunday afternoon. The church has stained-glass windows worth seeing and is open for Sunday services. Donations are appreciated.

Chappell Hill Lavender Farm. Dillard Road; (979) 251-8114; www.chappellhilllavender.com. Stroll through fragrant fields and cut your own fresh lavender. The farm has 3,000 plants, a gazebo, and a pond—a nice place for a picnic. The Lavender Patch Gift Shop also has lavender for use in cooking. The farm is open weekends March–October and weekdays by appointment. Free.

Chappell Hill Sausage Co. 4255 Sausage Lane (on westbound side of US 290, 3.5 miles east of Chappell Hill); (979) 836-5830; www.chsausage.com. Six different kinds of sausage are made here, primarily for supermarkets around the state. You can watch the sausage-making process and buy your favorite to take home. Closed Sunday.

The 1873 Providence Baptist Church. Notable for the stone baptistery under its pulpit, this handsome old building on the east side of Chappell Hill's main street sparkles with fresh paint, courtesy of its owners, the Chappell Hill Historical Society. Church doors are open to the public only during special events or for groups with advance reservations. For information call (979) 836-6033.

Old Masonic Cemetery. Turn west at the four-way stop at Main and Chestnut Streets in Chappell Hill, then right on the first road for 0.5 mile. At least twenty-four Confederate soldiers are buried here, along with assorted Crocketts and the son and daughter of William Barret Travis. The latter were longtime residents of Chappell Hill.

Cemetery lovers also will enjoy the old Atkinson Cemetery, south of town on County Road 87.

Rock Store Museum. 5070 Main Street (east side of Main Street near the bank); (979) 836-6033. The prime display is the town's history, embroidered and appliquéd on two 30-foot cloth panels. Open weekend afternoons in spring, when the locals feel like socializing, or by appointment. Donations are appreciated.

Texana Cigar and Coffee Company. 5080 Main Street (east side of Main Street); (979) 251-7500 or (888) 845-0853; www.texanacigar.com. A strong tobacco trade flourished in this Brazos River Bottom area during the plantation era, and this small shop recalls the tradition. Nonsmoker? Try their specialty coffees and pecan-smoked jerky, another local specialty. Open daily.

where to eat

Bevers Kitchen. 5162 Main Street; (979) 836-4178. This combination house and restaurant serves salads and sandwiches, homemade soup and chili, chicken and dumplings, and chicken-fried steak. Mexican dishes are added on Wednesday. Open for lunch through 3:00 p.m. Monday–Saturday. $–$$.

washington-on-the-brazos

From Chappell Hill continue north 18 miles on FM 1155 to Washington-on-the-Brazos. Early settlers used this same route. This portion of Texas was crossed by countless trails that were the interstate highways of the seventeenth and eighteenth centuries, and numerous historical markers presently comment on three major routes. The Old San Antonio Road ran to the Louisiana border and passed to the north of Bryan–College Station. The Coushatta Trail through Grimes County to the north was part of the Contraband Trace, used for smuggling goods from Louisiana into Spanish Texas. A third trail, La Bahia, went from Goliad to the lower Louisiana border, sometimes running in tandem with the Old San Antonio Road.

In 1821 one of Stephen F. Austin's first settlers started a small farm and ferry service where the busy La Bahia Trail forded the Brazos River. In 1835 the settlement was capitalized as the Washington Town Company, lots were auctioned, and the raw beginnings of an organized town began to emerge on the river's west bank. It was to become a pivot point for history.

March of 1836 was a fateful month for Texas. While Santa Anna was devastating the Alamo, fifty-nine men were creating a sovereign nation, the Republic of Texas, at the constitutional convention at Washington-on-the-Brazos. Washington later served twice as the capital of Texas but ultimately lost that honor to Austin. Later bypassed by the railroads, the original settlement faded into obscurity and then literally disappeared after the Civil War. Today, a state park (see below) on the site honors Washington's status as "the birthplace of Texas." A major expansion has added a second visitor center, interactive exhibits, a restaurant/conference center, and a living-history farmstead focused on the early Texas frontier.

There's a lot to see and do in the Washington-Brenham area, so consider making advance reservations for lodging. One choice is Barrington, built around the original steps of the Anson Jones home 3 miles west of the park (936-878-2844 or 866-828-8471; www.barringtonbb.com). For a complete list call the Washington County Chamber of Commerce at (888) 273-6426 or log on to www.brenhamtx.org.

what to do

Live Oak Ranch Family Nudist Resort. Off Highway 105 in Washington; (936) 878-2216; www.liveoakresort.com/. This pretty, twenty-five-acre facility is dedicated to "the Joy of Natural Living," which means no one wears clothes. All ages are welcome, and first-timers are permitted to remain clothed for a reasonable time until they feel comfortable being in the nude. Facilities include a swimming pool, a hot tub, a water slide, a clubhouse with a big-screen TV, volleyball courts, pool tables, dart machines, and so on. The resort also offers RV hookups, tent campsites, rental cabins, and a full-service restaurant. No overtly sexual behavior is tolerated, and "undue" demonstrations of affection are considered to be in very poor taste. If you've always wondered what it would be like to go skinny-dipping or live without the constraint of clothing, this is the place. After a few tough minutes of wondering where to put your eyes, the scene becomes very natural, almost asexual. Although there are no age limits (families very welcome), persons under twenty-one must be accompanied by their parents. Fee.

Rio Red Ranches. 16747 FM 1155 East, Washington; (936) 878-9997; www.rioredranches .com. The ranch breeds miniature horses. Call for visiting information.

Washington-on-the-Brazos State Historical Park. On FM 1155 at the Brazos River in Washington (follow signs); (936) 878-2214; www.tpwd.state.tx.us. Only a handful of relatively new buildings mark where the Republic of Texas began in 1836. However, a $4.3-million legislative grant has expanded this 154-acre park to "living plantation—circa 1830" status. Additional land has been purchased, a restaurant and visitor center have been opened, and both the Star of the Republic Museum and Anson Jones's historic homeplace, Barrington, have changed in many ways.

Start at the visitor center, and do bring a lunch hamper to enjoy the shady picnic grounds along the Brazos River.

All the following are within the park's boundaries:

Barrington Living History Farm. This re-creation of plantation life in early Texas (1850s) centers on Barrington (1844–45), the restored antebellum home of the last president of the Republic of Texas, Anson Jones. A costumed staff, working with tools and livestock common to that period, go about their daily lives as though the Civil War had never happened. Even the cookbooks used in the kitchen are from the 1830–50 period. Visitors are welcome to pitch in with the chores, the better to understand what life was like before the advent of the gasoline engine. The site includes a barn, log cabin slave quarters, a functional kitchen separate from the main farmhouse, a smokehouse, and a visitor center. Open Wednesday–Sunday, year-round.

Independence Hall. This simple frame building is a reconstruction of the original structure on this site, in which the signing of the Texas Declaration of Independence took place. Open daily year-round. Fee.

Star of the Republic Museum. Greatly benefiting from the historical park's multimillion-dollar rejuvenation, this outstanding place is full of exhibits. Children love the interactive experiences provided by the Showers-Brown Discovery Room, while adults become immersed in learning about the various cultures that shaped the Lone Star state. Open daily, except for major holidays. Fee. For more information contact Star of the Republic Museum, P.O. Box 317, Washington, TX 77880; (979) 878-2461; www.starmuseum.org.

continuing on

After exploring Washington, continue north on FM 1155 to the Highway 105 intersection, and turn right to Navasota.

navasota

Settlers responding to Stephen F. Austin's advertisements for colonists founded this town in the 1820s. A generation later cotton was king of the plantation economy, thriving here on the rich bottomland of the Brazos River.

The coming of the railroad in the 1850s brought even larger profits, and the wealthy farmers splurged on lavish townhomes in Navasota, many of which remain in fine shape today and are worth a "windshield" tour. Some line Washington Avenue (Highway 105) as it flows through town, and others require short detours onto Johnson, Holland, and Brewer Streets.

One of those mansions, LaSalle House at 400 East Washington (936-825-3865), is an 1897 Queen Anne Victorian that houses an antiques co-op; house tours (fee) are available on weekends. Shoppers will find numerous other antiques shops and malls scattered around town.

Groups of fifteen or more can tour several other historic structures in and around Navasota by reservation. Information and walking- and driving-tour brochures are available from the Grimes County Chamber of Commerce, 117 South LaSalle (P.O. Box 530), Navasota, TX 77868; (936) 825-6600.

Not too surprisingly, Navasota stood heart and soul with the South during the Civil War, but unpaid Confederate soldiers angrily burned much of the town in 1865. A yellow fever epidemic two years later dealt the final economic blow. This quiet community of 7,000 now lies in the heart of horse-farm country, its downtown a National Historic District.

Even fewer traces of the area's Indian and Mexican history survive, and visitors often are startled to find a statue of French explorer La Salle in the center of the main road. It memorializes his death nearby in 1687 at the hands of his own men.

what to do

Americana Alpacas. On FM 2988 in Whitehall; (936) 870-3887; www.americana alpacas.com. One of South America's most important animals have found a home in the heart of Texas. The laid-back cousins of the llama, alpacas are prized for their fleece. Paul and Robin Roberts keep more than seventy alpacas on their ranch and welcome visitors who call ahead.

Bank of Navasota. 109 West Washington Avenue. This 1880s building has been restored to its original look and use. Open Monday–Friday and Saturday morning.

Gibbons Creek Reservoir. On FM 244 in Carlos, approximately 20 miles north of Navasota via Highway 90; (936) 873-2424; www.gibbonscreek.com. Operated by the Texas Municipal Power Authority, this 2,500-acre lake draws heavy-duty fisherfolk from as far away as Oklahoma and Arkansas. It's stocked by Texas Parks and Wildlife, and bass, crappie, catfish, and perch thrive here. Boating, camping (primitive and RV sites available), and pic-nicking are allowed, and there's even a place for swimming. Fee.

Horlock History Center. 1215 East Washington; (936) 825-7055. Navasota's past is doc-umented in this restored 1892 Victorian house. Open for tours by appointment only. Free.

Navasota Livestock Auction Co. 7846 Highway 90 South; (936) 825-6545; www.navasota livestock.com. Three miles east of Navasota on Highway 90 (also see Cow Talk Steak House in "Where to Eat" listings). Ranchers from Grimes, Washington, and Brazos Counties bring their livestock here for sale, making this auction the state champ in terms of volume and dollars. Visitors are welcome to watch the action, but don't scratch your nose or tug on your ear—you may go home with a live calf as a souvenir. Saturday sales start at 11:00 a.m.

Navasota Theatre Alliance. 104 West Washington; (936) 825-3195; www.nta-stage.org. This local theater group uses professional directors and set designers for five or six quality productions by major playwrights each year at the Sonny Furman Theater. Call for schedule.

The Wood Factory. 111 Railroad Street; (936) 825-7233. *Victoriana lovers' alert:* This antique millwork business welcomes visitors to its showroom in what was Navasota's old P. A. Smith Hotel. Whether you need any gingerbread trim or not, take a peek; many pieces of their early-twentieth-century equipment are as old as the designs they produce. Open business hours on weekdays only.

where to eat

Cafe M. Bloomers. 8101 Highway 6; (936) 870-3277. Located inside Martha's Bloomers, a garden store, this pretty tearoom serves homemade soups, pasta salads, quiches, and sandwiches with genteel names such as the Azalea (smoked turkey and cheddar) and Buttercup (chicken salad on a croissant). Save room for the warm fruit cobblers that are always topped with Blue Bell ice cream. Wine, beer, and strawberry lemonade also are on the menu. Open for lunch Tuesday–Sunday. $–$$.

Cow Talk Steak House. 7846 Highway 90 South (at the Navasota Livestock Auction Company, 3 miles east of Navasota on Highway 90); (936) 825-6993. Nothing like going straight to the source for good hamburgers and steaks. Open for breakfast and lunch Tuesday–Saturday. $–$$. No credit cards.

La Casita Mexican Restaurant. 9416 Highway 6 Bypass; (936) 870-3040. Super clean and bright, this place serves authentic Mexican food. If you're traveling early in the day, stop here for breakfast. Open daily for breakfast, lunch, and dinner. $–$$.

Ruthie's Bar-B-Que Cafe. 905 West Washington; (936) 825-2700. This seemingly undistinguished barbecue place is a Texas classic—six kinds of meat pit-smoked over oak and mesquite. It's so good that it has been mentioned in *Texas Monthly* magazine. Open Wednesday–Saturday for lunch and dinner. $–$$. No credit cards.

Serendipity's. 114 Farquhar; (936) 825-0711. Need a little pick-me-up? Stop by this tearoom for a fresh cup of gourmet coffee and maybe a cup of freshly made soup. A salad bar, soups, and sandwiches will sate the hungry. And there's Breyer's ice cream and handmade fudge for those with a sweet tooth. Open for breakfast and lunch Monday–Saturday. $. No credit cards.

continuing on

From Navasota this day trip travels to the tiny town of Anderson, 10 miles northeast via Highway 90.

anderson

Time stopped here about 1932, and the entire town looks like a stage set for *Bonnie and Clyde.* Fact is, one member of the Barrow gang was tried here in the old courthouse, a tidbit duly noted on the building's historical medallion. But Anderson's history reaches back much further than the 1930s.

Established in 1834 as a stage stop on the La Bahia Trail, the town became an important assembly point and arms depot during the Civil War. Those days of glory live again during Texian Days in late September, when local folks don period costumes and open their homes to visitors. The entire town—everything you can see from the top of the courthouse—is listed on the National Register of Historic Places. Antiques stores have begun to fill some of the vacant buildings along Main Street. For information on the town, call Historic Anderson, Inc., at (936) 873-2662 or (936) 873-2111.

what to do

Baptist Church. East side of Main Street, 2 blocks south of FM 1774. Built of native rock by slaves in 1855, this handsome church still has regular Sunday services. LBJ's granddaddy once was Anderson's preacher.

Christmas Creek Nature Preserve. Near Richards; (936) 851-0114; www.christmascreek .com. Nature park and bed-and-breakfast inn. See Northwest Day Trip 1 for details.

Fanthorp Inn State Historic Park. South end of Main Street on the left; (936) 873-2633; www.tpwd.state.tx.us. One of the first stage stops in Texas and the seed that started the town, this old inn was built in 1834 and led to Anderson's being, for a time, the fourth-largest town in Texas. Owned by the Texas Parks and Wildlife Department since 1977, the inn has been restored and returned to a somewhat rumpled 1850s appearance; visitors have a sense that one stage has just departed and another is on its way. A barn of that period has been reconstructed to house a Concord stagecoach (reproduction) as well as exhibits describing the early stage routes across Texas. Staffed with an interpreter, the inn is open Friday through Sunday for self-guided tours. If you want to tour on Wednesday or Thursday, call ahead; there's usually someone there. Want to ride through the streets of Anderson in a horse-drawn stagecoach? Come for Stagecoach Days on the second Saturday of every month. And for a look at what holiday travel was like in the mid-1800s, don't miss the candlelight festivities on the Saturday of Thanksgiving weekend. *NOTE:* No overnight or dining facilities are available at the inn. Fee.

Grimes County Courthouse. Top of Main Street; (936) 873-2111. Built in 1894 of hand-molded brick with native limestone trim, this oldie has its original vault. Note the handsome pressed-tin ceilings with rounded cove moldings in the main hall. Open weekday business hours.

Historic Anderson Park. South of the intersection of FM 1774 and Highway 90; (936) 873-2553. Several architectural relics of Anderson's past are preserved here, including the Steinhagen Log Cabin, built in 1852 by slaves and notable for its walls of unspliced hand-hewn timbers; the Steinhagen Home, with a wing furnished to its 1850s period; and the Boggess Store, filled with early-twentieth-century merchandise. These old buildings can be toured only during special events or by arrangement.

New York Row. Parallels Main Street 1 block east. This is where the town swells lived during Anderson's heyday. That was a long time ago, so you'll need to use your imagination.

wandering the back roads

For anyone who likes country drives, getting to and/or from Anderson via FM 1774 is pure pleasure. While spring is prime because of the wildflowers, an autumn drive recalls the rolling hills of western Massachusetts. The oaks turn color with the first frost, and Anderson's lone church steeple pokes up through the landscape like a sentinel on a hill.

day trip 06

northwest

>>> **must be heaven:**
brenham, burton, dime box,
somerville, independence

brenham

If it wasn't a 72-mile commute on U.S. Highway 290 each way, Brenham would be overrun with refugees from Houston. This thriving community of slightly more than 12,000 is close to the ideal American small town—old enough to be interesting but enterprising enough to keep up with the times.

Shaded residential streets still sport a number of antebellum and Victorian homes, and many of the early-twentieth-century buildings downtown are spiffed up and in use. Designated a Main Street City by the Texas Historical Commission, Brenham underwent major renovation in the form of new pocket parks, benches, and sidewalks. You'll also find new businesses in some of the remodeled downtown buildings.

Just blocks away it's open country again—thousands of acres of beautiful farmland. In spring the bluebonnets and other wildflowers are magnificent, a carpet of color rolling to all horizons.

Founded in 1844 and settled by German immigrants over the ensuing two decades, Brenham was occupied and partially burned by Union troops during the Civil War. Most of the town's surviving history can be seen on a windshield tour, courtesy of a free map and visitor's guide available from the Washington County Chamber of Commerce, 314 South Austin, Brenham, TX 77833; (979) 836-3695 or (888) 273-6426; www.brenhamtexas.com. Call in advance to arrange a guided tour of the downtown historic district. Groups should

northwest day trip 06

inquire about tours and use of the Citadel, a former country club (circa 1924) that has been restored to *Great Gatsby* elegance. Highly visible on the westbound side of US 290, it looks like a massive plantation house sitting in the middle of a young vineyard 3 miles east of town.

Should you enjoy Brenham too much to leave, there are a number of bed-and-breakfasts in town. Among them are the highly regarded Ant Street Inn (800-805-2600; www.antstreetinn.com), Far View (979-836-1672; www.farviewbedandbreakfast.com), Mariposa Ranch B&B (979-836-4737; www.mariposaranch.com), and Ingleside B&B (979-251-7707; www.inglesidebb.com).

Nearby Burton (next stop on this day trip) also has bed-and-breakfast accommodations.

what to do

Ant Street Historic District. This downtown section of Brenham has been undergoing a colorful renovation for several years and now sports numerous fresh exteriors. The historic district extends to the old Savitall Market at Commerce and Baylor Streets, now handsomely renovated into the Ant Street Inn and Gallery (800-805-2600), a fourteen-room bed-and-breakfast similar in quality to the Tremont House in Galveston. If you're planning a big party or wedding, check out the ballroom; that space also is used for frequent antiques auctions.

Bassett & Bassett Banking House. Corner of Market and Main Streets. This vintage bank has been restored as part of a Main Street revival program and is open during normal business hours.

Blue Bell Creameries. Take the FM 577 exit from either US 290 or Highway 105 and go north on FM 577; (800) 327-8135; www.bluebell.com. If you want to tour the ice-cream plant, call ahead to confirm space; tours are not offered every day or on weekends, and reservations are required. Fee. The Country Store and Ice Cream Parlour (where you can buy a bowl of your favorite Blue Bell flavor) is open Monday–Saturday from 9:00 a.m. to 3:00 p.m., March–December.

Brenham Heritage Museum. 105 South Market; (979) 830-8445. Housed in the refurbished and quite grand Federal Building (1915), this museum offers artifacts and memorabilia dating from 1844, the year Brenham was founded. Displays change monthly, and an 1879 Silsby steam-powered fire engine resides permanently in an exterior showcase. Open Wednesday–Saturday; call for hours. Fee.

Ellison's Greenhouses. 2107 East Stone Street; (979) 836-6011; www.ellisonsgreen houses.com. Whatever the holiday, celebrate it early by touring this colorful wholesale nursery. Seasonally, some five acres of greenhouses are filled with poinsettias, tulips, Easter lilies, hydrangeas, and much more. Retail trade is welcome, and visitors love the unique accessories and gifts. Tours (fee) are given daily by appointment. Closed days prior to major holidays.

Nice to know: Ellison's is particularly spectacular during their annual poinsettia celebration (fee) on the weekend prior to Thanksgiving. More than 80,000 poinsettias fill several greenhouses with Christmas cheer, and some of those plants go on to grace the State Capitol, the governor's mansion, and the George Bush Presidential Library.

Fireman's Park. 900 block of North Park Street; (979) 836-3695. This shady city park has a fully restored C. W. Parker carousel, manufactured for carnival touring prior to 1913 and one of only a few antique merry-go-rounds remaining in Texas. Now visible behind protective glass panels, this wonderful antique operates by appointment and whenever Brenham has a civic celebration in the park.

Gerson Artworks. 307 West Alamo; (979) 836-4935. Only the colorblind will have trouble finding artist Alan Gerson's multitoned purple house with its front yard filled with crazy sculpture. Look closely, and you'll see that one of the huge pieces on display began its useful life as a Volkswagen trunk lid. Not sure if you've found the right place? Watch for a fried egg on the front walk and slashes of red and blue neon in the windows. Gerson also sculpted the horses that pull the city's old steam fire engine outside the Brenham Heritage Museum, 105 South Market. Gerson's gallery usually is open daily; call to make sure he'll be there.

Giddings-Stone Mansion. 2203 Century Circle (near South Market and Stone Streets); (979) 836-1690; www.brenham-mansion.com. This twelve-room Greek Revival home, with its imposing galleries, was built in 1869 on a hill in what was then south of town. Now owned by the local Heritage Society, it has been restored to its early-twentieth-century elegance and is considered by historical architects to be one of the ten most significant old homes in Texas. Tours (fee) are offered on weekends, April–June; groups by appointment. It also can be rented for special events such as weddings and meetings.

Giddings-Wilkin House. 805 Crockett; (979) 836-1690. Built in 1843, this is thought to be the oldest house still standing in Brenham. Now the property of the Heritage Society, it sometimes is open as a museum and can be toured by appointment.

Glasco's Gardens. 601 North Horton; (979) 836-3210; www.glascolandscape.com. This professional landscaping company welcomes visitors to its water and perennial gardens during business hours, Monday–Saturday. Tour groups welcome.

Miniature Horses at the Monastery of St. Clare. 9300 Highway 105 (9 miles northeast of Brenham via Highway 105); (979) 836-9652; www.monasteryminiaturehorses.com. The breeding, training, and sale of miniature horses are self-support ventures of this cloistered order, the Franciscan Poor Clares, and three of the nuns are permitted to show the public around this ninety-eight-acre facility. The grounds, chapel, and gift shop are open from 2:00 to 4:00 p.m. daily, plus there's a self-guided tour that shows off these pint-size animals. Spring visitors see twenty to thirty foals, each about 18 inches tall, cavorting in fields filled with wildflowers; there is a public show in September. Individuals and families are welcome year-round; bus tours only by advance reservation. You'll also find a picnic area here. Fee for guided tours; self-guided tours are free.

Nueces Canyon Ranch Resort and Equestrian Center. 9501 US 290 west (8 miles west of Brenham); (979) 289-5600 or (800) 925-5058; www.nuecescanyon.com. This well-designed horse show and training complex has something going on—cutting horse competitions, hunter/jumper shows, barrel racing, and so on—nearly every weekend. Passersby are welcome to watch the action and walk through the training barns, and there's a pretty area where you can picnic. Groups with advance arrangements can tour this working ranch (fee), which also offers bed-and-breakfast for both humans and horses.

Pleasant Hill Winery. 1441 Salem Road, Brenham; (979) 830-8463; www.pleasanthill winery.com. From US 290 turn south on Highway 36 (Belleville Road) to Salem. Tours (fee) of this vineyard follow the path of the grape as it makes its transition from vine to fruit to wine. You then get to taste the results. Open weekend afternoons year-round.

Unity Theatre. Corner of Church and Commerce Streets, Brenham; (979) 830-8358; www.unitybrenham.org. This nonprofit playhouse abandoned its spot on the city's popular square in the spring of 2002 for spacious new digs in a nearby historical warehouse. Combining professional and amateur talent, the company produces a variety of musicals and dramas throughout the year, and it generally plays to full houses. Call for a performance schedule, and consider overnighting at one of the area's bed-and-breakfasts. Performance tickets start at $18. Reservations are recommended.

where to eat

The Bread Basket. 210 East Alamo; (979) 836-9441. The staff at this gingham-decked cafe bakes fresh yeast rolls daily, and the blue-plate specials are substantial and popular with the downtown Brenham business community. Open for breakfast and lunch Tuesday–Sunday. $–$$. No credit cards.

Country Inn II. 1000 East Horton, across from the Washington County Fairgrounds on Loop 577; (979) 836-2396. Beef steaks with all the trimmings are the house specialty, generously cut with good ol' boys' hearty appetites in mind. The menu also offers fish, shrimp, and hamburgers. Open for lunch and dinner Monday–Saturday. $–$$.

Ernie's. 103 South Baylor; (979) 836-7545; www.erniesrestaurant.com. Downtown, this American bistro in an 1840s tavern has lunch specials, salads, and sandwiches. Evening fare includes fine wines, surprises such as Australian lamb and chicken saltimbocca, and Angus beef. Open for lunch and dinner Tuesday–Saturday; Sunday brunch. $–$$$.

Funky Art Cafe. 202 Commerce (inside the Pomegranate shop); (979) 836-1199. Need a coffee fix or a light lunch? This tiny spot serves salads, soups and sandwiches, and coffee drinks, along with biscotti, baklava, and a variety of gourmet foods and candies. Coffee bar open Monday–Saturday 8:30 a.m. to 5:30 p.m.; lunch served Tuesday–Friday 11:00 a.m. to 2:00 p.m. $.

Legends Billiards and Grill. 100 West Main; (979) 251-7665. A sports bar with big-screen TV, this spot also serves a variety of freshly grilled hamburgers. Open daily from 11:00 a.m. until midnight. $–$$.

Manuel's Mexican Restaurant & Taqueria. 409 West Main; (979) 277-9620. While handy with all the standards, this place is well liked locally for its weekday lunch buffet and chicken, pork, and beef fajitas. Open for lunch and dinner daily; breakfast Thursday–Sunday. $–$$.

Must Be Heaven Sandwich Shoppe. 107 West Alamo; (979) 830-8536; www.mustbe heaven.com/breakfast. These folks have a strong local following for their tasty cakes, pies, and other pastries. There's Blue Bell ice cream, along with homemade soups, salads, sand-wiches, and quiche. Open Monday–Saturday for breakfast and lunch (until 5:00 p.m.) and Sunday midday. $–$$. No credit cards.

Purcell's Country Style Buffet. 2800 Highway 36 South; (979) 836-9508. You pay first and then feast on all the food you want, served from the long steam tables in the center of this clean and spacious eatery. Entrees come multiple choice, from herbed chicken to carved beef and ham, plus there's a seafood buffet on Friday night. Open daily for lunch and dinner. $–$$.

The Southern Flyer. 3001 Aviation Way at the Brenham Municipal Airport; (979) 836-5462; www.brenhammunicipalairport.com. You don't need an airplane to take a trip here. Guests are transported to the 1950s the minute they step into this diner with its Formica tabletops, wall-mounted jukeboxes, and poodle-skirted waitresses. The food is as old-fashioned (and delicious) as the setting: hefty burgers accompanied by homemade onion rings; chicken-fried steaks served with buttery lima beans and corn casserole; and pasta topped with chicken parmigiana. And there's always a parade of private aircraft coming and going for entertain-ment. Open for lunch Sunday–Wednesday; lunch and dinner Thursday–Saturday. $$.

Tex's Barbecue. 4807 Highway 105; (979) 836-5962. When the thought of open-pit bar-becue stirs up an appetite, try here. If the weather's nice, try the picnic area or take-out serv-ice. Open for lunch Wednesday–Sunday. $. No credit cards.

Volaré. 102 South Ross Street; (979) 836-1514; www.volareitalianrestaurant.com. Chef Silvio DiGennaro brings the flavors of his native Sicily to numerous Italian entrees here. Housed in a New England salt-box-style building, it is a nice spot for lunch or dinner, Tuesday–Saturday. Closed between 2:00 and 5:00 p.m. Reservations recommended. $$.

burton

Continue west from Brenham on US 290 to visit the reviving small town of Burton, popula-tion 369. Founded in 1862 and named for an early settler, Burton's early success was due to its location along the tracks of the Houston and Texas Central Railway. Its rail station, opened in 1898, still can be viewed.

Enjoying yourself too much to leave? Consider overnighting at the Knittel Homestead (979-289-5102; www.knittelhomestead.com), which includes an 1870s building that origi-nally served as the town's post office.

what to do

Burton Cotton Gin and Museum. 307 North Main; (979) 289-3378; www.cottongin museum.org. When it was constructed in 1914, the Burton Farmers Gin represented the lat-est technology of its age. The cotton went from wagon to bale on a system of pulleys and conveyors all powered by a single engine. During its heyday, the Burton gin was only one of 4,000 gins operating in cotton-rich Texas. As the cattle industry grew, cotton farmers began to disappear. In 1974, its last year of operation, the gin produced just seven bales of cotton.

Now listed on the National Register of Historic Places as well as being designated a National Mechanical Engineering Landmark by the American Association of Mechanical Engineers, the gin has been lovingly restored and is the heart of a nine-acre museum com-plex. In addition to the gin and cotton-related farm machinery, visitors can see the restored Lady B, a Bessemer Type IV oil engine that powered the gin for thirty-eight years; the Wehring Shoe and Leather shop, which opened in 1923; and a circa-1919 car dealership and garage.

Each April the museum hosts Burton's Cotton Gin Festival, which celebrates small-town farm life. Activities include folk-life demonstrations, live music, and a parade.

The museum is open Monday–Saturday year-round, and guided tours are available. During the summer months, when temperatures inside the gin can reach more than one hundred degrees, tours are offered only in the morning. Call ahead to confirm business hours and tour availability. Fee.

where to eat

Brazos Belle Restaurant. 600 North Main; (979) 289-2677; www.brazosbelle restaurant.com. André Delacroix, a French-born chef (formerly at the Four Seasons Hotel in Houston), and his wife, Sandy, serve deliciously untrendy country food with French touches in one of Burton's most venerable buildings. Expect blue and white checkered place mats, fresh vegetables, exceptional breads, and a changeable feast of professional-quality art on the walls, most of which is for sale. Delacroix's skill shines in the Belle's signature dish, a grilled fillet of Norwegian salmon that's seasoned in a fresh lemongrass marinade and topped with a fresh tomato-caper sauce. You'll want to come back, as well, to sample other menu items such as large Gulf shrimp seasoned in a lavender marinade, a spicy cassoulet, and medallions of filet mignon. Open for dinner Friday and Saturday, brunch on Sunday. Reservations suggested. $$–$$$. No credit cards.

The Burton Cafe. 12513 Washington Street (on FM 390, behind the post office); (979) 289-3849. Homespun vittles and charm carry the day at this friendly place, considered by many people to be one of the best country cafes in the state. The roast beef platters are great, the homemade bread and veggies are locally produced, the pies are made from scratch, and the breakfasts are humongous. Want to know what's going on in the Brenham-Burton neighborhood? Just sit a spell and listen; you'll soon know as much as the locals. Open Monday, Thursday, Friday, and Saturday for breakfast, lunch, and dinner; Tuesday and Wednesday for breakfast and lunch. $–$$. No credit cards.

continuing on

From Burton you can complete this day trip by swinging northwest on FM 1697 and FM 141 to Dime Box and some areas of Lake Somerville. Or you can bypass Dime Box and reach Somerville by following FM 390 northeast to its intersection with either FM 1948 (turn north) or Highway 36 (turn northwest).

An alternative route follows Highway 105 northeast from Brenham to Navasota (see details under Navasota in Northwest Day Trip 5), or you can jog south from Brenham on Highway 389 (see West Day Trip 4).

dime box—old and new

The name alone of these two separate communities brings some explorers. Perhaps this explanation will save some time, gasoline, and tempers.

Old Dime Box is on Highway 21, sort of around the corner a few miles from new Dime Box on FM 141. The only things of visitor interest in both places are the historical plaques explaining that the town name comes from the old custom of leaving dimes in the community mailbox on the Old San Antonio Road (Highway 21) in return for items brought by rural delivery from Giddings.

If you do explore in and around Dime Box, you can get back on your original day-trip route by following Highway 21 northeast to Caldwell and then Highway 36 south to Somerville. Continuing on Highway 21 northeast from Caldwell brings you to College Station (see Northwest Day Trip 3).

somerville

Who would think that three little creeks could combine to form a 24,000-acre lake? Dammed in the early 1960s as a flood control and water conservation project, Lake Somerville has become a favorite water playground 88 miles northwest of Houston on Highway 36.

The town itself serves only as a gas and grocery supply depot—the lake is the big attraction. Popular with boaters, this lake offers excellent fishing for largemouth and white bass, white crappie, and channel catfish. Deer and other wildlife abound, particularly on the islands within this relatively shallow lake. Birding is varied enough to warrant a special brochure and field checklist, available free from the Texas Parks and Wildlife Department, Resource Management Section, 4200 Smith School Road, Austin, TX 78744; (800) 792-1112; www.tpwd.state.tx.us.

Campers, picnickers, boaters, hikers, and equestrians should investigate the following: *Rocky Creek Park, Yegua Creek Park,* and *Overlook Park,* operated by the U.S. Corps of Engineers (979-596-1622 or 979-596-2383); for campsite reservations sixty to ninety days in advance, call (877) 444-6777.

Welch Park, operated by the City of Somerville (979-596-1122).

Birch Creek Park (979-535-7763) and *Nails Creek Park* (979-289-2392), operated by the Texas State Park system (800-792-1112).

what to do

Somerville Area Museum. Highway 36 at Eighth Street; (979) 569-2383. The tiny town of Somerville isn't completely without indoor attractions. Supported by the Somerville Historical Society, the museum is housed in a one-hundred-year-old building that once was a saloon. Exhibits include American Indian and pioneer artifacts as well as photographs and memorabilia that trace the town's history. Open Saturday–Sunday and by appointment.

where to eat

Country Inn. 900 Avenue B (on west side of Highway 36 South on the southern edge of town); (979) 596-1222. This Aggie-land favorite serves many things but is known for its huge, tender steaks. The smallest is a one-and-a-half- to two-pound T-bone, and both the bounty and the doggie-bag hauls increase from there. Come hungry: The medium (two and one-half to three pounds) and the large (three and one-half pounds) sirloins literally fall off their serving plates. Open for lunch and dinner daily except Monday. Reservations are taken Tuesday–Friday but not on weekends. If the weather's nice, expect a very long wait for space in this sixteen-table spot. $–$$$.

continuing on

Your day trip continues south on Highway 36 from Somerville to FM 390. Turn northeast (left) to Independence. This scenic route (FM 390) follows portions of old La Bahia Trail, a prehistoric track that was by the 1830s one of three main highways in Texas. La Salle met his death on this trail (near Navasota) in 1687. Stephen F. Austin and his followers knew it well, and Davy Crockett used it to reach Goliad, en route to the Alamo. Today it's just a glorious country ramble, a two-lane exploration of horse ranch country that follows a high ridge through Washington and Grimes Counties. Take time to explore some of the side roads, and to admire the old Seward Plantation, a white ghost from the 1850s that crowns one oak-covered hill. A brochure covering other historic highlights is available from the Washington County Chamber of Commerce, 314 South Austin, Brenham, TX 77833; (979) 836-3695 or (888) 273-6226; www.brenhamtx.org.

independence

As far as Washington County is concerned, Independence is where it all started. Originally called Coles Settlement for its first pioneer, John P. Coles, the town changed its name in 1836 to celebrate Texas's independence from Mexico. Coles was a member of Stephen F. Austin's original 300 families, and his cedar log and frame cabin, built in 1824, stands just east of town at the entrance to Old Baylor Park. The town's interesting cemetery, about 2 miles north of the park entrance on County Road 60, is equally old.

When Brenham won election as the county seat by two votes, Independence began a century-long slide into obscurity. Today it is a mecca for Texana lovers because of its old stone church and historic ruins. The second house east of the FM 50/FM 390 intersection was the last home (circa 1863) of Mrs. Sam Houston; unfortunately, it currently is closed to the public. A second Houston homesite across from Old Baylor Park has a granite marker. For bed-and-breakfasts contact the Captain Clay Bed & Breakfast (979-836-5134; www.captainclaybnb.com) or Country Place Cottage (979-836-6429; www.countryplacebnb.com).

what to do

The Antique Rose Emporium. 9300 Lueckemeyer Road, Brenham (0.5 mile south of the FM 390 intersection on FM 50); (979) 836-5548 (retail) or (800) 441-0002; www.weare roses.com. More than 200 varieties of old garden roses, documented to have grown in Texas during its years as a republic, thrive here on the site of the Hairston-McKnight Homestead, settled in the 1840s. The remains of an old stone kitchen (circa 1855) have been restored as the center of a typical cottage garden of those times, a converted barn is now the office and bookstore, and an old corncrib has become a gift shop featuring rose-related items. There's also a selection of native Texas trees, shrubs, vines, wildflower seeds, and other plant species appropriate to the climate and locale. Open daily.

Independence Baptist Church. 10405 FM 50, Brenham (at the intersection of FM 50 and FM 390); (979) 836-5117. Organized in 1839, the church's present stone building was finished in 1872 and still hosts services every Sunday. Sam Houston saw the light here and was baptized in nearby Rocky Creek.

Old Baylor Park and Ruins of Old Baylor University. One-half mile west of the church on FM 390; (979) 830-0230. This birth site of Baylor University now is marked only by a few ghostly columns and some old oaks and is a good place to enjoy a picnic. It's also prime territory for bluebonnets in March and early April. The Coles Cabin has been relocated here and can be toured by appointment, as can a one-room schoolhouse. Tours also on weekend afternoons in March and April. Donation.

Seward Plantation. 10005 FM 390, Brenham (0.7 mile west of FM 50 in Independence); (979) 830-5388; www.independencetx.com/SewardPlantation.htm. The headquarters of a 1,000-acre plantation in the 1850s cotton era and on the Texas Register of Historic Sites, this handsome old place has been owned and occupied by the same family since its foundation was laid. This gracious piece of the past still has many of its original furnishings. The grounds also include log slave quarters and barns. Open only by appointment to groups of ten or more. Fee.

Texas Baptist Historical Center and Museum. 10405 FM 50, Brenham; (979) 836-5117. Adjacent to the Independence Baptist Church, this museum houses pre–Civil War artifacts as well as old church and family records. Mrs. Sam Houston (Margaret Moffet Lea) and her mother are buried in a somewhat unlovely site across the street. Open Tuesday–Saturday. Free.

Windy Hill Winery. 4232 Clover Road, Brenham; (979) 836-3252; www.windyhillwinery.net. August and Linda Meitzen built their small family winery on a hill with a view of the countryside. A gray tiger-striped cat guards the vineyard, and the couple—rightly proud of 1837 Texas family ancestry—use 100 percent Texas-grown grapes in Windy Hill wine. They invite you to stop by, relax, and sample the taste of true Texas wine. Open Friday–Sunday, with tours by appointment.

wandering the back roads

Independence is the last stop on this day trip, but you can easily extend your travels. Following FM 390 east brings you to Highway 105. Turn northeast (left) and you can tour Washington-on-the-Brazos, Navasota, and Anderson (see Northwest Day Trip 5). An alternative is to continue south from Independence on FM 50 to Highway 105 and Brenham, connecting there either with Highway 389 and West Day Trip 4 or with Highway 36 South to Bellville and home (see West Day Trip 4).

west

day trip 01

west

the way west:
west houston, katy, brookshire,
san felipe, sealy

west houston

Because this day trip begins with a drive west on Interstate 10, consider stopping on the western outskirts of town for one of the following activities:

what to do

Albert Alkek Velodrome. 19008 Saums Road in Cullen Park; (281) 578-0693; www .houstontx.gov/parks. Take the Barker-Cypress exit from I-10 and go north 1 mile to the park. Built for the 1986 U.S. Olympic Festival, this is one of only twenty Olympic-quality velodromes in the country and often the site of national cycling events. The overall program includes general riding sessions, developmental cycling classes for beginners, races for graduates of that program, and a Friday-night racing series open only to USCF-licensed riders. Helmets and track bikes can be rented on-site; spectating is free. Call for a brochure and seasonal schedule.

Flying at West Houston Airport. 18000 Groeschke Road, Houston; (281) 492-2130; www.westhoustonairport.com. Take Barker-Cypress exit from I-10 and follow the airport signs north to a left turn on Groeschke Road. You too can discover the wonder of flying in a four-seat Cessna. Discovery flights (thirty minutes) are $99 in this high-winged plane. Sightseeing and photography flights also can be reserved, starting at $110 per hour in the four-seater. Reservations required.

west day trip 01

Hot-air ballooning. Several companies will take you for a silent float over Houston for sixty to ninety minutes in a three-person basket suspended below a giant hot-air balloon. Most liftoffs are at sunrise to take advantage of the still air, and costs are in the range of $350 and up per couple, including champagne at the end of the trip. Pricey but worth it for a once-in-a-lifetime experience. Get the particulars from Airventure Ballooning, (713) 774-2359; www .txhotair.com.

continuing on

To continue this day trip, take I-10 West to the Katy exit.

katy

Founded as a rice and railroad town, Katy now is of interest to day-trippers primarily as a great spot to eat, play, shop, and experience China. You'll find a smattering of gift and antiques shops in "Old Towne" and several places to picnic. It's also a good food stop Tuesday–Saturday if you're returning to Houston on I-10 from points west.

what to do

Forbidden Gardens. 23500 Franz Road; (281) 347-8000; www.forbidden-gardens.com. From Houston take the Grand Parkway exit from I-10, turn north, then west on Franz Road; watch for orange pagoda roofs. Block some time for this handsome, forty-acre, open-air museum, which authentically replicates major scenes from China's history, starting in the third century B.C. Handmade in China by gifted artisans who then installed their work on the Katy prairie, the exhibits include a huge and intricate scale model of Beijing's Forbidden City, detailed models of Chinese palaces, a one-third-scale reproduction of the entire 6,000-piece terra-cotta army (no two soldiers are alike) found in burial pits of China's first emperor, and replicas of the weapons used by that first emperor to conquer and meld several warring states into one empire. Also here is a 100-foot-long model of Su Zhou, a city known as the Venice of China, detailed with various types of houses, shops, and temples as well as miniature figures of people going about their daily routines. Hourly guided tours are included in admission fee ($10 per adult, $5 for students and seniors, five and under free with a paid admission). Parking is free. Open Friday–Sunday 10:00 a.m.–3:30 p.m., weather permitting (call ahead to confirm times).

Katy Heritage Museum. 6202 George Bush Drive; (281) 391-4844. Opened in the spring of 2002, this museum pays tribute to Katy's farming roots. Among the exhibits here are a 1914 Model T roadster, a 1925 truck once used to haul rice to market, and artifacts from the old Robertson Store, including a coffee grinder, scale, and rice shovel. Next door to the

Heritage Museum is the Veteran's Memorial Museum, known locally as the "G.I. Joe Museum." Free. Open Tuesday and Thursday 10:00 a.m.–2:00 p.m.

Katy VFW Veterans Memorial Museum and Community Park. George Bush Drive and Avenue D; (281) 391-8387; www.ci.katy.tx.us/museums.html. This oak-shaded retreat offers picnic tables, a small playground, and indoor exhibits focused on America's participation in foreign wars. Free. Park is open daily; call for museum's open days and hours.

Mary Jo Peckham Park and Katy City Park. 5597 Gardenia Lane; (281) 391-4482. These blended play spaces offer miniature golf, playgrounds, picnic areas, a fishing lake, a caboose, and the old Katy Railroad depot. Open daily.

Nelson Water Gardens. 1502 Katy Fort Bend County Road; (281) 391-4769; www.nelson watergardens.com. Where else in the Houston area can you find acres of exotic goldfish amid blooming lotus and water lilies? The shop sells everything needed to rejuvenate or create your water garden, but visitors are welcome to just browse among the thirty production ponds out back. These folks also publish a large color catalog and even mail goldfish. Open daily in summer, Monday–Saturday in winter.

Waterfowl hunting trips. For guided hunts on the Katy and Eagle Lake prairies, call (281) 392-8999 or (281) 391-6100.

where to eat

John & Ann's Pie Shoppe. 5608 Fifth Street; (281) 391-8088. Need a box lunch to eat here or to go? For $6.50 you get a great sandwich, chips, drink, and a slice of their super homemade pie. This tiny spot also makes a special quiche daily as well as fruit, cream, and specialty pies to order. Prefer sugar-free? Just let them know. Open Tuesday–Saturday for lunch. $–$$. No credit cards.

brookshire

Brookshire's history is brief. This small community was established in the early 1880s by the MKT Railroad to serve a rich agricultural area. Its ethnic past ranges from Polish to German, Greek to Czech, Swiss to Armenian. The Waller County Festival is an energetic melding of these cultures every October.

what to do

Blue Barn Fun Farm. On FM 1458, approximately 0.5 mile west of FM 359; (281) 375-6669; www.bluebarnfunfarm.com. This ten-acre country learning experience is run with loving care by longtime farmers Dan and Paula Brubaker to educate children about country life.

Following a basic program set up with the assistance of Texas A&M, pint-size visitors learn how to milk a cow and get to try the hands-on method themselves. They also pet calves, baby chicks, and a soft-shell turtle; jig for crawfish; and get up close to doves, bullfrogs, pigs, deer, geese, ducks, quail, golden pheasants, bobwhite quail, guinea hens, ring-necked pheasants, rabbits, goats, chickens, and turkeys. A small plastic horse is used to teach children how to mount and rope. A tractor-drawn hay wagon then hauls everyone to a picnic area shaded by huge oaks, so pack a picnic hamper when you come; cold drinks are sold on the premises. July visitors are given free watermelon, August visitors get stone-ground cornmeal and a recipe for corn bread, October and November visitors receive free pumpkins, and December visitors go home with candy canes. Cost is $6 per person in groups of twenty or more; $7 per person (including children) for individuals. Open daily. Absolutely no admittance without advance reservations.

Bomber Field. FM 1887, Monaville, between Hempstead and Brookshire; (281) 471-6762; www.bomberfieldusa.com. See Northwest Day Trip 4 for details.

The Brookwood Community. 1752 FM 1489, 1 mile south of I-10 (signs); (281) 375-2100; www.brookwoodcommunity.org. This handsome, 475-acre country facility is a privately funded community for functionally disabled adults (mentally and/or physically handicapped), aided in part by volunteers. Institutional gloom is not found here, however. Brookwood looks like the home most people only dream about and functions like a successful company. Their bedding and potted plants and art are sold not only on the premises but also through Brookwood's four retail outlets in the Houston area. Tours are given the first Wednesday of every month by appointment. In addition to lunch in the Brookwood Cafe (see "Where to Eat"), visitors can purchase Brookwood's original ceramics, garden sculptures, silk-screened notes and cards, and plants at the Garden Center, open Monday–Saturday 9:00 a.m. to 4:30 p.m. and Sunday noon to 4:30 p.m.

Dewberry Farm. 7705 FM 362, 7 miles north of Brookshire; (281) 934-3276 or (866) 908-3276; www.dewberryfarm.com. Meet barnyard animals, ride a barrel train, or get lost in a corn maze at this cheery agricultural-themed playground. Many activities are seasonal, so call ahead to see what's happening on the farm. Fee.

The Waller County Historical Museum. 906 Cooper; (281) 934-2826; www.wlrctyhistsoc .org. Built in 1910, this nice old home houses period furnishings, historical artifacts and documents, and some interesting vintage photos. Free, but donations are welcome. Open Wednesday–Friday and Saturday midday. Call for hours.

where to eat

Brookwood Cafe. 1752 FM 1489; (281) 375-2400. When you want a midweek lunch prepared by a chef trained at the Culinary Art Institute and formerly with Maxim's, call in advance for reservations here. The menu offers hot entrees, salads, and desserts. Open for lunch only, Tuesday–Sunday. $$.

wandering the back roads

If you are coming from the FM 1960/Highway 6 area of Houston and prefer back roads, swing west on FM 529 and then south on FM 362 to Brookshire. Going home, just reverse those directions to miss the traffic crunch on Highway 6 near Bear Creek.

If you love country drives, save some time for wandering south of I-10 on FM 1489. This is horse and cotton-growing country, and the ranches and farms are beautiful. The road passes through the small communities of Simonton, Wallis, and East Bernard, an excellent route into the southwest sectors described in this book.

continuing on

To find San Felipe either drive west from Brookshire on I-10 for 8 miles and watch for the exit signs to Stephen F. Austin State Park, or follow the country route via FM 359 northwest to Pattison and then west on FM 1458. The latter is a great country ramble along the route of the pioneers.

san felipe

Alas, how fleeting is fame. From 1823 to 1836 San Felipe collected enough "firsts" to secure its niche in Texas history. Then known as San Felipe de Austin, it was the original settlement and capital of Stephen F. Austin's first colony. It also was the site of the first Anglo newspaper and postal system in the territory and the founding spot of the Texas Rangers. The town was burned in 1836 to prevent its use by the advancing Mexican Army. Although rebuilt later in that decade, San Felipe never regained its earlier momentum.

In addition to visiting the oldest post office in Texas, visitors today find some pieces of San Felipe's past in and around the state park. Stop first at the small historical park where FM 1458 crosses the Brazos and search for the still visible traces of wagon ruts that lead to the old ferry crossing. A dog-trot log cabin replicates Austin's headquarters, and the J. J. Josey Store, built in 1847, has been restored as a museum. Unfortunately, neither is open very often. Bring a lunch; there's a shady picnic ground along the river on the other side of the road.

Stephen F. Austin State Park (979-885-3613 or 800-792-1112; www.tpwd.state.tx.us) is nearby and open daily, year-round; watch for the Park Road 38 turnoff from FM 1458. This park offers an outstanding eighteen-hole golf course, as well as picnicking, camping, fishing, and numerous other family activities. As an oak-shaded retreat, it's wonderful on warm weather weekends. Fee.

continuing on

After enjoying San Felipe and the park, resist the temptation to take back roads to Sealy. The route that forks to the right immediately outside the park gate is frustrating and non-scenic. Instead, return to I-10 and continue west to the Sealy exit.

sealy

San Felipe sold a portion of its original 22,000-acre township to the Gulf, Colorado, and Santa Fe Railroad in the 1870s to create the town of Sealy in 1879. That town now bills itself as the "Best Little Hometown in Texas" and collects a few more refugee Houstonians every month.

Is there any connection with the Sealy mattress? Yes, indeed. A Sealy businessman named Haynes made the first tufted mattress early in the twentieth century, and folks referred to it as "that mattress from Sealy."

Visitors enjoy a drive down Sealy's oak-shaded Fifth Street, with its early-twentieth-century homes, and a walk around the downtown area, which is being restored to its original appearance. There are numerous antiques shops, most of which have free walking maps of the town.

For information on Sealy, San Felipe, or Frydek, contact the Sealy Chamber of Commerce, 309 Main Street, Sealy, TX 77474; (979) 885-3222; www.sealycvb.org.

what to do

Haynes Mattress Factory. 109 North Hardeman; (979) 885-3222. Discover Sealy's connection to a good night's sleep. Daniel Haynes used his expertise as a cotton-gin builder to create a machine that compressed cotton for use in mattresses. Haynes started his mattress-making business in 1885 and later patented his machine in 1889. One early national ad campaign featured the slogan: "Sleeping on a Sealy is like sleeping on a cloud." The factory with its original equipment is open for tours the third Thursday of each month or by appointment. A donation is appreciated.

Lonestar Motorsports Park. 120 Old Columbus Road; (979) 877-0922; www.lonestar motorsportspark.com. Coming from Houston, take exit 713 from I-10, go over the interstate, and turn right on the feeder road; the race track will be on your left. Motorcycles, modified cars, and dragsters (some with drivers in the eight-to-sixteen age category) test their stuff on this 0.8-mile dragstrip; spectators are welcome. Open weekends year-round, weather permitting. Call for race information. Fee.

Port City Stockyards. North of Sealy on Highway 36; (979) 885-3526; www.port-city.com. This is one of the largest cattle auction operations in America, and visitors are welcome. Cattle are auctioned on Wednesday afternoon year-round.

Santa Fe Park Museum. On Main Street; (979) 885-3222. Includes artifacts from the early days of Sealy and Austin County. Just look for the small tin building with bright flowers, a flagpole, and a grader in the front yard. Open by appointment.

Thomas Family Berries. 12753 Hahn Road; (979) 865-9796; www.myspace.com/thomas familyberries. In season, this farm produces blackberries. Call for information.

where to eat

Hinze's Bar-B-Que. 2101 Highway 36 South; (979) 885-7808. Well known for outstanding meats and sauce, this spot has been featured several times in the *Houston Chronicle* and was voted one of the ten best barbecue restaurants in the state by the readers of an Austin newspaper. Open daily for lunch and dinner. $–$$.

Tony's Restaurant. 1629 Meyer (Highway 36); (979) 885-4140. Breakfast anytime and a full menu and noon buffet make this a popular eatery. Open daily for breakfast, lunch, and dinner. $–$$.

day trip 02

west

heart of history:
columbus, frelsburg,
new ulm, cat spring

columbus

Some 56 miles west of Houston's city limits via Interstate 10, Columbus is in one of the old-est inhabited areas of the state. The early Spanish maps of Texas marked this as a sizable Indian village known as Montezuma, and Stephen F. Austin's first colonists called it Beason's Ferry. Now, as Columbus (population 4,800), it is one of the prettiest and most historic towns in Texas. As you stroll through the shady town square, it's hard to believe that the busy interstate zips by less than 1 mile to the south.

Back in 1823 Stephen F. Austin brought a survey party to this fertile land looped by the Colorado River, thinking it would make a fine headquarters and capital for his first settle-ment. The river was deep enough for commerce, and the busy Atascosito Trail crossed the river nearby. But this was Karankawa country—the Karankawas were a fierce Indian tribe labeled by history as cannibals—and the threat made San Felipe a better choice.

Some of Austin's colony did settle here, however, and a tiny village named Columbus was laid out in 1835. Its life was brief. In March 1836 Gen. Sam Houston and his Texian forces retreated from Gonzales and camped in Columbus on the east bank of the Colorado River. The pursuing Mexican Army settled in on the west bank, where it soon was reinforced by additional troops.

Knowing his position was weak and that an attack on the Mexicans would be suicide for both his men and the cause of Texas independence, Houston elected to retreat farther.

west day trip 02

Moving to Hempstead (see Northwest Day Trip 4), he ordered all the buildings in and around Columbus burned so that they would be of no use to the Mexicans. Caught in the middle, the local residents fled east to safety, a migration termed by history as the "Runaway Scrape."

Houston's strategy was vindicated by his victory over Santa Anna and the Mexican Army at San Jacinto the following month, and slowly Columbus began to build again. Today it is a delightful small town full of live oak and magnolia trees. If you're into superlatives, drive by the massive oak at 1218 Walnut, the second largest in the state. Thanks to large natural deposits of sand and gravel, Columbus literally is where Houston comes from—approximately 90 percent of the aggregate used to construct Houston's skyscrapers was excavated nearby.

The town's mainstay always has been the river on its doorstep. Early settlers floated their construction lumber downstream from pine forests near Bastrop, and by the mid-nineteenth century paddle wheelers were making regular runs between Columbus, Austin, and Matagorda. Dressed up with names such as *Moccasin Belle, Flying Jenny,* and *Kate Ward,* these flat-bottom boats also carried cotton from large plantations south of town to the shipping docks at Matagorda Bay (see Southwest Day Trip 1).

The river still figures in the town's life, as a source of natural beauty and recreation. A 6-mile stretch of it has been designated an Inland Paddling Trail by Texas Parks and Wildlife. To enjoy it, put in at the North River Bridge (Highway 71 North) and take out at historic Beason's Park near the East River Bridge (U.S. Highway 90). Local canoe rentals and livery service are available (see "What to Do"). Beason's Park is a year-round rallying point for cyclists and runners and is the site where Gen. Sam Houston's army camped prior to declaring victory over the Mexican Army at San Jacinto.

Wide and smooth (and usually opaque with sediment), with only a few small rapids, the Colorado River at Columbus is relatively safe for novice canoeists. The numerous long sandbars make night floats a timeless experience. Moonlight glows from these freshwater beaches, and the wildlife show is fascinating as the river comes alive with beaver, deer, and raccoons.

Exploring Columbus and its numerous heritage medallion homes is easy with the *Historical Talking Houses Audio Tour,* prepared by the Columbus Convention and Visitors Bureau and available weekdays at 435 Spring Street, across from Courthouse Square. It's also available by mail: P.O. Box 98, Columbus, TX 78934. Call (979) 732-8385 or (877) 444-7339 for information. The CCVB also can advise you in regard to the historical homes offering bed-and-breakfast and on the best wildflower routes in spring. Check those out at www.columbustexas.org.

what to do

Alley Log Cabin. 1224 Bowie. Built in 1836 by Abraham Alley, one of Stephen F. Austin's original "Old Three Hundred" colonists, this square-notch oak cabin was moved into town in 1976 from its original site at the Atascosito crossing of the Colorado River. Open Monday–Friday.

Canoeing. Howell Cone Livery (528 Jackson Street; 979-732-3816) rents canoes, inner tubes, and kayaks. He provides shuttle service, organizes special river-based events, and said, "Recently, Texas Parks and Wildlife designated six miles of the river as an Inland Paddling Trail." It also has a picnic area. Open sunrise to sunset.

Colorado County Courthouse. Bounded by Spring, Milam, Walnut, and Travis Streets on Courthouse Square. Built in 1890–91, this is the third courthouse on the same site and still the county seat. The four-faced clock is original, but its steeple fell in a 1909 hurricane and was replaced by a neoclassic dome. A full restoration completed in 1980 uncovered a handsome stained-glass dome above the district courtroom, hidden for generations behind a false ceiling. The courthouse is open Monday–Friday.

Take special note of the stump of the famous Courthouse Oak, 2,000 years old and the site of the first district court held in 1837. At that time the first courthouse on this site had been burned by Houston's forces, and a second one had yet to be built. Judge R. M. Williamson, known as "Three-Legged Willie" because of his false leg, elected to hear cases under this tree.

Columbus Opry. 715 Walnut Street (the Oaks Theatre); (979) 732-9210 or (979) 732-6510; www.columbusopry.com. Named the best of its kind in the nation in 1996, 1997, and 1998 by the Country Music Association, this bit of Nashville in the heart of Texas showcases outstanding local and regional country-western talent and regularly draws professional scouts on Saturday nights. There's lots of audience-performer interaction and a wholesome "no alcohol, no smoking" environment suitable for families. Fee; free for children under six.

Confederate Memorial Museum and Veterans Hall. On the southwest corner of Courthouse Square; (979) 732-8385. This old water tower was built 400,000 bricks strong in 1883. Dynamite didn't dent it in a later demolition attempt, so the United Daughters of the Confederacy decided it was a safe repository for their treasures. The exhibits feature clothing, small possessions, articles, documents, and pictures of early Columbus, including artifacts from the "Old Three Hundred," as Stephen F. Austin's first colony was known. Donation. Open during the May homes tour and for groups by prior arrangement.

Dilue Rose Harris House. 602 Washington; (979) 732-8385. Built of tabby in 1858, this house museum is filled with Texas primitives and early Victorian furniture. Open during May homes tour and by private arrangement.

1886 Stafford Bank and Opera House. 425 Spring Street (across from Courthouse Square); (979) 732-8385. Built by millionaire cattleman R. E. Stafford in 1886 for a reputed $50,000, this elegant old building originally housed Stafford's bank on the first floor and a 1,000-seat theater upstairs, where such headliners as Lillian Russell and Al Jolson performed. Today the showbiz names may not be so grand, but the theater is, thanks to an eighteen-year, $1.5-million restoration financed entirely by local residents. The original 15-foot chandelier and the first elaborate stage curtain have been reproduced, and a variety of entertainments once again bring up the footlights. There are monthly dinner theater performances September–July. Don't miss either the museum on the first floor or the unusual marble cornerstone. The opera house also is open to visitors Monday–Saturday and during the homes tour in May. Fee for tours.

Fishing. Bass and catfish await in the Colorado River. You'll find a public boat ramp at the North River Bridge.

Grave of the Infidel. Odd Fellows Cemetery on Montezuma Street. Like all frontiers, the Columbus area attracted characters. Back in the 1890s Ike Towell made a name for himself as an outspoken atheist. The town marshal, he also was instrumental in the establishment of Jim Crowism in the area. He wrote his own funeral service, and his tombstone reads HERE LIES IKE TOWELL, AN INFIDEL, WHO HAD NO HOPE OF HEAVEN OR FEAR OF HELL.

"Gunsmoke" at the Brune Land and Cattle Company. Take the Highway 71 (Austin) exit from I-10 for 7 miles, turn left on FM 1890, and watch for signs. A nonprofit organization that promotes the sport of cowboy action shooting and safe gun handling, the Texas Historical Shootist Society holds cowboy shoot-outs here every third Sunday of the month. The society also hosts "Trailhead," a yearly shoot-out and gathering for society members on the fourth weekend of March that includes a trail ride through bluebonnet country, shooting competitions, a vendors' row, games, crafts, a campfire sing-along, liar's contest, and so on. Visitors are welcome to come and watch, but no children under eight, please. For information write the Texas Historical Shootist Society, P.O. Box 216, Barker, TX 77413, or log on to www.thss.org.

Hunting. Colorado County is happy hunting grounds for deer, quail, dove, and geese. Every winter it becomes the goose capital of the world because of its location on the central flyway. Arrangements to hunt can be made through the Clifton Tyler's Goose Hunting Club (goose and wild duck guide, day and season hunting; 103 Mesquite Street, Columbus, TX 78934; 979-732-6502; www.texasgoosehunt.com).

Live Oak Arts Center. 1014 Milam; (409) 732-8398. Housed in a historic building, this gallery's exhibits change monthly and feature both local and internationally known artists. Open Wednesday–Saturday.

Nesbitt Memorial Library. 529 Washington; (979) 732-3392. Root-tracers prize this library's archives room for its regional genealogical information. Children and collectors love it for its antique doll and toy collection. Open weekdays, Saturday until 4:00 p.m.

Preston Kyle Shatto Wildlife Museum. 1002 Milam; (979) 732-5135; www.pkswildlife museum.com. Animal trophies from around the world are shown here in simple dioramas. Open 10:00 a.m. to 2:00 p.m. on the first and third Thursdays, September–June. Call ahead to confirm operating hours. Donation.

Santa Claus Museum: The collection of Mary Elizabeth Hopkins. 604 Washington; (979) 732-5135. A walk through twentieth-century American pop culture, this museum features more than 2,000 representations of the jolly elf in every form imaginable. The collection dates from 1913 and features artifacts distributed by the world's most recognized manufacturers, retailers, and artists: Thomas Nast, Norman Rockwell, Steiff Co., Coca-Cola, Neiman Marcus, and more. Open Monday and Thursday. Fee.

Splashway Family Waterpark. P.O. Box 85, Sheridan, TX 77475; (979) 234-7718; www.splashway.org. Can't stand the heat? Cool off at this four-and-a-half-acre water park. Among its attractions are a 100-foot water slide, a 900-foot rolling river, and a high-thrill wave pool. Play beach volleyball or water volleyball, or just watch the toddlers splash in the children's wet playground. Call for directions. Fee.

where to eat

Mikeska's Barbeque. Located at exit 698 in Columbus; (979) 732-3101; www.jerry mikeska.com. Known as the barbecue king of the Southwest to local folks, Jerry Mikeska not only sells his tasty ribs, sausage, and brisket in Columbus but also caters for events as far away as Washington, D.C. Open for lunch and dinner daily, with a buffet on Sunday morning. $. No credit cards.

Schobel's Restaurant. 2020 Milam; (979) 732-2385. Convenient from I-10, this family restaurant cuts its own steaks, grinds its own hamburger meat, and makes its own pies. The menu also includes seafood and Mexican dishes, and there are large buffets at the daily lunch and on Friday night. Open daily for lunch and dinner. $–$$.

continuing on

Columbus is the gateway to all of Austin and Fayette Counties, rolling farmland that still looks much as it did when it was settled by Polish, German, and Czech immigrants in the 1800s. FM 109 North continues this day trip through that territory to the small German communities of Frelsburg and New Ulm.

frelsburg

When you stop to chat in this region, don't be surprised to hear strong German accents. The ethnic heritage of this community, 12 miles north of Columbus via FM 109, runs deep. The town is named for John and William Frels, who settled here in the 1830s.

You'll see Saints Peter and Paul Catholic Church on a hill as you approach on FM 109. Although this particular Catholic sanctuary was built in 1927, the parish it serves was organized in 1847 and is the oldest in Texas. Visitors are welcome either to celebrate Mass or to view the three carved wood altars. Nearby and a bit more humble in its architecture, St. John's Lutheran Church (1855–56) and its churchyard look like New England transplants.

Heinsohen's General Store has served this area for generations. If you stop in to buy a cool drink, you'll find it stocks everything from the latest in electronic games to pegged pants. Don't leave without buying some of the home-done pickles.

The big doin's in Frelsburg is the annual Fireman's Picnic on the second weekend in June. A fund-raiser, it also is an enjoyable look at a small, still very German community in the heart of Texas.

what to do

Raisin' L Ranch. Off FM 2503 in Ellinger; (979) 732-9511; www.raisinlranch.com. Calling itself a quail hunting plantation, this operation offers day hunts for beginners and experienced sports shooters. An experienced guide and hunting dogs are part of the package, as is lunch and trap shooting. Fee. Call for reservations.

Texas Falls Golf and Country Club. Three miles east of FM 109 via Dr. Neal Road, between Frelsburg and New Ulm (watch for signs); (979) 992-3123; www.thefallsresort.com. The golf course of this large real estate development is ranked highly in Texas among golf pros, a demanding eighteen holes designed by Jay Riviere and Dave Marr. Expect bent-grass greens, a series of clear-water lakes, and numerous waterfalls. Golf fees vary; call for tee times three days in advance if possible. The resort's restaurant is open on weekends ($–$$). Two-bedroom villas with kitchens and swimming pool privileges also are available for overnight guests. Closed on Tuesday.

continuing on

From Frelsburg continue north on FM 109 to the more sizable community of New Ulm, population 650.

new ulm

Also founded by Germans and Czechs in the early 1800s, New Ulm soon may be in for its second golden age. Back in the 1940s the entrepreneurial Glenn McCarthy made some Texas-size bucks in the nearby Frelsburg oil field and brought lots of his Hollywood friends to the quiet streets of New Ulm. New wells are hinting at another wave of prosperity sometime in the future. In the meantime enjoy the simplicity and old-time rural architecture of this crossroads settlement as part of a country drive. This also is spectacular wildflower territory in the spring.

where to eat

Texas Star Cafe. 24131 Bastrop Street; (979) 992-3522. Big portions, plate lunches, a fresh salad bar, and homemade desserts like tres lesches cake and buttermilk pie distinguish the Star. Its 16 oz. T-bone steak deserves attention, too. Advice for first-timers at lunch: Come early because those plate lunches sell out fast. Open for breakfast, lunch, and dinner Monday–Saturday. $–$$.

wandering the back roads

This day trip continues on to Cat Spring via FM 1094 East. Other options from New Ulm include taking FM 109 North to Industry and then jogging either northwest on FM 1457 to Winedale and Round Top or turning east on Highway 159 to Bellville. All are part of West Day Trip 4.

cat spring

When the wildflowers bloom in late March and early April, this tidy crossroads community looks like a calendar picture. As you come into town on FM 1094 from Frelsberg, watch for an unusual twelve-sided building on a rise to the left. This is the Cat Spring Agricultural Society Hall, built in 1902 and still the heart of community activities.

The Cat Spring Agricultural Society was founded in 1856 and is considered the forerunner of today's Texas Agricultural Extension Service. Early German and Czech farmers pooled their knowledge through this society, keeping explicit planting and production records of their small cotton and grain farms in a central book. All entries were written in German until America entered World War I; the practice was then deemed unwise, and all records thereafter were written in English. They are still used as a reference by local farmers.

If you want to use Cat Spring as a touring base, consider overnighting at Southwind Bed and Breakfast (979-992-3270; www.catspringbnb.com), a working spread for registered Texas Longhorns. If you have a horse and would love some country riding, bring it with you; Southwind has an old restored barn with twelve stalls.

what to do

Rancho Texcellente. Paso Fino Road; (979) 865-3636; www.paso.net. This 250-acre working ranch holds open house on Saturday for visitors interested in Paso Fino horses (appointments preferred). They love to show off their beautiful stock and even offer riding lessons ($30 per hour) to visitors who would like to saddle up for a guided trail ride. Also here: stock-tank fishing and bed-and-breakfast accommodations for those who want to experience ranch life. Call for directions.

where to eat

Carol's in Cat Spring. 10745 FM 949; (979) 865-1100. This elegantly casual restaurant has become a destination for Houstonians enamored with chef Doug Atkinson's imaginative regional fare. Try the oysters with a chipotle rémoulade, the grilled salmon topped with mango and black bean salsa, or the fettuccine with bison, sun-dried tomatoes, basil, garlic, olive oil, capers, and pecans. Desserts are outstanding, and the wine list is better than many found in the big city. Whether you're a banker from the city or a rancher from over the hill, owner Carol Davis will make you feel at home. Open for dinner Wednesday–Sunday and lunch/brunch Saturday–Sunday. $$–$$$.

Cross Road Tavern. At the corner of FM 949 and FM 1094; (979) 357-4808. This gasoline station also sells hamburgers at lunch daily and puts on all-you-can-eat catfish fries on Friday nights. $–$$.

wandering the back roads

From Cat Spring you have several choices. A turn southeast on FM 1094 takes you to Sealy and access to I-10 east for a swift return to Houston. If, however, you want to journey on, swing northeast on FM 2429 to connect with Highway 36 North to Bellville (see West Day Trip 4).

Yet another alternative is to head home the slow way, taking in some sights as you go. To do the latter from Sealy, take FM 3013 southwest 11 miles to the Attwater Prairie Chicken National Wildlife Refuge (979-234-3278). This 8,000-acre preserve is the happy "booming" grounds (mid-February through April) for the nearly extinct Attwater's prairie chicken. Each male prairie chicken has his own domain and protects it with a war dance, a real sight to see. Rangers may restrict public access, however, to protect the birds, so inquire before you make this jaunt. Day visitors usually can drive 5 miles of road through this preserve, plus there are two walking trails; binoculars are highly desirable. This refuge also has a high resident bird population and harbors migratory flocks in winter as well. More than 250 species of flowering plants have been recorded here, which makes a spring visit exceptional. This refuge is open year-round, with some picnic facilities, but call in advance for advice.

A second option from Sealy follows Highway 36 south to Wallis and a visit to Guardian Angel Catholic Church, one of the most beautiful painted churches in the state. Watch for signs to the church. Organized in 1892 by several Czech families, this church's interior and stained-glass windows rival those found near Schulenburg (see West Day Trip 3). The church doors normally are open during the day.

From Wallis FM 1093 East more or less parallels I-10, ultimately becoming Westheimer Road in far west Houston.

The area around Cat Spring is threaded with small country roads, and rambling is a joy. Be sure, however, that you have a good state highway map in hand if you care where you end up.

day trip 03

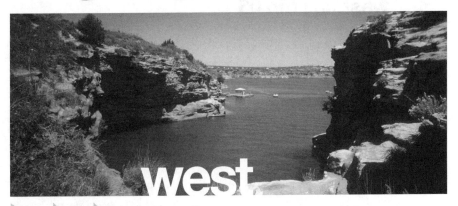

west

the painted churches:
schulenburg, la grange, fayetteville

schulenburg

Begin this trip by driving due west from Houston on Interstate 10 to the Schulenburg exit and turning south on U.S. Highway 77.

Like Sealy, this is a railroad town, created in 1873 when the fledgling Galveston, Harrisburg, and San Antonio Railroad purchased a right-of-way across Louis Schulenburg's farm and built a station. Folks living in nearby High Hill used log rollers pulled by oxen to move their homes and business buildings 3 miles south to the new town site, and Schulenburg began to thrive.

Local residents still tell time by train whistles, and day-trippers find an architecturally interesting Main Street (particularly the 400–600 blocks), numerous historic sites, and a string of "painted churches" beautifully representative of the area's strong Czech, Austrian, and German heritage.

Strong ethnic traditions make the Schulenburg Festival a big event the first full weekend in August. For additional information and a driving-tour map, contact the Schulenburg Chamber of Commerce, 618 North Main, Schulenburg, TX 78956; (979) 743-4514; www.schulenburgchamber.org.

west day trip 03

what to do

Itsy Bitsy Burro Company of Cedar Grove Farm. North of Schulenburg; call (979) 247-4965 for an appointment and directions; www.lildonk.com. Basically a breeding farm for miniature donkeys, this place also has Norwich terriers, and cattle fields line the long drive up to the 1860s ranch house. This is an ideal place to show off the best of country life to children, but appointments are required.

The Old Anderson Place. 510 South Main Street. Built before 1857 and later the home of Louis Schulenburg, this is thought to be the oldest occupied house in the area. Privately owned, it is not open for tours. Do not disturb the occupants.

Painted Church Driving Tour. An interesting map to the rural countryside around Schulenburg is available from the chamber of commerce. It will lead you to the tiny Czech settlement of Dubina and its beautifully frescoed Saints Cyril & Methodius Catholic Church, to Ammannsville and the unusual stenciled Gothic interior of St. John the Baptist Catholic Church, to Praha and the painted murals of the Blessed Virgin Mary Catholic Church, and to High Hill and the painted murals of St. Mary's Catholic Church. En route and worth seeing are a Russian-styled house and (near Dubina) a century-old iron bridge over the Navidad River. Most of the churches are still in use and may or may not be open; best consult in advance with the Schulenburg Chamber of Commerce, which also provides guided tours by advance appointment.

Stanzel Model Aircraft Museum. 311 Baumgarten; (979) 743-6559; www.stanzel museum.org. This petite but first-rate museum focuses on the mechanical and marketing genius of native sons Victor and Joe Stanzel, whose toy factory operated in the area for more than fifty years. The brothers held more than twenty-five patents, including one for a rocket-inspired carnival ride. A must-stop for flight and toy enthusiasts. Closed Tuesday and Thursday September–June. Fee.

Von Minden Hotel. 607 Lyons; (979) 743-3714. The hotel, which was completed in 1929, is a rare example of what was a very popular combination in the Northeast in its day: the hotel with "cozy theater." It was a wedding present to Ruby and Ben Speckles by Ruby's parents, the Von Mindens. Ghost enthusiasts flock to the hotel hoping for a sighting of Ben and Ruby, who ran the hotel/theater for more than fifty years and are said to haunt the place. Stop by the hotel's pizza restaurant, if you dare.

where to eat

Frank's Restaurant. At the intersection of I-10 and US 77; (979) 743-3555. A favorite stop for travelers roaming between Houston and San Antonio, this spot has been serving up Texas standards since 1929. Open daily for breakfast, lunch, and dinner. $–$$.

Kountry Bakery. 110 Kessler (US 77 North); (979) 743-4342. While a great spot for home-made breads, cookies, pies, sweet rolls, and the like, this fragrant place also serves salads, breakfast tacos, stew, chili, soups, burgers, sandwiches, and daily specials. Check the blackboard for the cook's selections. Closed on Wednesday. Open other weekdays from 5:30 a.m. to 5:00 p.m., Saturday until 2:00 p.m. $. No credit cards.

Oakridge Restaurant & BBQ Smokehouse. At the intersection of US 77 and I-10, exit 674; (979) 743-3372 or (800) 320-5766; www.oakridge-smokehouse.com. This long-established family restaurant smokes its own meats and makes its own sausage, but you'll find chicken, burgers, fish, and buffet offerings here as well. In addition to patio dining on nice days, there's a small playground for children and a gift shop. Open daily for breakfast, lunch, and dinner. $–$$.

wandering the back roads

If you want to explore farther, consider deviating briefly from this day trip itinerary to visit Flatonia, 12 miles farther west and well beyond the 110-mile limit of this book. While I-10 and U.S. Highway 90 are hardly back roads, they are time-savers and the most direct routes. Another railroad town, Flatonia was established in 1875 and is where many of the eggs sold in Houston are laid. Prime sights include a historical museum in the old Flatonia Bank Building, an 1886 mercantile (open daily except Sunday), and the oldest operating newspaper (1875) in the county. For information call the Flatonia Chamber of Commerce at (361) 865-3920 or log on to www.flatonia-tx.com.

While you're in the territory, visit Praha on FM 1295, off US 90, 3 miles east of Flatonia. The first Czech settlement in Texas, this tiny community and its large church host Czechs from all over America for homecoming in mid-August, a festival that began in 1856.

la grange

There are two ways to get to La Grange from Houston, but they both follow I-10 West some 56 miles to Columbus. There you can either take Highway 71 northwest 26 miles to La Grange or continue on the interstate another 21 miles to the US 77 exit, then go north 16 miles to your destination.

Long before TV personality Marvin Zindler focused the bright lights of TV publicity and traditional morality on Miss Mona and her Chicken Ranch on the outskirts of town (*Best Little Whorehouse in Texas*) some years ago, La Grange had a colorful personality. A bear of a man known as Strap Buckner was running an Indian trading post here by 1819, and local legend says he cleared the site of La Grange in a wild wrestling match with Satan.

Whatever the truth, a small community began about 1831 where the La Bahia Trail crossed the Colorado River, and some of Stephen F. Austin's first colony helped tame the land. By 1837 the town known as La Grange was the seat of government for Fayette

County. The courthouse, built in the 1890s, stands in the town square, and its original clock still chimes the hour.

Pause for a moment under the once glorious Muster Oak on the square's northeast corner. Through six conflicts starting with the Mexican attack of 1842, La Grange's able-bodied men have gathered here with their families before leaving for battle. The tradition took a 1990s twist during Iraq's occupation of Kuwait. When area army reserve units came through La Grange, they found Muster Oak wrapped with a giant yellow bow.

La Grange is a nerve center for wildflower tours in the spring, and the local chamber of commerce will help you plan a driving route. Whenever you come, spend some time exploring the city's historical square, slowly being restored to old-time character via the Main Street Program. Walking-tour brochures as well as guides to area antiques shops and cemeteries are available at the chamber of commerce, 171 South Main, La Grange; (979) 968-5756 or (800) 524-7264; www.lagrangetx.org. Those offices are housed in what was the old Fayette County Jail, built in 1883 and used until 1985. Now renovated, the old jail serves also as a tourist information center and as a museum displaying relics and memorabilia of former law enforcement officers.

Should you decide to linger, you'll find bed-and-breakfast at Big Tin Flag Bed & Breakfast (866-405-1158; www.bigtinflag.net), Blue Willow Farm Bed & Breakfast (979-968-5964; www.faycovet.com/BB.html), and Brendan Manor (866-658-1100; www.brendanmanor.com).

what to do

Fayette County Heritage Museum and Library. 855 South Jefferson Street (across from the Faison home); (979) 968-6418. A local bicentennial project, the museum has changing exhibits and special humidified archives to preserve historic documents. Open Tuesday–Sunday, but hours vary.

Hermes Drug Store. 148 Washington (across from the courthouse); (979) 968-5835. Established in 1856, this is the oldest drugstore in continuous operation in Texas. Visitors expecting a vintage site will be disappointed, however; although many of the original fixtures and beveled mirrors remain, the interior otherwise is very much of our times. Open Monday–Friday, Saturday until noon.

Holy Rosary Catholic Church in Hostyn. From La Grange take US 77 South approximately 5 miles, and then turn west on FM 2436 for 1 mile. Even non-Catholics enjoy strolling on this hilltop, noted for its large stations of the cross, grottoes, shrines, Civil War cannon, and replica of the first log church on this site.

The Jersey Barnyard. 3117 Highway 159; (979) 249-3017; www.texasjersey.com. More than 300 cows are milked at this dairy twice a day, and you're welcome to see how it's done. This guided educational tour includes a tractor-pulled hayride to the milking barns, a milking demonstration, plus the chance to pet or feed goats, chickens, fish, calves, cows, pigs, ducks, bunnies, and a donkey. *Fun to know:* This is home to "Belle, the Singing Cow" of Blue Bell ice cream commercial fame. Open daily except Wednesday by advance appointment only. Fee.

KatySweet Confectioners. 4321 West Highway 71; (979) 242-5172; www.katysweet .com. If you call in advance for reservations, these folks will show you how they make bonbons, pralines, fudge, and other indulgences; tastes are part of the tour. Open weekday business hours.

Monument Hill and Kreische Brewery State Historical Park. 414 State Loop 92 (2 miles south of town off US 77); (979) 968-5658; www.tpwd.state.tx.us. Even after the Texans' historic victory at San Jacinto, the Mexican Army continued to raid this portion of Texas through the following decade. The tragic 1842 Dawson Massacre near San Antonio and the ill-fated Mier Expedition are the focus of this memorial. Both are lesser-known but interesting chapters of Lone Star history. This popular picnic site, high on a bluff overlooking the Colorado River, features a nature walk through the woods and one wheelchair-accessible trail. The view north from the overlook includes the old La Bahia Trail crossing on the river.

In 1978 the adjacent Kreische Brewery and home site were added to the facility and subsequently restored. Kreische was a skilled stonemason and brewer from Europe who established this first brewery in Texas between 1860 and 1870 below his home on what is now Monument Hill. Ultimately it became the third-largest brewery in the state, and his product, a dark beer called Frisch Auf, was sold at his beer garden. The restoration has cleaned out the springs that provided water for the brewery and stabilized the old buildings. Guided tours down to the brewery are given on weekends. Open daily. Fee.

Mountain Biking at Bluff Creek Ranch. 537 Owl Creek Road, Warda; (979) 242-5894; www.bcrwarda.com. From the Columbus exit on I-10 West, take Highway 71 North to La Grange, turning north on US 77 for 10 miles to Warda. Turn right on Owl Creek Road (Fayette County Road 152) and go 0.5 mile to a red and white sign. This private, 200-acre longhorn cattle and Arabian horse ranch offers 10 miles of challenging mountain bike trails through meadows and creeks as well as forested and hilly terrain. Rated intermediate to expert, some of the hard dirt trails are easy enough for new riders. Bluff Creek hosts several major races annually. Bikers also can camp here—there are restrooms with showers—and recently they added a rustic bunkhouse. There are rental bikes and a shop on-site. Fees.

N. W. Faison Home and Museum. 822 South Jefferson Street; (800) 524-7264. The nucleus of this gracious frontier home is a two-room cabin built of pine around 1845. Bought in 1866 by N. W. Faison, a Fayette County clerk and land surveyor who survived the Dawson Massacre, the home remained in the Faison family until 1960. Open only for group tours by prior arrangement. Fee.

St. James Episcopal Church. 156 North Monroe; (979) 968-3910. Built in 1885 and still painted its original rust and cream, this small church has retained its original furnishings, handmade by the first rector and his congregation. Visitors are welcome at the 10:00 a.m. Sunday service and by appointment.

Texas Czech Heritage & Cultural Center. 250 West Fairgrounds Road; (979) 968-9399 or (888) 785-4500; www.czechtexas.org. The first Czech immigrants arrived in Fayette County in the 1850s, and by 1900, more than 9,000 immigrants from the present-day Czech Republic or former Austria-Hungary had settled in the surrounding counties of central Texas. This center is dedicated to telling their story. Open weekdays and weekends by appointment.

where to eat

Bistro 108. 108 South Main Street; (979) 968-9108; www.bistro108.com. The scent of fresh-baked French bread is not necessary to draw diners in for the popular early bird dinner specials at the Bistro. A fine-dining menu of seafood, pastas, steaks, chicken, and pork and thirty choices of wine encourage patrons to crowd into this cozy restaurant. Open for lunch and dinner Monday–Saturday and Sunday brunch. $–$$$.

Bugle Boy. 1051 North Jefferson; (979) 702-9310; www.thebugleboy.com. A World War II army barrack, originally at Camp Swift in Bastrop, has been converted to a hip coffee shop that features live music, as well as an expansive menu of caffeinated beverages. Beer and wine also are available. Open Tuesday–Saturday. $.

Frank's Place. 235 West Travis; (979) 968-3759. A varied selection of steaks and seafood here, with a salad bar. Although no mixed drinks are sold, take note of the 200-year-old bar. Open for breakfast and lunch Tuesday–Friday and breakfast on Saturday. $$.

Holman Valley Steakhouse. 10204 FM 155 (9 miles south of La Grange in the crossroads community of Holman); (979) 263-4188. Judy and David Hajovsky have turned this old country store and meetinghouse into an excellent and much needed eatery for the region. In addition to steak, the menu includes seafood and chicken. Open for dinner Wednesday–Saturday. Reservations advised. $–$$. No credit cards.

Prause's Market. 253 West Travis (on the town square); (979) 968-3259. Fresh and smoked meats here, as well as barbecue to eat on-site or take out. Open Monday–Friday and on Saturday morning. $. No credit cards.

Weikel's Bakery. 2247 West Highway 71; (979) 968-9413; www.weikels.com. Don't leave La Grange without trying some authentic Czech pastries. This bakery has been selling its kolaches and other snacks since the early 1980s. Consider a traditional kolache filling such as prune or poppy, or go with the cream-cheese-filled Danish. The bakery's pigs-in-the-blanket are stuffed with pork sausage and jalapeño cheese. Open daily. $.

wandering the back roads

Before continuing on from La Grange to Fayetteville and the conclusion of this day trip, consider a detour north/northwest to the tiny community of Serbin. Settled from 1854 through 1900 by Wends (Sorbs) from Lusatia in East Germany, this is the only Wendish village in Texas where you can still hear the Wendish language occasionally. Sights include St. Paul's Lutheran Church (979-366-9650), completed in 1871 and still in use, and the Texas Wendish Heritage Museum (979-366-2441), open Tuesday–Sunday (fee). The latter exhibits Old Country folk dress, manuscripts, personal papers, photographs, and painted Easter eggs in addition to two log buildings built in the 1850s. Group tours that include a Wendish meal can be arranged by calling the museum. To reach Serbin, take US 77 North from La Grange for approximately 7 miles and turn west (left) on FM 153 for 8 miles. Turn north (right) on FM 448 and go 9 miles to FM 2239; Serbin then is 2 miles west (left). You'll be driving through lovely countryside all the way.

If hunger strikes, you're out of luck in Serbin. The closest food source is a true taste of rural Texas: the Warda Store (and post office, gas station, restaurant, and bar; 979-242-3366). Located in Warda on US 77 about halfway between La Grange and Giddings, this spot is locally famous for its "Warda-burgers." Open daily (call for hours), but only after 4:00 p.m. on Sunday.

Delaying an exploration of Fayetteville for another day, you'll also find road food as well as a picturesque 1899 octagonal courthouse in Giddings, about 5 miles northeast of Serbin via FM 448. From Giddings it's a straight shot home to Houston via U.S. Highway 290 East, unless you detour just east of Carmine onto Highway 237 South, which connects you with West Day Trip 4.

continuing on

If you do not jaunt off to Serbin, your next stop on this day trip is Fayetteville. From La Grange follow Highway 159 northeast 15 miles on its zigzag course through the countryside.

fayetteville

If you like the big time and bright lights, move on. This small town keeps a low profile, tucked away in the rolling farmland east of La Grange. If too many folks fall in love with it, it's bound to change, and that would be a pity.

Some of Austin's first colonists were sharp enough to settle here in the early 1820s, and by 1833 the tiny community was a stage station on the old San Felipe Trail, with service to Austin via Round Top and Bastrop. The town officially was mapped in 1847, and the next decade saw extensive German and Czech immigration, an ethnic blend that continues.

In the town's settlement days, free food was served to all comers, but occasionally the vittles ran out before the customers did. Late arrivals were told to "lick the skillet," and Fayetteville was nicknamed Lickskillet as a result. The town celebrates the Lickskillet Festival the third weekend of October with parades, fun, and a big meal (not free!) in the town square.

Fayetteville looks much as it did at the end of the nineteenth century: a series of 2- and 3-block streets in a grid with a central square. The town's pride and heart is the rare Victorian precinct courthouse in the center of that square, a small wooden structure built in 1880 for the heady sum of $800. The four-faced clock in the steeple resulted from a ten-year fund-raising effort by the Do Your Duty Club and was installed with much civic horn-tooting in 1934.

City folks cherish this small town as a wind-down place. The best way to get on Fayetteville time is to pick up a walking map from one of the stores and take a slow stroll around town. While Fayetteville retains its sleepy charm, its days of relative obscurity are numbered. Houstonians are buying Fayetteville's old homes as country getaways, and many of the vintage buildings around the square are metamorphosing into Victorian-style shops, galleries, or lodgings.

Fayetteville's shops usually are open Tuesday–Sunday. For information contact the Fayetteville Chamber of Commerce, 115 West Fayette, Fayetteville, TX 78940; (979) 378-4021; www.fayettevilletx.com. For additional overnight options in the region, consult the Round Top (see West Day Trip 4), Brenham (see Northwest Day Trip 6), and La Grange (mentioned earlier in this day trip) sections of this book.

what to do

Art Guild of Rural Texas. 114 North Live Oak; (979) 378-2113. Artists near and far show their work in a variety of media. Exhibits change monthly. Open Monday–Saturday 10:00 a.m. to 2:00 p.m.

Citywide Garage Sale. Dozens of families participate in Fayetteville's Citywide Garage Sale each July. A free map pinpoints their locations. Call (979) 378-4021 for more information.

Fayette Area Heritage Museum. 117 Washington Street (on the square); (979) 378-2210. Lots of local lore here, with docents to add the human commentary. Open Monday–Saturday, or by appointment.

Fayette Lake. From Highway 159 bass fishermen may want to detour east on County Road 196 to this 2,400-acre lake, the cooling pond for the Fayette Power Project. Open year-round, it offers fishing, camping, swimming, and powerboating from both Park Prairie (979-249-3344) and Oak Thicket Parks (979-249-3504). Bait and tackle shops dispense necessities and advice at the entrances to both. Fee.

Texas Pickin' Park. On the square in Fayetteville; (979) 378-2753. The music starts in April, and the pickin' goes on each Saturday through November. Fayetteville welcomes all acoustical musicians to play their favorites for local and visiting fans of old-time music.

where to eat

Joe's Place at Baca's Saloon. On the square in Fayetteville; (979) 378-9035; www.joes placeatbacasaloon. Travelers have been discovering Baca's (pronounced *Batchas*) for a century. Barbecue's a big hit, along with steaks, pizzas, and salads. Open for lunch and dinner Wednesday–Sunday. $–$$.

Keilers Restaurant. On the square in Fayetteville; (979) 378-2578. Take your pick: In addition to daily lunch specials, the menu offers fried catfish, steaks, hamburgers, and seafood platters. Save room for the homemade pies. Open for lunch and dinner Wednesday–Saturday. Lodging rooms upstairs. $–$$. No credit cards.

Orsak's Cafe. On the square in Fayetteville; (979) 378-2719. There's nothing fancy about this clean and basic cafe, but the food is acceptable and affordable. In addition to daily lunch specials and a regular menu, Wednesday night brings fried chicken; Thursday night, pork chops; Friday night, seafood; and Sunday, barbecue. You'll want to linger long enough to visit with local residents—nearly everyone who comes to town drops in for at least a cup of coffee, to pick up messages, and otherwise to stay in touch. Open Tuesday–Sunday for breakfast, lunch, and dinner; until 2:00 p.m. on Monday. $–$$.

wandering the back roads

After touring Fayetteville you can continue east on Highway 159 to Bellville and then home (see West Day Trip 4). Or you can reverse the order of this day trip, touring Fayetteville first and then continuing to La Grange. See the map with this section for your route options. It's also easy to connect with tours of Round Top and Winedale (see West Day Trip 4) or Brenham (see Northwest Day Trip 6), if you prefer.

If you are traveling in any part of this territory from late March through May, contact the La Grange Chamber of Commerce in advance. It scouts the best routes for color during the wildflower season. For information call (800) 524-7264.

day trip 04

west

antiques and pie:
ledbetter, round top, winedale and
industry, bellville

ledbetter

Begin this day trip by driving northwest from Houston on U.S. Highway 290 to Ledbetter, 25 miles west of Brenham. If it's Saturday, antiques shoppers will want to spend some time in the whistle-stop town of Carmine, a few miles east of Ledbetter.

Both Carmine and Ledbetter are railroad towns, the latter platted in 1870 by the Texas and New Orleans Railroad. Folks anticipated big things—those old plats show a big depot from which wide streets with pretty names stretched in all directions. The depot did become a reality, the first and largest in Fayette County. The town, however, maxed out at about 1,000 residents in 1900 and began a steady decline after World War II. The last passenger train whistled through in 1952, the last freight in 1979. Now even the tracks are gone, and Ledbetter has a permanent population of approximately one hundred souls. Perhaps the town is best defined by what it doesn't have: gas stations, fast-food franchises, supermarkets, traffic lights, noise, and crowds—in short, Ledbetter is a perfect pause in another era.

what to do

Stuermer's General Store and Working Museum. 100 FM 1291, Ledbetter (at the intersection of US 290 and FM 1291); (979) 249-5642 or (979) 249-3066. No one knows exactly when this old place was built, but the two antique bars (one dated 1836 on the back) were part of a saloon established here by the owner's great-grandfather in 1890. Today Chris Jervis

west day trip 04

and her mother, Lillian Stuermer Dyer, sell sandwiches and Blue Bell ice cream from those bars, and the rest of the two-story store is filled with memorabilia and antiques (not for sale), along with those sundry items no one can do without. Kids love this place; the jukebox and pool table are free. This is the oldest flag stop on the Kerrville bus route, and when the shutters are closed, the store is closed. When the shutters are open, usually Monday–Saturday, come on in.

Jay and Chris Jervis also have six bed-and-breakfast lodgings, one in a charming 1880s country cottage known as Granny's House. All the units have private baths and mini-kitchens, $60–$105. Guests also have access to a party house, complete with indoor swimming pool.

where to eat

Monzi's Fine Cuisine. 155 West Austin (US 290), Giddings (about 10 miles west of Ledbetter on US 290); (979) 542-2201; www.monzis.com. Housed in an 1870s building, this elegant dining room is where the locals head for special occasions. The menu features a nice variety of regional favorites, including blackened catfish and grilled USDA Choice steaks. Sunday brunch is a real treat with selections such as rack of lamb, eggs Benedict, and Belgian waffles. Open for breakfast, lunch, and dinner Wednesday–Saturday, brunch and lunch on Sunday. $$$.

continuing on

To reach Round Top, take either FM 1291 South from Ledbetter or Highway 237 South from Carmine.

round top

When it comes to vintage Texas villages that have retained the essence of their past, Round Top is the champ. Officially founded in 1835 by settlers from Stephen F. Austin's second colony, it was first called Jones Post Office and then Townsend, after the five Townsend families who established plantations in the area. The name of Round Top originally applied to a stage stop 2 miles north, a landmark by 1847 because it had a house with a round top. When the stage line between Houston and Austin moved its route slightly south, the town and the name followed.

Driving into Round Top is like passing through a time warp. A small, white meeting-house in the middle of the village green is part of the town's charm. In fact, Round Top is so small, so compact and neat, that visitors often feel like giants abroad in Lilliput.

Those first Anglo settlers were followed by Germans, many of whom were intellectuals oppressed in their native country. Others were skilled carpenters and stonemasons whose craftsmanship marks numerous area buildings that survive today. A drive on the lanes around Round Top is a lesson in enduring architecture.

Nice to know if you hate to leave: The numerous bed-and-breakfast lodgings in the Round Top area include Briarfield at Round Top (979-249-3973; www.briarfieldround top.com), Cole Cottage (888-922-4179), Gaste Haus (979-249-3308; www.texaspioneer arts.org), A Light unto My Path (979-249-5620; www.alightuntomypath.com), Oak Grove House (800-716-3931; http://oakgrovehousebandb.com), Outpost at Cedar Creek (979-836-4975; www.outpostatcedarcreek.com), Round Top Cottages (877-756-2681; www.round topcottages.com), and Anderson's Round Top Inn (979-249-5294; www.andersonround topinn.com).

With its current population of less than one hundred, Round Top holds two distinctions. Not only is it the smallest incorporated town in the state, it has what many think is the oldest Fourth of July celebration west of the Mississippi. Local folks have been kicking up their heels on Independence Day since 1826, and the annual tradition now runs to orations, barbecues, a trail ride, and the firing of the cannon in the town square.

Whenever you visit, just park your car near the square and walk around. Round Top folks welcome visitors and have lots of tales to tell, so stop and chat as you explore. Unless you are passionate about country antiques and/or folk art and don't mind major crowds, avoid coming to Round Top on the first full weekend of both April and October, when literally thousands of people attend the Round Top Antiques Fair, one of the finest events of its kind in the world. More than 270 dealers from all parts of the country participate in this blue-chip show, but that's not all. Riding the fair's coattails is a seemingly endless antiques and flea market scene along many of the region's roads. Farmers rent field space to all comers, and hunting for bargains and treasures is the rule of the day. Nerve center for the latter scene is Warrenton, 3 miles south of Round Top on Highway 237 (toward La Grange), and the action begins the weekend prior to the Round Top show.

For information on the area, contact the Round Top Chamber of Commerce, P.O. Box 216, Round Top, TX 78954; (979) 249-4042; www.roundtop.org. If you're already in town and need information, stop at the Round Top Visitors Center, 203 Washington, just off the square. A display of local heritage and attractions, it's open mornings only, Monday–Saturday.

what to do

Bethlehem Lutheran Church. Up the hill from Moore's Fort and 1 block southwest. This sturdy stone church was dedicated in 1866 and is still in use. The front door usually is unlocked, so enter and climb the narrow wood stairs to the loft. Not only will you get a strong feeling for the simplicity of the old days, but you'll see an unusual cedar pipe organ, one of several built by local craftsman Johann Traugott Wantke in the 1860s for area churches. The old churchyard cemetery is charming and ageless, enclosed by a hand-laid stone wall reminiscent of New England.

Henkel Square. On the square in Round Top; (979) 249-3308. Back in 1852 a German immigrant named Edward A. Henkel bought twenty-five acres in Round Top to establish a mercantile store. The following year he built a two-story home that now is the keystone of Henkel Square, a historical open-air museum operated by the Texas Pioneer Arts Foundation.

Dedicated to preserving the history of this region, Henkel Square is a collection of sixteen historically important structures scattered across eight acres of pasture in the heart of town. The docents are local women who explain each home or building, its furnishings, and how it fit into early Texas life. Don't miss the old Lutheran church, which doubled as a school. Its painted motto translates from German to "I call the living to my church and the dead to their graves," a reference to its two-clapper bell. One rings; the other tolls.

Five of the buildings were moved to Henkel Square from sites in surrounding communities, and the lumber needed for restorations was cut in the local woods, just as it was in pioneer times. Using old tools and techniques, present-day craftsmen have kept each structure faithful to its period, an attention to authenticity that has won Henkel Square awards for restoration excellence.

The entrance is through the Victorian building that once housed Round Top's apothecary, and several of the homes have outstanding wall stenciling and period furniture. Open Thursday–Sunday afternoons year-round, except for major holidays. Fee.

International Festival-Institute at Round Top (Festival Hill). P.O. Box 89, Round Top, TX 78954-0089 (on Jaster Road, off Highway 237, 0.5 mile north of the town square); (979) 249-3129; www.festivalhill.org. What once was rolling open pasture graced only by birdsong is now a mecca for music lovers throughout the world. Back in 1968 noted pianist James Dick performed near Round Top and fell victim to its bucolic charm. Returning in 1971, he held the first of his musical festival-institutes in Round Top's tiny town hall, a venture that has grown into permanent quarters on Festival Hill. Every summer sixty young professional musicians from various parts of the world attend master classes taught by a professional guest faculty and perform with internationally known musicians in a series of public concerts.

Two handsome old homes have been moved onto the Festival Hill grounds. The William Lockhart Clayton House, built in 1870 in La Grange, is now staff living quarters, and the C. A. Menke House, originally an old ranch house in Hempstead, is used as a conference center.

An Early Music Festival on or near Memorial Day weekend kicks off a series of summer concerts (through mid-July) in the modern and air-conditioned Festival Hall, and monthly afternoon performances are offered from August to April. Tickets can be ordered in advance or purchased at the box office prior to curtain. There usually is a free concert for children in mid-June, as well as assorted educational museum forums at various times of the year.

Picnic facilities are free for the summer concerts, and you can even leave the food packing to someone else. Both Royers' Round Top Cafe (979-249-3611) and Klump's Country Cooking Restaurant (979-249-5696) prepare box picnics to go if you call in advance. During the August-to-April series you can reserve a Saturday night preconcert dinner at Festival Hill ($$$). Limited overnight accommodations also are available by advance reservation during those months. Extensive herb gardens amid rock and cloisters adjacent to Menke House are open daily. For a guided tour (fee), call (979) 249-3129.

Also available to groups for seminars and conferences, Festival Hill houses extensive art, notably the David W. Guion Americana Collection and the Anders and Josephine Oxehufwud Swedish and European Collection. Guided tours ($5 per person) can be arranged by calling (979) 249-3129.

Moore's Fort. On Highway 237, 2½ blocks south of Round Top's square. This double log cabin with an open dog-trot center was the frontier home of John Henry Moore. Built about 1828 near the Colorado River in La Grange, it was used primarily as a defense against Indians. The fort is not open to the public.

Round Top Area Historical Center. 304 North Washington (Highway 237 North); (979) 249-3042; www.texaspioneerarts.org. Housed in the town's former blacksmith shop, this young but growing museum displays regional memorabilia from 1820 through the 1850s. This also is a good source for local genealogical information. Currently open from noon to 3:00 p.m. on Friday and Saturday, or by appointment.

Round Top General Store. On the Highway 237 side of the town square; (979) 249-3600. Stop at this circa 1847 store for antiques, gifts, and fudge. Open Saturday–Sunday afternoons.

Sterling McCall Old Car Museum. 4212 Highway 237, Warrenton, about 5 miles southwest of Round Top; (979) 249-5089; www.oldcarcountry.com. This nonprofit museum displays more than eighty-eight cars built between 1909 and 1959. Among its treasures: a hand-built 1956 Lincoln Mark II, Arthur Godfrey's 1956 Studebaker, and the re-creation of a 1950s-era service station. Open Thursday–Sunday and by special appointment. Fee.

where to eat

Chef Pasquale's Steak and Seafood. 109 Bauer Rummel Road, 3 blocks south of the square on Highway 237; (979) 249-5044; www.chefpasquales.com. Born in Rome and trained as a chef in Italy, Ricciardi Pasquale was executive chef at both Nino's and Vincent's restaurants in downtown Houston before opening this charming place in Round Top in 2003. Expect fine food in an only-in–Round Top setting: an 1870s dog-trot-style house, flanked by historic Moore's Fort (circa 1828; see "What to Do"). The latter is used for private parties. Open for dinner Wednesday–Saturday and brunch on Sunday. (Open daily for lunch and dinner during Antique Week). $$–$$$.

Klump's Country Cooking Restaurant. On the west side of the square in Round Top; (979) 249-5696. House specials run to Mexican food on Wednesday night, fresh catfish fillets on Friday night, and fried chicken at Sunday noon. Owner Liz Klump also offers memorable apple pie, barbecue, steaks, and hamburgers for lunch and dinner Wednesday–Saturday; breakfast and lunch (until 2:00 p.m.) on Tuesday and Sunday. $–$$.

The Oaks Restaurant. 5507 Highway 237, Warrenton, 3 miles south of Round Top; (979) 249-5909; www.oaksfamilyrestaurant.com. A local favorite, it serves most of the Texas standards as well as steaks, Italian, pizza, sandwiches, and daily specials. *Tip:* Sunday often brings all-you-can-eat cold shrimp (you peel). Open for lunch and dinner Thursday–Sunday. $–$$. No credit cards.

Royer's Round Top Cafe. On the square in Round Top; (979) 249-3611; www.royers roundtopcafe.com. Owned by Bud and Karen Royer and operated by their adult children, this small spot has been justly praised by numerous food writers and publications and is now a destination in itself—a very good reason to make a day trip to Round Top. Originally the menu was "the kind of food you come to the country for," and that still predominates. However, the taste bar has been raised to include more sophisticated offerings. Winners range from a luscious fresh salmon to the pricey but perfect Angus tenderloin. Royer's also serves a unique BLT layered with one-quarter pound of grilled shrimp. One off-menu item, Bud's fork-tender chicken-fried steak, is pure country and worth what is often a two-hour wait for seating; folks usually just settle down on the hay bales out front.

Good to know: There are two exceptions to Royer's "no reservations/no credit cards" rule. On nonevent weekends you can phone ahead and Bud will put your name on the seating list (a move that usually results in a shorter wait), and on event weekends you can guarantee your arrival at a certain time via a credit-card deposit. You will still have to pony up the price of your meal via cash or check, however.

Sweet frills run to Blue Bell ice-cream cones (vanilla only) and homemade desserts. Real apples and pumpkins go into the pies—no canned or processed fillings are used—and if you are lucky it will be dewberry cobbler day. The pies are available to go—they sell several hundred every weekend—so call ahead to reserve your favorite. Royer's normally is open Thursday–Saturday for lunch and dinner and Sunday noon to 3:00 p.m. The days and hours of operation change seasonally, however, so call. For example, this cafe is open on Wednesday in March and April, but closed on Sunday during Antique Week and on Easter, Mother's Day, and Memorial Day. $–$$$. No credit cards.

continuing on

To visit Winedale, take FM 1457 North for 4 miles to FM 2714 and turn northeast.

wandering the back roads

If you have lingered too long in Round Top and now must head home, why not take the scenic route? Highway 237 South (connecting to Highway 159 South) to La Grange (see West

Day Trip 3) is one of the nicest country rambles in the state. Take a few minutes to travel east or west of the highway on the many graded county roads. You'll pass gracious old homes, log cabins, churches flanked by tiny cemeteries, and numerous historical land-marks. As you enter Warrenton on Highway 237 South, watch for a large two-story rock house on the west side of the road. This is the Neece House, built in 1869 and now avail-able for special events. You'll also pass St. Martin's, locally called the smallest Catholic church in the world. It holds only twelve people. Concurrent with the Round Top Antiques Fair on the first full weekends in April and October, Warrenton blossoms into a giant antiques, crafts, and collectibles market, with plenty of hearty country food on the side. Warrenton's old grocery store has been renovated into a bed-and-breakfast, Warrenton Inn (979-249-3074). If you're wandering here on a weekend, have a look at the Sterling McCall Old Car Museum on Highway 237 (fee; 979-249-5089). (See a description earlier in this day trip.)

From La Grange follow Highway 71 southeast to Columbus (see West Day Trip 2) and I-10 east to Houston.

winedale and industry

Winedale provides another look at yesterday's Texas. The settlement is blink-small: a gas station and a few homes tucked into a valley threaded by Jack's Creek. That old-style split-rail fence on the right, however, encircles one of the most ambitious restoration projects in the state, the Winedale Historical Center (www.cah.utexas.edu/museums/winedale).

Administered by the University of Texas Center for American History, this 225-acre out-door museum illustrates many pages of the past. The basic farmstead was part of a Mexican land grant to William S. Townsend, one of Austin's second colony of settlers. He built a small house on the land about 1834 and in 1848 sold the farm to Samuel Lewis. He in turn expanded the home and the plantation, and by the mid-1850s this old farmhouse was a stage stop on the main road between Brenham and La Grange.

Although Winedale's grounds are open daily for wandering, and the visitor center is open Monday–Friday, guided tours (fee; weekends or by appointment only) are the only way to access the buildings. Starting at the visitor center, the first stop is a simple 1855 farm building known as Hazel's Lone Oak Cottage, often used as a gallery for an exhibit on Winedale's history. From there the tour moves to the focal point of the entire museum com-plex, the Lewis-Wagner House. This two-story farmhouse is notable for its authentic Texas primitive furnishings and beautiful wall and ceiling frescoes painted by a local German artist of the time, Rudolph Melchior. Other rare examples of Melchior's art can be seen in several of the Henkel Square houses in Round Top.

The Winedale complex also has assorted dependencies, such as a smokehouse and pioneer kitchen. The old barn, built in 1894 with cedar beams salvaged from an early cot-ton gin, now rings with the ageless words of Shakespeare in July and August, courtesy of

University of Texas English students. The performances are Thursday–Sunday evenings, seats must be reserved in advance (fee), and an inexpensive hunter's stew dinner is served before the Saturday-evening show. You also are welcome to bring a picnic basket and blanket and feast in the field. For picnics to go contact either Klump's or Royer's eateries, listed in the Round Top section of this trip.

A ten-minute trek through the back pastures of Winedale leads to the McGregor-Grimm House, a two-story Greek Revival farmhouse built in 1861 and moved to Winedale from Wesley in 1967. As the Lewis-Wagner House represents the earlier, rather simple plantation home of the area, the McGregor-Grimm House is more gracious and elaborate, typical of pre–Civil War cotton-boom wealth.

Winedale hosts numerous special fests, symposia, and exhibitions throughout the year, many of which focus on early Texas antiques and crafts. The complex also includes a nature trail and herb garden. Picnickers are welcome. For more information call (979) 278-3530, or write the Winedale Historical Center, P.O. Box 11, Round Top, TX 78954.

continuing on

From Winedale turn southeast (left) on FM 1457 and go approximately 9 miles to the intersection with Highway 159. Turn east (left), and it's then 19 miles to Bellville—beautiful country all the way.

En route take a few minutes to explore Industry, settled in 1831–33 and the oldest German community in Texas. An 1838 Republic of Texas post office still stands, now surrounded by Friedrich Ernst Memorial Park just north of the Highway 159/FM 109 intersection. Stop also at Lindemann's General Store, in business since 1884 and a great place to buy local sausage, custom-cut meat, and cold drinks (open daily). The current building, however, is a relative newcomer—it's only about twenty years old. The original Lindemann's Store on Industry's old Main Street (2 blocks west of the intersection of FM 109 and Highway 159) has a historical marker, and the building itself now houses the Lindemann Store Museum. Several other vintage buildings, including an 1860s church that's still used for services once a month and at Christmas, an 1920s doctor's office, and the 1899 Welcome Hall, can be visited by advance appointment (call 979-357-2772). The latter was originally called Halle Das Welcome Maennerchor (Hall of the Welcome Men's Choir) and served as Industry's social center for generations.

The old Welcome Store (979-836-7378), a landmark in the area since 1890, is 4 miles north of Industry on FM 109. You'll find cut tree trunks neatly holding up the porch's shed roof, enough groceries on the shelves to keep locals from having to drive into Brenham, and some friendly old farmers probably playing dominoes. Alas, age claimed the traditional pot-bellied stove some time back. Open daily; call for hours.

wandering the back roads

An alternative route from Winedale to Bellville follows FM 1457 only as far as the tiny town of Shelby and then angles north (left) on Highway 389. At the intersection with FM 2502, turn right and go 3 miles to Wesley, an early Czech-Moravian settlement. Watch on the east side of the road for the turnoff to the community's historic church, the first church of the Czech Brethren faith built in North America (1866). This simple structure's rock foundation is original, and a huge oak log (visible from the rear) supports the center of the building. Unfortunately, this small sanctuary usually is locked, preventing visitors from viewing its hand-painted interior decorations.

From Wesley you can either connect with Brenham (see Northwest Day Trip 6) by returning north on FM 2502 to Highway 389 and then turning northeast (right), or you can continue on this day trip to Bellville. To do the latter, go south on FM 2502 to Highway 159 and turn east (left).

bellville

Settled in 1848 and the Austin County seat, Bellville was named for Thomas Bell, one of Stephen F. Austin's "Old Three Hundred," as his first colony has been labeled by history. The best time to visit is during the spring Country Livin' Festival, when nature lines the routes into the town with bluebonnets and Indian paintbrush. During that festival the chamber of commerce sets up roadside booths where you can get maps and directions to the best flower displays. They also sell packets of bluebonnet seeds in the hope that you will sow some of next year's color yourself. For information on Bellville, including antiques shops, galleries, and such, contact the chamber of commerce, 4 West Main (P.O. Box 670), Bellville, TX 77418; (979) 865-3407; www.bellville.com.

Restoration is bringing back the architectural integrity of the old town square. Numerous building fronts have been returned to their original design, and more than a dozen house antiques stores. There also are boutiques and art galleries, most of which open on Sunday afternoon. Plan your trip to take in Market Day on the Square on the first Saturday of the month March–December.

Karmel House (979-865-3363; www.karmelhouse.com) provides an in-town bed-and-breakfast experience, and three others are more rural: Somewhere in Time (979-865-9547; http://somewhereintimebb.com), on five acres west of town; Outpost at Cedar Creek (979-836-4975; www.outpostatcedarcreek.com), a restored German farmstead on thirty acres; and Lonesome Pine Ranch (979-865-3647; www.texasranchlife.com). The latter is a 1,100-acre cattle ranch between Chappell Hill and Bellville with six historical cabins, all comfortably furnished with antiques or period reproductions. The bed-and-breakfast fee includes catch-and-release bass fishing on thirty-five lakes, excellent birding opportunities, and all of the ranch atmosphere you care to absorb. Wagon rides and trail rides carry additional fees, as do the March and September cattle roundups, which are offered on a day-visit basis.

what to do

Bluebonnet Farms. Near Bellville; (979) 865-5051. This hundred-acre farm breeds, raises, and trains American saddlebred horses and has several national champions in its paddocks. Visitors are welcome only if they have a sincere interest in the riding and training of horses. No sightseers or casual drop-ins, please. Appointments required.

The 1896 Jailhouse Museum. 36 South Bell Street; (979) 865-9116. The sheriff's office and county jail (with original gallows) have been furnished to their early-twentieth-century look, and monthly exhibits include artifacts from the Texian Army encampment at Raccoon Bend as well as assorted weapons, many of which were confiscated from prisoners during the jail's serious years. Open Saturday 11:00 a.m. to 3:00 p.m. Donations appreciated.

The Turnverein (dance hall). On FM 529 in the city park, immediately east of Bellville. Bellville's dance hall was the first (1897) of five wooden pavilions in Austin County attributed to Joachim Hintz, a German immigrant carpenter. Still in continuous use, this quaint, twelve-sided hall has hosted many an oom-pah band and schottische as well as countless county fairs, antiques shows, and so on. Other examples of Hintz's dance halls include the Sealy Liedertafel Hall on Main Street in Sealy (circa 1914); Peter's Hacienda Schuetzen Verein (circa 1900), 5 miles north of Bellville on Highway 36, then 1 mile west on Trenckman Road; the Coshatte Turnverein (circa 1928; call the Bellville Historical Society at 979-865-9116 for directions); and the Cat Spring Landwirth Schaftlide Verein (circa 1902), on FM 1094 in Cat Spring.

where to eat

Granny's Bar-B-Q. 515 East Hellmuth Street (½ block off Highway 6); (979) 865-5752. Real pit barbecue here, with all the fixings. Open for lunch and early dinner Monday–Saturday. $–$$. No credit cards.

The Hill. 758 West Main; (979) 865-3607; www.thehillrestaurant.com. Clean and crisp to look at with its red-black-white color scheme, this hamburger spot seems one of the best of its genre. No surprises here—but do try the shakes, malts, and floats. Open for lunch and dinner Monday–Saturday. $. No credit cards.

Latigo. 412 East Main; (979) 865-9066. This cafe serving Lone Star cuisine is in a lovingly restored historical building that once housed a Dr Pepper bottling company. Former Houston chef Atkinson has added his own twist to Texas favorites, burgers, sandwiches, and entrees, and the bakery includes interesting fare as well, such as jalapeño cheesecake and chocolate chip banana bread pudding. Open for lunch and dinner Monday–Saturday and lunch Sunday. $–$$.

Manuel's Mexican Restaurant. 1416 South Front (Highway 36 South); (979) 865-8408. Fajitas and shrimp enchiladas are two of the house specialties. Open daily for lunch and dinner. $–$$.

Newman's Bakery. 504 East Main; (979) 865-9804. This coffee shop is a local favorite for breakfast as well as soup and sandwiches for lunch. Open Monday–Friday 4:00 a.m. to 5:30 p.m., Saturday–Sunday 4:00 a.m. to 5:00 p.m. $.

wandering the back roads

To return to Houston from Bellville, you again have a choice. FM 529 East is a rural route that intersects Highway 6 north of the Bear Creek business area in northwest Harris County. If you live in south Houston, your best bet from Bellville is Highway 36 South 15 miles to Sealy (see West Day Trip 1), then east on I-10 toward home.

southwest

day trip 01

southwest

birding mecca:
wharton, el campo, edna, palacios and
blessing, matagorda, bay city

wharton

The trip through Wharton, El Campo, Edna, Palacios and Blessing, Matagorda, and Bay City covers a lot of territory, so you may want to make a weekend out of it with an overnight in Palacios. Take your fishing and crabbing gear and have fun.

Start your trip via U.S. Highway 59 South to Wharton. While not a gee-whiz destination in itself, Wharton offers several pleasures. This rich agricultural land drew Stephen F. Austin's early settlers, and Wharton County and the town were formed when the Republic of Texas joined the United States. The town square with the county courthouse in its center has access to the Colorado River below the square. *Fun to know:* Playwright Horton Foote, winner of the 1995 Pulitzer Prize for *The Young Man from Atlanta* as well as two Academy Awards at various times in his career, is a Wharton native and still maintains a home here. Many of his plays take place in "Harrison," a thinly disguised stand-in for his hometown.

Although no homes are open to the public on a regular basis, it's pleasant to drive down Wharton's oak-shaded streets. For information on local events as well as a list of antiques shops and an interesting driving map of "the Caney Run" through Wharton, Colorado, and Matagorda Counties, contact the Wharton Chamber of Commerce, 225 North Richmond Road, Wharton, TX 77488; (979) 532-1862; www.whartontexas.com.

southwest day trip 01

Houston

949
San Felipe
Cat Spring
1458
Brookshire
Katy
10
6
1093
6
0
Beltway 8

3013
Sealy
1458
359
Clodine
1393
723
1489
Fulshear
Simonton
Eagle Lake
Wallis
36
Rosenberg
Richmond
59
762
Brazos R.
(Tadpole Rd.)
288
Alvi

950
102
60
1161
FM-360
Needville
1994
762
1462
Woodrow
Rosharon

Egypt
540
Hungerford
71
Colorado R.
Glen Flora
Wharton
1301
Boling
New Gulf
36
Holiday Lakes
Da

El Campo
1301
Pledger
East Columbia
Angleton

59
60
West Columbia
Richwood Village
523

Danevang
35
Brazoria
322
Lake Jacks
Clute
Edna and Lake Texana
71

521
2918
Jones Creek
Bay City
521
2918

Blessing
616
San Bernard National Wildlife Refuge
Gulf of Mexico

35
Wadsworth
521

Palacios
Matagorda

0   10   20 miles

what to do

Cotton ginning. There are not many places left in Texas to watch a cotton gin do its thing. If you are interested and plan to visit Wharton during the August–October ginning season, you can visit the Moses Gin through advance arrangement with the Caney Valley Cotton Co., Box 470, Wharton, TX 77488; (979) 532-3522.

Geese and duck hunting. Numerous outfitters guide visitors to excellent shooting on this region's vast prairies. For a list contact the Wharton Chamber of Commerce at the address previously given.

Peachland (Gundermann's) Orchard. Take the Eagle Lake exit from US 59 South and follow FM 102 North into Glen Flora (watch for signs); (979) 677-3319. If tornadoes, freezes, and droughts have left the crops intact, visitors will find organic veggies here, fresh from the field. Open daily May–July, weather permitting. Country arts and crafts and sometimes cider also are sold here. Call for crop information.

Riverfront Park at the Port of Wharton. This seventeen-acre civic project has a playground, picnic tables, walking trails, restrooms, and a deck overlooking the river. Concessionaires are often here during summer, offering rental canoes, paddleboats, and bicycles; check the current situation with the Wharton Chamber of Commerce. Stop here with your picnic, and then tour the nearby Monterey Square in front of the 1888 courthouse. The square is one of the Main Street projects fostered by the National Trust for Historic Preservation.

The Strawberry Patch. Wharton County; (979) 531-0048; www.texasberrypatch.com. Call for location and other information. This farm produces strawberries and peaches.

Wharton County Farmers Market. Corner of Houston and Milam Streets in Wharton. Open Saturday from 9:00 a.m. to noon. For information call the chamber of commerce, (979) 532-1862.

Wharton County Historical Museum. 3615 Richmond Road; (979) 532-2600. Some interesting bits and pieces of Wharton's past are gathered here. Farm and ranch exhibits focus on early settlement days, and the childhood home of a local boy who made the big time, former CBS news anchor Dan Rather, was moved onto the museum grounds in 1992. Call for times of guided tour. The museum also sponsors living-history events and historical reenactments several times a year. Call for dates. Open daily Monday–Friday and on Saturday and Sunday afternoons. Fee.

where to eat

Fibber's Cafe. 315 East Milam; (979) 532-8761. You'll find freshly ground hamburgers here, along with steaks, seafood, and a buffet lunch with daily specials and fresh veggies. Open daily for breakfast and lunch. $–$$.

Hinze's Bar-B-Que. 3940 US 59 Loop; (979) 532-2710. Local folks think this family-run place has the best pecan-smoked, succulent barbecue in the region, not to mention the homemade chocolate, coconut, and pecan pies. Try Hinze's for takeout. Open for lunch and dinner daily. $–$$.

Pat A Cake on the Square. 119 South Fulton; (979) 282-8000. Chef Jonathan Jones, formerly of Houston's acclaimed Riviera Grill, abandoned the city grind for the slower pace of a country cafe. But what a country cafe. Jones is reinventing Texas Gulf Coast classics such as chicken-fried steak, brine-cured pork chops, and fried shrimp. Handmade dishes feature seasonal delicacies as the cafe prides itself in working with local farmers, fishermen, and ranchers. Open for lunch only on Monday, lunch and dinner Tuesday–Saturday. $$–$$$.

wandering the back roads

Wharton is surrounded by vast cotton, corn, and rice fields, and the early spring months along any rural road in the area produce a vision of fresh green punctuated by bright wildflowers. Local folks think there is no prettier drive in Texas than FM 102 from Wharton north to Eagle Lake. Another nice rural drive is along the Spanish Camp Road, FM 640.

To continue this day trip, follow US 59 South to El Campo and Edna.

el campo

This spreading town, 68 miles south of Houston on US 59, sits in the middle of a vast coastal grass plain used for open cattle range from the early 1800s. By the 1850s this area was the starting point for cattle drives across east Texas on the Opelousas and Atascosito Trails, heading for the railroad terminals at New Orleans and Mobile.

The railroad eventually made it to this part of Texas, and by the early 1880s the area had an official railroad name, Prairie Switch. Mexican cowboys handling the large herds would camp nearby—thus the name El Campo, which was officially adopted in 1902 when the town was incorporated. Early settlers came from Germany, Sweden, Czechoslovakia, and Ireland, an ethnic mix still found in the area. As you drive around checking out the antiques and crafts stores, watch for the twenty-three murals on assorted downtown buildings. Taken from old photographs, each depicts some phase of El Campo's early days and has an explanatory plaque. For information contact the El Campo Chamber of Commerce, Box 1400, El Campo, TX 77437; (979) 543-2713; www.elcampochamber.com.

what to do

El Campo Museum of Natural History. 2350 North Mechanic (inside the civic center on Highway 71 North at FM 2765); (979) 543-6885; www.elcampomuseum.com. The main attraction at this extensive, well-done museum is the big-game trophy exhibit, a donation in 1972 from a local family. Over the years numerous other exhibits have been added, including displays on Africa, waterfowl, the Arctic, the jungle, the Alaskan brown bear, and animals native to south Texas. There's also a clown collection and displays of shells and rocks. Interactive computers and information boxes make this an in-depth educational experience. Open Monday–Saturday; call for hours. Donation appreciated.

where to eat

Greek Bros. Oyster Bar and Saloon. 133 South Mechanic; (979) 543-1757; www.greek bros.com. One of the most popular eateries in the region, this large and lively place puts some tasty twists on seafood, chicken, and other Texas standards. Oysters are always on the menu and are prepared several different ways. Although there's a full bar as well as dancing (live band on Thursday, Friday, and Saturday nights), this is a family kind of place. Open for dinner Monday–Saturday. $–$$$.

Los Cucos Mexican Cafe. 805 East Jackson; (979) 578-0612. One of several Los Cucos restaurants in the greater Houston area, this spot has more than one hundred items on its menu. Specialty dishes include beef or chicken served with seafood toppings of shrimp, crawfish, and crabmeat. Open daily for lunch and dinner. $–$$.

Mikeska's Bar-B-Q. 218 Merchant (downtown, across from the police department), (979) 543-5471; and a second location on US 59/Blue Creek Road on the northern outskirts of El Campo, (979) 543-8252; www.mikeskabbq.com. These spots are two of the reasons why Wharton County is considered by many to be the International Capital of Barbecue. Both are good sources for picnic sandwiches, and both are open daily (until 2:00 p.m. on Sunday). $–$$. Only the US 59 location accepts credit cards.

Pincher's Cajun and Seafood Restaurant. 104 East First Street; (979) 541-5211. This family-style place occupies nicely revamped quarters in the back of a historic brick building that housed a hardware store from 1905 to 1983. In addition to the expected étouffées and gumbos, the menu usually includes sourdough hamburgers, steaks, king and snow crab, fresh fried shrimp, oysters, scallops, freshwater catfish, and numerous selections featuring crawfish. Open for lunch Monday–Friday, dinner Monday–Saturday. Closed midafternoon. $–$$.

Prasek's Smokehouse. Route 3, Box 18, El Campo (on US 59, 4 miles west of El Campo); (979) 543-8312; www.praseks.com. Using an old family recipe, Mike and Betty Jo Prasek turn out memorable smoked sausage and both beef and turkey jerky, as well as baked goods. If you call at least a day ahead, they'll have sandwiches ready to go when you arrive. Open daily from 7:00 a.m. (8:00 a.m. on Sunday) until early evening. $–$$.

edna

Once known as "Macaroni Station," because that's all the New York, Texas and Mexican Railroad commissary on this site stocked, Edna is home to some 7,000 persons and is a commercial center for livestock, oil, and agriculture. It's important to day-trippers primarily as the gateway to beautiful Lake Texana (see "What to Do").

Interesting to know: That lake now covers the old town site of Texana, which was a well-established Indian village at the time of La Salle's expedition in the area in 1685. In 1832 it became the first town founded in Jackson County, and a few years later the Allen brothers decided Texana would be the ideal location for their dream city because of its location on the Navidad River, which provided deepwater access to the Gulf of Mexico. Anticipating that it would be a great port, they offered $100 in gold for the land. When the owner demanded $200, the Allen brothers moved northeast and ultimately bought a tract of land in Harris County upon which they founded their dream city—Houston.

Artifacts from Texana's early days were uncovered by archaeologists before the site was inundated with water. They now are on display at the Lavaca-Navidad River Authority headquarters, north of Palmetto Bend Dam on FM 3131. Free and open weekdays. Another bit of interesting salvage, the Texana Presbyterian Church, which predates the Civil War, now sits on Apollo Drive, next to the Edna Presbyterian Church.

For area bird lists as well as information on Lake Texana, the town of Edna, and assorted historical sites, more than thirty of which have historical markers, contact the Jackson County Chamber of Commerce, P.O. Box 788 (317 West Main), Edna, TX 77957; (361) 782-7146; www.ykc.com/jccc.

what to do

Lake Restaurant. Twenty-one miles southwest of El Campo via US 59; 6.5 miles east of Edna via Highway 111 South. Formed by the Palmetto Bend Dam, which backs up the Navidad River for 18 miles, this 11,000-acre lake is noted for its catfish and bass, plus there are good camping, fishing, and picnicking under shady oaks. Much of this mixed oak-and-pecan woodland is usually kept neatly trimmed by resident deer. All water sports are here, either at Lake Texana State Park (361-782-5718 or 800-792-1112) or at Lake Texana Marina and Brackenridge Plantation Campground (361-782-5456; www.bracken ridgepark.com). You can rent paddleboats and canoes. Birding is excellent in the state park, so much so that it's a stop on the Great Texas Coastal Birding Trail. For information on the latter, call the Houston Audubon Society at (713) 932-1392 or log on to www.houston audubon.org.

Texana Museum. 403 North Wells (Highway 111 North); (361) 782-5431. Exhibits here include old volumes of medicine formulas, a rosewood Chickering piano more than 130 years old, a much older violin, artifacts pertaining to the settlement of Jackson County, and a jail out back, built in 1922, complete with hangman facilities. The museum is open Tuesday–Friday afternoons. The old jail now houses the Otto Lawrence Children's Museum. This hands-on experience opens the doors of a vintage country schoolroom, store, and post office. Dress-up clothes and accessories plus old-time games are part of the fun. Open by appointment. Free.

where to eat

Dos Hermanos Mexican Restaurant. 106 East Houston Highway (US 59 frontage road; exit 111); (361) 782-3372. If you hanker for Tex-Mex while roaming this way, try here. Open for lunch and dinner daily. $–$$.

Frontier Restaurant. 608 North East Street; (361) 782-5270. This local favorite does the standards well. Open for lunch daily, dinner Thursday–Saturday. $–$$. No credit cards.

Palmetto Restaurant. 906 West Main; (361) 782-2471. American and Mexican standards here, along with a good noon buffet and salad bar. Don't pass up the homemade rolls. Open for breakfast, lunch, and dinner Monday–Saturday; breakfast and lunch on Sunday. $–$$.

continuing on

To reach Blessing and Palacios from Edna, take Highway 111 East from Edna for 29 miles (you'll cross Lake Texana) to Highway 71; turn south (right) 4 miles, then west (right) on Highway 35 for 2 miles to Blessing, 13 miles to Palacios.

palacios and blessing

When you want to get away from it all, take Highway 71 South from El Campo to the sleepy fishing community of Palacios. Whatever you want to escape, it isn't here. The big activity for visitors is walking from the Luther Hotel to downtown's eateries, with a short stroll along the refurbished bayfront thrown in for excitement.

The area was named Tres Palacios several centuries ago by shipwrecked Spanish sailors who claimed they saw a vision of three palaces on this bay. Although the tiny town that began here around the turn of the twentieth century doesn't quite live up to the vision, for day-trippers Palacios is the perfect low-key escape.

There are two lighted fishing piers (bring your own bait and gear), numerous other jetties out into the bay, a nice shell beach, plus several public playgrounds, marinas, piers, and boat ramps. A 1.5-mile lighted walkway curves along the seawall, and a newer, rather grand public beach area starts just south of the Luther Hotel.

The old town of Blessing, 13 miles north of Palacios via Highway 35, is a real piece of the past. When the tracks of the New York Central (Missouri Pacific) Railroad and the Southern Pacific Railroad finally crossed on the Texas prairie in 1902, legend says that developer J. E. "Shanghai" Pierce said, "Thank God," and set aside 640 acres for a town of that name. The post office demurred, and "Blessing" was chosen as a compromise. Pierce's burial site is here in Hawley Cemetery, along with his likeness atop a 10-foot column so that he could continue to oversee his lands even after death.

For information on the Palacios/Blessing area, contact the Palacios Chamber of Commerce, 312 Main, Palacios, TX 77465; (361) 972-2615 or (800) 611-4567; www .palacioschamber.com.

what to do

Birding. More than 450 bird species, including brown pelicans and black skimmers, have been spotted along this portion of the Texas coast, making Palacios an important stop on the Great Texas Coastal Birding Trail. There are five birding sites in the city and six others nearby. For a map to major birding sites, contact the Palacios Chamber of Commerce.

Great outdoors. You may want to overnight to take advantage of these opportunities. For scuba diving equipment and scuba instruction, call Don's Diving Service (361-972-2177). For fishing charters call Lost Anchor (361-972-6325) or Capt. Hank Huitt at Palacios Guide Service (361-972-6393).

Palacios Area Historical Museum. 401 Commerce, Palacios (at Fourth Street). Housed in a 1902 building, this collection of artifacts and antiques covers the period from 1902 through World War II. For information call the Palacios Chamber of Commerce, (362) 972-2615.

Texas State Marine Education Center. 102 Marine Center Drive, Palacios; (361) 972-3774. Basically an educational facility designed to handle large groups of students, this operation is of interest to individuals and family visitors only for its 700-foot-long pier (strolling is fine, but no fishing) and its self-guided, 1.2-mile nature trail through a coastal marsh. Pick up a trail guide at Hulin House to fully appreciate the trail's abundant freshwater and saltwater wildlife. Birding platforms overlooking the marsh also are accessible, so bring binoculars. Guided group tours that include parts of the educational facility area are available only by advance appointment. Open weekdays only.

where to eat

Blessing Hotel Coffee Shop. Avenue B and Tenth Street, Blessing; (361) 588-6623; www.hotelblessing.com. Built in 1906, the hotel now is owned by the Blessing Historical Foundation and is under slow restoration. What was the hotel's ballroom is now a coffee shop with a well-earned reputation of its own. You pay your money and fill your plate from pots of delicious country-style food lined up on top of old stoves. The breakfasts are incredible, and the lunches are large enough to satisfy a hardworking field hand. No cutesy quiches here; the noon meal on Sunday is like Thanksgiving all year long. Open daily until 2:00 p.m. $. No credit cards.

Outrigger Restaurant. 515 Commerce, Palacios; (361) 972-1479; www.outrigger restaurant.com. Easy to find—it's opposite the park gazebo—this place offers the Texas standards: seafood, burgers, and chicken-fried steak. Open for lunch and dinner daily. $–$$.

Palacios Mexican Restaurant. 511 Main Street, Palacios; (361) 972-2766. Seafood gets an olé touch at this eatery. Locals also recommend the chiles rellenos as well as the fajitas. Open daily for lunch and dinner. $–$$.

where to stay

Bed-and-breakfast seems a growth industry in the Palacios area. If that's your choice for an overnight, contact the following: the Getaway (361-972-2177), a three-bedroom cottage; the Main Bed & Breakfast (361-972-3408); and the Peaceful Pelican (888-972-0317). The chamber of commerce can provide an extensive list of vacation rental properties.

The Luther Hotel. 408 South Bay Boulevard, Palacios (on the bay between Fourth and Fifth Streets); (361) 972-2312. Quality lasts, and this rambling white frame hostelry has survived many a storm since its construction in 1903. Sited with dignity on a large lawn, this is the kind of place where you contentedly watch twilight creep across Palacios Bay while lounging in a chaise on the front porch. Resort it isn't; relaxing it is. Members of the Luther family still run this historic hotel and suggest you have reservations, as they hang out the NO VACANCY sign with regularity. The rooms are plain but comfortable, with air-conditioning and private baths. Be warned, however: There are no in-room telephones, and two rooms have no television sets. Several of the rooms have kitchens, plus there's a third-floor "penthouse" if you feel like splurging. Except for a complimentary continental breakfast, no food is served at the hotel.

wandering the back roads

The main route into Palacios is Highway 71 and Highway 35 South from El Campo. En route a short turn east on County Road 46 (11 miles south of El Campo) brings you to Danevang Lutheran Church and a memorial to the Danish pioneers who settled here in 1894.

continuing on

To reach Matagorda from Palacios, take Highway 35 North approximately 6 miles. Then turn east (right) on FM 521 for 17 miles to the Highway 60 intersection at Wadsworth. Turn south (right) on Highway 60 for approximately 11 miles to Matagorda. Across the cotton fields you'll glimpse the Houston Light & Power Company's South Texas Nuclear Plant, which produces enough electricity to power more than one million homes. Before the events of 9/11, the plant offered tours. Since then, its visitor center has closed and its security beefed up so much so that its Web site (www.stpnoc.com) brags of the plant's SWAT-like security personnel, all expert marksmen. While driving FM 521 near the power project, watch on the north side for tiny St. Francis Catholic Church and cemetery. Part of an early Polish settlement, only the church was rebuilt after the 1895 hurricane swept all else away.

matagorda

Founded in 1829 with Stephen F. Austin as one of its original proprietors, Matagorda thrived as the Colorado River's port on the Gulf of Mexico and was the third-largest town in Texas by 1834. One of the early freight routes that supplied central Texas with the basics of life ran between Matagorda and Austin. Wagons left both cities on the first and fifteenth of every month.

The railroad steamed across Texas by 1853 and bypassed Matagorda in favor of Bay City. A hurricane in 1854 dealt another blow, and Matagorda never regained its early prominence.

Visitors now find two historic churches (1838 and 1839; both thought to be the first of their denominations in Texas), an 1830 cemetery, several homes with historical markers, and a double lock system operated by the U.S. Army Corps of Engineers on the Intracoastal Canal.

If it's crabbing, seining, picnicking, or beaching you want, turn south on FM 2031 (locally called River Road) in the center of town and follow it to the Gulf. There are many fine crabbing and fishing holes along the way, and the road ends at a county park (picnic and restroom facilities) and 20 miles of beach stretching as far as you can see. Pink granite jetties poke out into the Gulf, ideal for fishing. For the latest information contact the Matagorda Chamber of Commerce, (979) 863-2920; www.matagordachamber.com.

what to do

Birding. More than 300 species of birds have been spotted in the Matagorda area thanks to its diverse habitats. The Matagorda Bay Nature Park bird count has led the nation in the largest number of species counted since 2000. During a one-day bird count in 2003, 231 species were identified by birding enthusiasts. Contact the Matagorda Chamber of Commerce for a map of prime viewing areas, as well as information on seasonal birding tours and events.

Boating. Exploring the serene Colorado River and wildlife-filled Matagorda Bay by kayak and canoe is highly recommended. Kayakers have five public access areas, many with picnic sites, camping, fishing piers, and group pavilions. For rental equipment call Freebird Kayak & Canoe Adventures at (979) 863-7926.

Fishing. There are several charter fishing operations offering excursions on the Colorado River, Matagorda Bay, and the Gulf of Mexico. Contact the chamber of commerce for a list of fishing guides and charters.

LCRA Matagorda Bay Nature Park. Located where the Colorado River meets the Gulf of Mexico; (800) 776-5272; www.lcra.org. The park has a beach area with a fishing pier, and a group pavilion and picnic shelters. Situated along the river channel, the Conservation Center has an interpretative center open to the public, two more fishing piers, and a seventy-site RV park with full hookups. A half-mile section of Gulf beach next to the Conservation Center is closed to vehicles, but the remaining 23 miles is a driving beach with good shelling.

where to eat

River Bend Restaurant & Tavern. On the River Road (FM 2031), 1 mile south of the Intracoastal Canal; (979) 863-7481. Sit on the outdoor covered deck overlooking the Colorado River, if weather permits. The seafood platters and dinners are primarily fresh caught, and the half-pound burgers are a local favorite. At sunset, watch wild hogs feed on the other side of the river. Open for lunch and dinner Wednesday–Sunday. $–$$.

continuing on

To reach Bay City from Matagorda, take Highway 60 North. For miles on either side of Highway 60 you'll see ranches and farms, including many deep green fields that are turf farms providing Houstonians with the makings for enviable lawns.

bay city

The county seat of Matagorda County, Bay City is one of Texas's oldest communities. Founded in 1894 just 25 miles from the Gulf of Mexico, it was known then as Bay Prairie. Today it is a center for farming and ranching, as well as nuclear energy.

Fishing, water sports, and other outdoor pursuits are luring more weekenders from the big city. Another draw is the monthly Market Day, which draws hundreds of vendors from across the state. Held on the town square, Market Day is the third Saturday of each month.

For more information contact the Bay City Chamber of Commerce & Agriculture, P.O. Box 768, Bay City, TX 77404-0768; (979) 245-8333; www.baycity.org.

what to do

Matagorda County Birding and Nature Center. Located about 1.7 miles west of the city on Highway 35; (979) 245-3336; www.mcbnc.org. As birding tourism has taken flight, so has Bay City. In the fall of 2002 the city opened this inviting thirty-five-acre preserve on the banks of the Colorado River. The center spotlights three ecological zones with nature trails, six specialty gardens, and a variety of educational programs. Make time for chatting with the helpful volunteers at the park's office. They can provide details on the most recent bird sightings, as well as offer tips on birding destinations outside the city.

Matagorda County Museum. 2100 Avenue F; (979) 245-7502. Housed in a 1917 postal building on the town's historical square, this museum showcases a variety of fun exhibits, ranging from a look at Karankawa Indian lore and cowboy life to the story of the *LaBelle,* French explorer LaSalle's ship that sank in Matagorda Bay in 1686. The shipwreck was discovered in 1995, and many of the relics recovered have found their way here. The museum also offers interactive exhibits for children that look at frontier life on the Texas coast. Open afternoons Wednesday–Saturday. Fee.

Riverside Park. Located on FM 2668, just south of Bay City; (979) 245-0340. This woodsy park is a one-stop destination for family fun. Nestled along the Colorado River, it offers fishing and boating opportunities, jogging and nature trails, picnic areas, a Xeriscape garden, a shuffleboard court, a driving range, and a playground. If you want to overnight, there are forty campsites with full-service RV hookups.

where to eat

K-2 Steakhouse. 1701 Eighth Street; (979) 245-6936. Steaks broiled, grilled, or chicken-fried are favorites here, and the western salad bar tops most. Other good dining choices are grilled shrimp or gumbo. Open daily for lunch and dinner. $–$$$.

day trip 02

southwest

gator country:
angleton, brazosport, east and west
columbia, richmond and rosenberg

angleton

Two routes—Highway 288 and Highway 35—come south from Houston and meet in
Angleton before continuing to the Brazosport area as Highway 288. You'll pass the old
Brazoria County Courthouse in Angleton, built in 1896 and expanded in 1916 and again in
1927. It now houses the Brazoria County Historical Museum.

If you enjoy canoeing, explore Bastrop Bayou, about 5 miles south of Angleton via
either FM 523 or Highway 288. The best put-in for this 5-mile float is at the FM 2004 bridge,
south of the intersection with FM 523. The best takeout is 2 miles (by road) farther at the
old Highway 288 bridge (watch for a railroad track). Even better, float as far as you want,
and then turn around and paddle back to your car. The current generally is not a problem.
For information call the Greater Angleton Chamber of Commerce at (979) 849-6443.

what to do

Brazoria County Historical Museum. 100 East Cedar (at intersection with Velasco
Street); (979) 864-1208; www.bchm.org. A general store and a doctor's office from Brazoria
County's past are re-created here, along with a plantation bedroom, dioramas, and eco-
nomic exhibits. A sixty-eight-panel exhibit on the Austin Colony illustrates "Where Texas
Began" and includes artifacts from early settlement days, books, documents, and furnished
replicas of a log cabin and an antebellum room. Other areas show items salvaged from the

southwest day trip 02

Houston

Rosenberg
Richmond
George Ranch
762
(Tadpole Rd.)
762
1462
Rosharon
Brazos River County Park
Needville

Brazos R.

1093
1464
90 alt.

288
35

36
East Columbia
West Columbia
Holiday Lakes
Angleton
35
Richwood
Brazoria
322
523
Lake Jackson
Clute
Oyster Creek
Brazoria National Wildlife Refuge

San Luis Pass County Park

521
2918
Jones Creek
Surfside Jetty County Park
Freeport
Quintana Beach County Park

San Bernard National Wildlife Refuge

Gulf of Mexico

0   10   20 miles

blockade runner *Acadia,* a Civil War ship that lies in a watery grave in San Luis Pass. If you're tracing your Texas roots, check out the "Old Three Hundred" genealogical database here. This spot is also worth a stop to shop in the museum's interesting store. Donation requested. Open Tuesday–Saturday. Call for hours.

Brazos River County Park. From Highway 288 north of Angleton, turn west on County Road 44, south on FM 521, then west on County Road 30. This seventy-five-acre park on the banks of the Brazos River has picnic sites with grills, pavilions for groups, 0.5 mile of surfaced trail, a man-made lake with a duck island, a two-story observation tower, and a large, well-equipped playground. Lots of small wildlife here, including rabbits, squirrels, and deer. For information or group reservations, call (979) 849-5711, ext. 1541.

where to eat

Bo's Barbeque. 2024 East Highway 35; (979) 849-0781. If you need a steak or barbecue fix, try here. Open for lunch and dinner daily. $–$$.

Smithhart's. 2440 North Velasco; (979) 848-1320. Serving numerous Texas standards, this bar and grill has a strong local clientele. Open for lunch and dinner daily. $–$$.

continuing on

From Angleton Highway 288 South takes you into the heart of Brazosport.

brazosport

It's rare to find the name Brazosport on current maps, but that's because it really is nine communities in southern Brazoria County: Brazoria, Freeport, Lake Jackson, Quintana, Richwood, Surfside, Oyster Creek, Jones Creek, and Clute. Their common bond is the mighty (and usually muddy) Brazos River as it empties into the Gulf of Mexico.

Local folks say that the name has its origins on seventeenth-century nautical charts to mark where the Brazos meets the sea, and Brazosport today is the only mainland community actually on the Gulf-front coast of Texas.

This is historic country—many people from Stephen F. Austin's first colony settled here—but there is little physical evidence left to provide tourist interest. The area's biggest draws are the free and unrestricted beaches. Any sunny weekend finds thousands of cars lined up on the sand, boom boxes and barbecues going full blast. Most of the beach-related businesses shut down after Labor Day, and Brazosport quickly reverts to the industrial and refining community it basically is.

There's something going on in at least one of the nine towns nearly every month of the year. For a schedule of special events as well as information on marinas, vacation rentals, deep-sea charter and party-boat fishing, and so on, contact the Southern Brazoria County

Visitors and Convention Bureau, 420 West Highway 332, Clute, TX 77531; (979) 265-2505 or (800) 477-2505; www.brazosport.org. For local weather information call (979) 798-1212; for surf and tide conditions, call (979) 233-5301; for a fishing report call (979) 233-7351.

exploring the outdoors

Beaches. The old mouth of the Brazos River becomes, through engineering, the Brazos Harbor Channel and is framed by two jetties ideal for fishing and crabbing. This channel divides the beaches. Northeast to San Luis Pass via FM 3005 and the Bluewater Highway (County Road 257) are Surfside and Follets Island beaches (14 miles of sand). Southwest of the channel are Quintana Beach and Bryan Beach State Park, both accessed via Highway 288 South (Brazosport Boulevard) and FM 1495. You could become "shell shocked" on these beaches, where 600 known species have been found.

The latter's 878 acres are undeveloped but good for fishing, beachcombing, and bird-watching. Use four-wheel drive and keep a wary eye on the tide, or you may be stranded by raising water. Quintana Beach has an excellent county park that includes two restored historic houses, a shore ecology lab, picnic pavilions, restrooms with showers, a fishing pier, a playground and sports courts, World War II gun mounts, and both primitive camping and RV sites. The latter require reservations (call 979-233-1461). Fee. Take notice, however, of the park's warning signs regarding snakes, and be aware that there is often storm debris on the beach.

With the exception of Quintana and a small section of Surfside, automobile traffic is allowed on all beaches. Camping generally is where you wish. There are no hookups, and public restroom facilities are extremely limited. If it's solitude you seek, Bryan Beach is your best bet. For additional information call (979) 265-2508.

Big Boggy National Wildlife Refuge. On the northern shore of East Matagorda Bay. Difficult to get to, this wild area is open for seasonal waterfowl hunting and special activities. Call the Texas Mid-Coast National Wildlife Refuge Complex for details; (979) 849-6062.

Birding. The diversity of the habitats in the Brazosport area has made it ground zero for birding enthusiasts, whose hobby is the United States' fastest-growing outdoor activity. With an average of 217 species spotted, Freeport generally ranks in the top three areas nationally in the Annual Christmas Bird Count, an event sponsored by the Audubon Society that draws more than 55,000 participants in North America.

Brazoria National Wildlife Refuge. On the north shore of West Galveston Bay. From Highway 288 South in Lake Jackson, turn east on FM 2004 for 5 miles, go right on FM 523 for 8 miles, and follow the signs. This 42,338-acre reserve is the winter home to more than 100,000 snow geese and sizeable populations of Canada and white-fronted geese. What's good for the goose is also good for roseate spoonbills, pintails, northern shovelers, mottled ducks, and stately sandhill cranes. The park is open sunrise to sundown daily. There's hiking trails and a 6-mile auto tour that traverses numerous habitats. And mind the warnings to stay on the trails—alligators prowl the refuge year-round. (See the Texas Mid-Coast National Wildlife Refuge Complex listing for contact information.)

Fishing charters and party boats. Amberjack, red snapper, shark, bluefish, and Spanish mackerel are some of the species anglers can pluck from the waters surrounding the reefs, oil platforms, and wrecks in the Gulf. Action Charters (979-265-0999; www.actioncharter fishing.com) operates four boats for parties of eight to twenty-four people. Freeport native David Smith (979-297-4410; www.davidsdeepseacharters.com) takes anglers fishing for ling and dorado about 40 miles into the Gulf aboard his boat, *Rock Bottom.* Both of these charter firms provide equipment, bait, and expertise. Reservations are a must; call for rates. For a list of other fishing charter operations, call the Brazosport Chamber of Commerce at (979) 265-2505 or log on to www.brazosport.org.

Gulf Coast Bird Observatory. 103 West Highway 332, Lake Jackson; (979) 480-0999; www.gcbo.org. Dedicated to the conservation of birds and their habitat in and around the Gulf of Mexico, this research center and interpretive center welcomes visitors interested in learning more about birding. Trails wind through much of this forested thirty-six-acre site, plus this is a good source for the upper Texas coast version of the Great Texas Coast Birding Trail map. Open weekdays during business hours, but ask about special events.

Longhorn cattle. Dow Chemical has developed a 600-acre greenbelt and stocked it with Texas longhorn cattle. Best viewing is in the 1200 block of Highway 332 West.

Quintana Neotropical Bird Sanctuary. Cross the Intracoastal Waterway on FM 1495, then travel east 2.1 miles on County Road 723. Managed by the Houston Audubon Society, this compact sanctuary is a rewarding stop for both the novice and expert birder. The trails are dotted with park benches from which visitors can spy hummingbirds, flycatchers, and tanagers. Nearby is Xeriscape Park, which features a nature trail and hummingbird garden. Both are open daily. For information call Quintana City Hall at (979) 233-0848 or log on to www.quintana-tx.org.

Recreational vehicles. Two county parks have been designed for outdoors enthusiasts who like to bring their "homes" with them. San Luis Pass County Park and RV Campground is one of the hottest fishing spots on the Gulf coast. Day-use facilities include fishing piers, a boat ramp, a playground, and a visitor center with a deck overlooking the water. The RV area has full hookups as well as a bathhouse with showers and laundry facilities. For reservations call (979) 233-6026. Anglers, birders, and picnickers also will find good facilities at Surfside Jetty County Park on the Brazos River Harbor Channel. This Gulf-front park features a deck and patio with picnic tables, restrooms, showers, lighted volleyball courts, and an observation tower. Handrails and a paved walkway allow for easy fishing from the jetty.

San Bernard National Wildlife Refuge. Ten miles west of Freeport. From Highway 36 South turn southwest on FM 2611, left on FM 2918, and then right on County Road 306. This 23,445-acre prairie and marsh preserve can be reached by boat from the Intracoastal Waterway and by car via FM 2004 West from Highway 288 in Lake Jackson. Established as a quality habitat for wintering migratory waterfowl and other birds, the refuge has recorded more than 400 species of wildlife and is the winter home to more than 90,000 snow geese. Birding, wildlife observation, hiking, photography, fishing, and waterfowl hunting are the major activities. One loop road encircles Moccasin Pond for auto tours, and there are three walking trails, including one that is wheelchair accessible. These trails are generally rich with birds. The park is open sunrise to sundown daily. (See the Texas Mid-Coast National Wildlife Refuge Complex listing for contact information.)

Scuba diving. One hundred miles off the Texas coast is Flower Garden Banks National Marine Sanctuary, a 42-square-nautical-mile underwater paradise where divers can see twenty-one species of coral and more than 300 species of fish, including tiger shark, conger eel, and southern stingray. For information about the sanctuary, write them at 4700 Avenue U, Building 216, Galveston, TX 77551; call (409) 621-5151; or log on to www.flower garden.nos.noaa.gov/. Three vessels moored at Freeport—MV *Fling* or MV *Spree,* and *Seasearcher II*—make two- and three-day diving trips to the sanctuary. Diving trips must be booked through dive shops, which can be identified by the following charter firms: Gulf Diving (MV *Fling* or MV *Spree;* 979-233-4445; www.gulf-diving.com) and Advanced Diving (*Sea Searcher II;* 800-396-3483; www.seasearcherii.com).

The Texas Mid-Coast National Wildlife Refuge Complex provides some of the nation's best birding opportunities. The complex comprises three refuges—Big Boggy, Brazoria, and San Bernard—that are home to more than 300 bird species. The ecosystems represented range from coastal prairie and bottomland forest to saltwater marsh and muddy bayou. Savvy outdoors enthusiasts know that when visiting wildlife refuges, you should always have sturdy footwear, sunscreen, and insect repellent. And don't forget the binoculars and camera. For information contact the refuge office at 1212 North Valasco, Suite 200, Angleton, TX 77515; (979) 849-6062; www.fws.gov/refuges.

Valasco Riverside Park. Avenue A at Highway 288, Freeport. This tiny park on the bank of the Old Brazos River offers a lush, shady spot for a picnic or just a place to collect your thoughts. A paved hiking/biking trail that runs alongside the river is easily accessed here.

what to do

Brazosport Center for the Arts and Sciences. 400 College Drive, Clute (on the Brazosport College campus off Highway 288); (979) 265-7661; www.bcfas.org. This 40,000-square-foot cultural complex is of interest to day-trippers primarily for the gem of a natural science museum it contains. Exhibits at the Brazosport Museum of Natural Science interpret this coastal region through shells, plants, animals, fossils, minerals, and Indian artifacts. The shell exhibit, the most extensive in the southern United States, is particularly well done and will turn your beach trips into expeditions. The Brazosport Nature Center and Planetarium has a star show for the public on most Tuesday evenings. A self-guided nature trail along Oyster Creek reveals more than 200 species of river-bottom vegetation. Closed Monday. Fee for special programs.

Brazoria Civic Center Historical Museum. (979) 236-0241. Brazoria was an important settlement during the early days of Anglo Texas, and this small museum has artifacts dating from 1827 as well as an interesting re-creation of Dr. Sofie Herzog's medical office. Herzog was the county's first woman doctor and the first female railroad surgeon in the world. At press time, the Brazoria Heritage Foundation has completed partial restoration of the old Brazoria Elementary School building at 214 West Smith Street in Brazoria, which has become the museum's new headquarters. The train museum, formerly in Lake Jackson, will be relocated here as soon as its area in the school building is renovated. The train exhibit focuses on Brazoria County in the year 1955 via a 21-by-32-foot layout in HO scale. The exhibit literally covers the territory—from rivers and bridges to farms, animals, and homes. Call for days and hours of operation.

Girouard's General Store. 626 West Second Street, Freeport; (979) 233-4211. When *Texas Monthly* magazine labels something the best in the state, it's worth a good look. You'll find the wrenches over the bread, plumber's helpers near the piñatas, and nearly everything else tucked somewhere. This is an outstanding example of a nearly extinct type of store. If you forgot your crabbing or seining gear, just stop here. Open Monday–Saturday.

Lake Jackson Historical Museum. 249 Circle Way, Lake Jackson; (979) 297-1570; www.lakejacksonmuseum.org. This well-done look at the past focuses on the four heritages of the local area. Starting with the Karankawa Indians, the exhibits continue through the mid-nineteenth-century plantation era, the beginnings of the petrochemical industry in 1940, and the subsequent creation of Lake Jackson as a Dow Chemical company town. One of the big attractions here is the Windecker Eagle, a revolutionary airplane invented by a Lake Jackson dentist in the early 1950s. Built of glass and epoxy resins and therefore invisible to radar, it served as the forerunner for today's Stealth aircraft. Suspended here as if ready for takeoff, this is one of nine remaining originals. Open Tuesday–Sunday. Fee.

Sea Center Texas. 300 Medical Drive, Lake Jackson; (979) 292-0100; www.tpwd .state.tx.us. Technically the largest red drum (redfish) hatchery in the world, this $13-million facility is reason enough to journey to southern Brazoria County. The 15,000-square-foot visitor center has a large touch pool where folks can handle marine animals such as clams, snails, anemones, crabs, starfish, and urchins; an impressive coastal bay aquarium where Gulf species such as red drum, speckled trout, and snook cruise through 2,200 gallons of water; a 5,000-gallon jetty exhibit with a variety of fish zipping in and out of wooden pilings and rocks; a 5,000-gallon artificial reef that replicates those found in the open Gulf; and a 1,000-gallon Gulf of Mexico aquarium, where 500-pound Gordon the Grouper swims amid tarpon, redfish, and circling sharks.

Visitors also can tour the brood fish tanks in an adjacent hatchery building and explore several outside culture ponds and a five-acre marsh area. The latter has elevated walkways, interpretive signing, and viewing platforms. Open Tuesday–Friday from 9:00 a.m. to 4:00 p.m. Free.

Surfside Beach Museum. 1304 Monument Drive, Surfside; (979) 233-1531. Housed in a 1915 Coast Guard station, this small but interesting collection is worth a look. Open business hours on weekdays.

where to eat

Cafe Annice Kitchen & Art Space. 24 Circle Way, Lake Jackson; (979) 292-0060. If beautifully prepared and presented food is high on your list of personal pleasures, make a special trip to this eatery. Owners Leonard and Janel Botello have created a visual cross between a California-style cafe and contemporary Italian trattoria, complete with coffee bar, a challenging menu, and vivid abstract art on the walls. Top honors go to the Texas blue crab cakes, the pasta caliente with jumbo shrimp, and the grilled-chicken Caesar salad. Open Monday–Saturday for lunch and dinner (closed midafternoon). $–$$.

Dido's. County Road 519, Brazoria; (979) 964-3167. From FM 521 in Brazoria, turn left on Highway 36, right on FM 311, and right on FM 519 to the river. Dido runs his own shrimp boats, which makes for good eating, either in the air-conditioned dining room or on the outside deck. For groups of ten or more, Dido's also operates the *Velasco Princess,* a 72-foot paddle wheeler, on the San Bernard River in southern Brazoria County. Open for lunch and dinner; closed Monday. $–$$$.

D.J.'s Bar-B-Que. 906 West Plantation, Clute; (979) 265-6331. This longtime local favorite is open Monday for lunch only; Tuesday–Saturday for lunch and dinner. $. No credit cards.

On the River. 919 West Second Street, Freeport; (979) 233-0503. The fried, boiled, blackened, or baked fish is great here (particularly the stuffed shrimp and catfish), plus there are plenty of steaks and chicken selections as well. The location is a 1910 building, cozied up with antiques. Open for lunch and dinner Monday–Saturday, dinner only on Sunday (5:00 to 9:00 p.m.). $–$$.

The Picket Fence. 708 Dixie Drive, Clute; (979) 297-7234. If you're hunting for a tasty, home-style lunch, give this popular place a try. Choices include freshly made soups, casseroles, salads, sandwiches, and desserts. Open Monday–Saturday for lunch. $.

Red Snapper Inn. 402 Bluewater Highway, Surfside; (979) 239-3226. Locals love this place for its inventive way with fresh fish. Try snapper a la grecque, the shrimp baked with feta cheese and fresh tomatoes, or the sautéed fillet of fresh flounder topped with fresh mushrooms and artichoke hearts, and you'll probably agree. Save room for a slice of house-made cheesecake or apple pie. Open daily for lunch and dinner. $–$$. No credit cards.

Windswept Restaurant. 105 Burch Circle, Oyster Creek; (979) 233-1951. One of the favorite seafood restaurants in the Brazosport area, this place specializes in fresh shrimp dinners and whole flounder. To get here, drive east on Highway 332 in Surfside, left on FM 523, right on Linda Lane, right on Duncan Drive, and right again on Burch Circle. The restaurant is behind the Oyster Creek water tower. Open for lunch and dinner daily. $–$$$.

continuing on

From Brazosport and environs this day trip continues north to East and West Columbia. Although Highway 36 is the swiftest route, you might prefer to mosey a while along the old river road that runs beside the Brazos from Jones Creek to Brazoria. To do the latter, start north on Highway 36 at Freeport, turn east (right) on County Road 400, and continue northwest along the river. At the intersection with FM 521, turn west (left) for about 0.75 mile to intersect Highway 36 and the original routing for this trip.

wandering the back roads

As you pass through Brazoria, take time to explore. Most of the original town has been flooded by the river, but there are a growing number of antiques stores as well as several historical markers worth a read. As an alternative to continuing on Highway 36 to the Columbias, you can follow FM 521 West and Highway 60 South to Matagorda (see Southwest Day Trip 1).

east and west columbia

As you drive into these two small towns on Highway 36 and Highway 35, it's hard to believe they were among the most thriving communities in the state in 1836. East Columbia originally was Bell's Landing, a small port on the Brazos River established in 1824 by one of Austin's first colonists, Josiah H. Bell. Today East Columbia is almost a ghost town, with only a few fine old homes to hint at its early importance.

West Columbia was another enterprise of Josiah Bell. In 1826 he cut a road across the prairie on the west side of the Brazos and created a new town called Columbia. Within three years it was one of the major trading areas in Texas, and by 1836 some 3,000 people lived here, the rich river bottomland nurturing a thriving plantation economy.

After Sam Houston's victory over Santa Anna at San Jacinto, West Columbia really came into its own. The most powerful men in Texas came here, designated it the first state capital, created a constitution, and elected Sam Houston the first president of the new republic.

Such glory was short-lived. The town wasn't big enough to house everyone who came to the governmental proceedings, and in 1837 the legislature moved to Houston. But West Columbia had snagged its place in history, and visitors find several interesting sites as well as antiques shops along Brazos Street. For maps and advance information, contact the West Columbia Chamber of Commerce, 247 East Brazos, West Columbia, TX 77486; (979) 345-3921; www.westcolumbia.org.

what to do

Ammon Underwood House. On the river side of Main Street in East Columbia. Built about 1835 as a pole cabin and enlarged twice, this stately old home has been surprisingly mobile. It has been moved three times to save it from tumbling into the Brazos. Currently owned and restored by the First Capitol Historical Foundation of West Columbia, this is the oldest house in the East Columbia community. Many of the furnishings and some of the wallpaper are original, and one room has been left unfinished to show early construction techniques. A log cabin built prior to 1850 has been moved onto the land beside the Underwood home. Open during the San Jacinto Festival and by appointment through the West Columbia Chamber of Commerce (979-345-3921).

Columbia Historical Museum. 247 East Brazos, West Columbia; (979) 345-6125; www.westcolumbia.org/museum.htm. Local antiques, plus exhibits on area ranching, the oil boom days of the 1920s, and present times are the focus here. Children enjoy the display of Indian arrow and spear points and the metal bell once used on a Brazos River steamboat. Open 10:00 a.m. to 2:00 p.m. Thursday–Saturday, or by appointment.

Hanson's Riverside Park. On the San Bernard River, 2.5 miles west of West Columbia on Highway 35. This picnic spot has grills, a playground, a fishing pier, and an old-fashioned swimming hole.

Replica of the First Capitol. On Fourteenth Street, behind the First Prosperity Bank; (979) 345-3921. This successful bicentennial project re-creates the small clapboard building that served as the first capitol of Texas. The original building was a store, which subsequently had a variety of tenants before it was destroyed in the 1900 storm that devastated much of the Texas coast. The shed room to the right as you enter is thought to replicate Stephen F. Austin's office when he served as the first secretary of state for the republic, and the furnishings of the building, while not original, are antiques from that period. Open Monday–Friday by appointment.

The Varner-Hogg State Historic Park. P.O. Box 696, West Columbia, TX 77486-0696 (1 mile north of Highway 35 on FM 2852); (979) 345-4656; www.tpwd.state.tx.us. This land was one of the original land grants from Mexico, part of approximately 4,500 acres given to Martin Varner in 1824. Varner built a small cabin, began running stock, and in 1826 built a rum distillery on his holdings. Stephen F. Austin termed the results of this last enterprise the first "ardent spirits" made in the Texas colonies.

Varner sold his holdings in 1834, and the next year the new owner built a two-story brick house that survives today. Varner's original cabin is believed to be incorporated into the house. The bricks of the existing house were made by slaves from clay found in the nearby Brazos riverbed. By the late 1800s this plantation was prospering with sugar cane, cotton, corn, and livestock. In 1901 the first native-born governor of Texas, James Hogg, bought the plantation and regarded the house as the first permanent home his family had. In 1920 the four Hogg children began remodeling the old house. Donated to the state in 1958, it was further restored in 1981. There is a shady picnic area, and house tours are given whenever a small group forms. The park is open daily; the plantation house is open 9:00 to 11:00 a.m. and 1:00 to 4:00 p.m. Wednesday–Saturday and 1:00 to 4:00 p.m. Sunday. Fee.

where to eat

Cowgirl's Kitchen. 333 West Brazos; West Columbia; (979) 345-2776. Ask for a large chef's salad at Cowgirl's, and you are served a Calamity Jane. If you order a Marshal, that's the chicken-fried steak. Many folks riding the range like catfish; for it, try the Deputy. The menu's fun, but the kitchen's cowgirl food is seriously good. Open weekdays for breakfast, lunch, and dinner. $–$$.

Elmo's Grill. 454 South Seventeenth Street (Highway 35), West Columbia; (979) 345-5127. If you're looking for fast, low-cost, no-surprises food, consider this local favorite. No menus here—just bulletin boards listing the normal burgers and Mexican offerings as well as at least one daily special. Open daily for lunch and dinner. $. No credit cards.

Lucy's Mexican Food. 1017 South Columbia Drive, West Columbia; (979) 345-5300. The Tex-Mex here is so popular with local residents that you may have to wait for a table. Both the fajitas and the chicken-fried steak come highly recommended. Open for lunch and dinner Monday–Saturday. $–$$.

richmond and rosenberg

Enjoy Richmond while you can. Within a decade it may be swallowed by Houston's urban creep, a historic oasis amid acres of subdivisions. For now, just getting to Richmond and its sidekick city of Rosenberg is a pleasure, whether you come north via Highway 36 from the

Columbias or west on U.S. Highway 90A from Houston. The countryside primarily is farms and ranches, shaded by mature pecan trees and pleasant to pass by any time of the year.

Richmond flows into Rosenberg, the larger of the two towns. An early shipping site on the Brazos, Rosenberg really boomed in 1883, when the railroad came to town. While it remains the commercial center, the two towns have shared a common history for the past century. For day-trippers Richmond is the more historically interesting destination.

In Texas time Richmond is very old, one of the first permanent settlements of Stephen F. Austin's original 300 colonists. For centuries the Brazos River had made a big bend here, each flood leaving more rich soil in its wake. Shortly after Christmas Day 1821, five men staked their fortunes on this fertile land, building a two-room fort just below the bend, thus the name Fort Bend County. Today a marker stands on this site, almost lost between the eastbound and westbound bridges of US 90A as they span the Brazos.

The settlement thrived with the addition of Thompson's Ferry, northwest in the bend of the river, and in 1837 the town of Richmond was formally laid out on the site of the old fort. By 1843 a sugar mill was in operation at nearby Sugar Land, the forerunner of the Imperial Sugar plant, and sugar cane plantations were thriving throughout the area by the 1860s.

Richmond had a number of now-famous residents, among them Mirabeau Lamar, Deaf Smith, and Jane Long. Carrie Nation ran a hotel on the corner of Fourth and Morton Streets before she took up her hatchet-wielding crusade against demon rum.

Visitors find several reminders of Richmond's colonial past, but the overriding feeling is that of exploring small-town America, circa 1940. Somehow it is reassuring to discover a corner drugstore and other small businesses within the shadow of an old-fashioned courthouse. A walk along Richmond's main drag, Morton Street, is a visual antidote to Houston's skyscrapers.

A detailed map guides you along the oak-shaded streets to all the historic sites, courtesy of the Fort Bend County Museum. The maps are available at the museum (see "What to Do") or from Rosenberg Tourism Development, P.O. Box 32, Rosenberg, TX 77471; (832) 595-3520; www.rosenbergtourism.com.

what to do

Brazos Bend State Park. 21901 FM 762 (Tadpole Road), Needville (20 miles south of Richmond); (979) 553-5101; www.tpwd.state.tx.us. Turn south on the Crabb River Road exit from U.S. Highway 59 South and follow signs. One of the newest parks in the system, this is 5,000 acres of wild beauty along Big Creek, a tributary of the Brazos. Overnight facilities include screened shelters, trailer sites with hookups, tent sites with water, and primitive sites with no water that require a hike in; almost all are shaded by massive oaks. In addition to two large fishing piers where you can angle for bass, catfish, or crappie, there are hiking/biking and nature trails, several large playing fields, seven photography platforms for "focusing on" the park's exceptional wildlife, and an interpretive center. Rangers lead daily programs, so the center should be your first stop to see what's going on. *Of interest:* Children under seventeen do not need a license to fish in this park. *Caution:* This is alligator country; no one can enter any of the park waters for any reason. All visitors are given a list of alligator etiquette rules when they arrive. A nature trail designed for all, including those with vision, hearing, or mobility challenges, now circles the park's Creekfield Lake. Flat and paved, the trail is 0.5 mile long and has tactile interpretive panels that explain the wetlands ecology. A taped audio tour can be checked out at the park's visitor center. Fee.

Also in the park is the George Observatory, a satellite facility of the Houston Museum of Natural Science that opens at 3:00 p.m. on Saturday. General public viewing through the large telescope is possible from dusk to 11:00 p.m. on summer Saturdays, dusk to 10:00 p.m. in winter. Passes are given out on a first-come, first-served basis beginning at 5:00 p.m. (arrive no later than 4:00 p.m. or you won't get a pass). Several smaller telescopes on the top deck of the planetarium are available for persons without passes. Fee. Adjacent to the observatory, the Challenger Learning Center offers space lore, including a simulated mission to the moon. For information call (979) 553-3400.

Decker Park. North of the railroad tracks at Sixth and Preston Streets, Richmond; (281) 342-2849. Two buildings moved here mark the very slow beginning of a living-history museum: a 1902 railroad depot and the 1850s McNabb House, once owned by Carrie Nation's daughter. The Victorian brick relic across Preston Street was the county jail from 1896 to 1948. It now has been restored to its former architectural splendor and functions as a museum and offices for the Richmond Police. Call for hours and jail tour information.

The Fort Bend County Courthouse. Fourth and Jackson Streets, Richmond. This fifth courthouse was built with an air of majesty in 1908 and was so well refurbished in 1981 that it was cited by the Houston chapter of the American Institute of Architects. It also is the only public building in Fort Bend County listed on the National Register of Historic Places. Notable features are the three-story rotunda, the mosaic tile floors, and the rich woodwork on the stairs and in the main courtroom. Open Monday–Friday. Free.

Fort Bend Museum. 500 Houston Street, Richmond (at Fifth Street); (281) 342-6478; www.fortbendmuseum.org. Just about every aspect of "Life along the Brazos" between 1820 and 1930 is covered in this complex comprised of three historic homes, with displays including items and manuscripts of Mirabeau Lamar, Jane Long, and Austin's first colony. One diorama tells the harrowing tale of early railroad crossings on the Brazos, and special artifacts include the hatchet Carrie Nation used on a Houston saloon in 1905. On the grounds are the Long-Smith Cottage, a Greek Revival house furnished to reflect a typical middle-class home circa 1850–60. The home was bought in 1860 by Julia Beale Bassett Smith, who lived there for thirteen years along with her husband and ten children. Also here is the John M. Moore House, a gracious old home that looks as though it will stand for several more years. Originally a Gothic Victorian home with a domed tower, it was built in 1883 by the Moores, a ranching family whose patriarch was elected to the U.S. Congress in 1905. Following that election, the home was remodeled to its current Greek Revival style. The decor offers a look at life in Richmond in the early 1940s. Not open for tours, the third historic home is the McFarlane House, which was constructed in 1882.

The museum staff also gives demonstrations of frontier skills and guides historical tours of Richmond for groups by advance notice. Closed Monday.

The George Ranch Historical Park. 10215 FM 762 (P.O. Box 1242, Richmond, TX 77406), 8 miles southeast of Richmond; (281) 545-9212 or (281) 343-0218; www.george ranch.org. What was life like in rural Texas between 1890 and 1930? This 470-acre living-history project (part of a 23,000-acre working ranch) turns back the years and lets you participate as well. Costumed actors re-create Victorian life at the J. H. P. Davis Home (1896) and more modern times at the George ranch house (1930s); cowboys rope and ride; ranch hands demonstrate cattle-dipping, blacksmithing, woodworking, and so forth; and tractor-drawn carryalls haul you around the grounds. The 1820s Jones Farmstead, an authentically re-created working farm, includes a furnished dog-trot cabin, a barn, a corncrib, croplands, an orchard, and a garden.

Nearly every weekend between Memorial Day and Labor Day has a special theme. Don't miss Texian Market Days the fourth weekend of October. Special events such as rodeos and trail rides can be arranged year-round for corporate meetings, conventions, and private groups. Although there's a small eatery on-site, picnickers are welcome. Open daily. Fee.

Glider rides. This glorious, silent sport is now available in nearby Wallis. For information call Thrilling Adventures at (800) 762-7464.

Morton Cemetery. On Second Street, north of Jackson Street, Richmond. Used during the 1838–41 period, this is the last resting place of Mirabeau Lamar and the "Mother of Texas," Jane Long.

Museum of Southern History. 14080 Southwest Freeway, Sugar Land; (281) 269-7171. The South *may* rise again. This collection includes muskets, rifles, guns, uniforms, furniture, pictures, money, letters, and other memorabilia relating to both Jane Long and the Civil War. Other exhibits show ship models, maps, and prints. Open Tuesday–Friday and on weekend afternoons. Fee.

Old Rosenberg. Located from Fourth Street to First Street, Rosenberg; (281) 342-5464. From Avenue H (US 90A) start at First Street and go from there. It's 5 blocks deep and 3 blocks wide and thrives with antiques shops, boutiques, the civic center, and the Rosenberg Railroad Museum. Picnic at Seabourne Creek Park, an official birding site (but swimming is not allowed).

Rosenberg Railroad Museum. Corner of Third and Avenue F, Rosenberg; (281) 633-2846; www.rosenbergrrmuseum.org. Housed in a replica of an 1883 depot, this family-friendly museum traces the history of Fort Bend County, once home to eight rail lines and a major player in the cattle and cotton industries. Open Tuesday–Sunday. Fee.

Seabourne Creek Park. Highway 36 South, 0.25 mile south of US 59; (832) 595-3520. Whenever there's a big celebration in Rosenberg, this 164-acre park plays host. Opened in spring 2001, the park features a four-and-a-half-acre stocked lake with fishing platforms, a 700-foot boardwalk accessing a wetlands basin, and hiking and biking trails. Sorry, no swimming.

Skydive Spaceland. 16111 FM 521, Rosharon; (281) 369-3337; www.skydivespaceland .com. Been there? Done that? Discover the rush of jumping out of a plane at 14,000 feet. The staff at Skydive Spaceland can get you in the air and out of the plane in less than half an hour. That is, if you don't mind a tandem jump, where you're strapped to a professional jumper. There's a prejump class where you learn how to pull the ripcord, how to steer, and how to land safely. Then you take wing. The jump includes a sixty-five-second free fall before you glide down to earth. A videographer catches all the action so that if you desire, you'll have a record of your adventure. Fee.

where to eat

Italian Maid Cafe. 300 Morton Street, Richmond; (281) 232-6129; www.italianmaid cafe.com. Delicious pastas, done with an Old Country touch and served with either salad or soup, are the big draws here. Alternates include daily specials, several unusual soups and salads, and a long list of sandwiches that makes you hungry just to read it. Open for lunch Monday–Friday, dinner Tuesday–Saturday. $–$$.

Karl's at the Riverbend. 5011 FM 723, Richmond; (281) 237-9300; www.karlsrb.com. If it's fine food you seek, come here. The mix of American and continental standards range from beautifully prepared game to a memorable Wiener schnitzel, prime rib, and fish. There's usually a low-cost midweek menu as well as some daily specials. Open for lunch and dinner Tuesday–Saturday and for Sunday brunch. $$–$$$.

Sandy McGee's. Two locations: 314 Morton, Richmond (281-344-9393), and 1207 Sixth Street, Rosenberg (281-341-9151; www.sandymcgees.com). If inventive salads, sandwiches, and daily specials sound appealing, don't miss these charming cafes. Save room for dessert. Open for lunch on weekdays. $–$$. No credit cards.

wandering the back roads

An alternate route from Houston to Richmond forsakes US 59 and US 90A and instead rambles west out Westheimer (FM 1093) past its intersection with Highway 6 and then turns south (left) on FM 1464. Continue south on FM 1464 for approximately 8 miles to its intersection with US 90A. A turn west (right) then takes you directly into Richmond's historic district.

To roam among pastures and pecan orchards, go north from Richmond on FM 359 (Skinner Road), and when it curves to the left, stay straight. That puts you on Skinner Lane, one of the prettiest drives around.

Another country ramble takes the long way home. From Richmond turn south on FM 762 (Eleventh Street/Thompson Road) and follow its zigzag southeasterly course through the countryside. Just beyond Crabb, FM 762 turns farther south as the A. P. George Road. Stay on FM 762 as it jogs onto Tadpole Road. At the intersection with FM 1462 at Woodrow, turn east (left) to intersect Highway 288 and then north (left) toward Houston and home.

northeast

day trip 01

northeast

humble beginnings:
humble, cleveland, coldspring

humble

As with the small town of Spring in north Harris County, there are two Humbles—old and new. The new is easy to find, a plastic forest of franchise signs and shopping centers around the U.S. Highway 59/FM 1960 interchange. Old Humble lies quietly behind, east of the railroad tracks and south of FM 1960.

Back in 1865 a fisherman named Pleasant Smith Humble established a small ferry across the San Jacinto River near where US 59 crosses it today. Things remained quiet until the railroad arrived in 1878, and Humble became a flag stop on the narrow-gauge HE&WT line, running between Houston and Shepherd. Settlers came, and by 1886 Humble was officially a town.

Rich with timber, Humble fed a growing logging industry. Back in 1887 a local lumberman, Jim H. Slaughter, rafted logs down the San Jacinto for milling. Pulling into a small backwater to make an overnight camp, he noticed bubbles seeping along the riverbank. When his match brought a flame, he recognized the presence of natural gas and subsequently bought sixty acres of land in the area. Although he personally didn't profit greatly, this was the beginning of the oil fields in Humble and Harris County.

The first wells came into production in 1904, and by mid-1905 the field was producing more barrels per day than any other in the state. The Moonshine Hill area east of town soon had a population of 25,000, and Humble got busy earning a reputation as one of the tough-

northeast day trip 01

est towns in Texas. The Texas Rangers often had to be called on to keep some semblance of law and order.

In 1909 the Humble Oil and Refining Company was formed in a small, tin-roofed building on Humble's Main Street, one of its organizers being the local feed store owner, Ross Sterling. The company was successful and ultimately became part of the Exxon we now know. Sterling didn't do badly either. He soon bought the Humble State Bank and carved a niche in the state's history as a newspaper publisher, oilman, and governor of Texas from 1931 to 1933.

As quickly as it had come, the oil boom disappeared—no new wells were coming in—and by 1915 Humble once again was a small, quiet community strongly dependent on lumber and agriculture for its financial base. A second oil strike at greater depth in 1929 brought new life, and Humble was chartered as a city in 1933.

Humble's Main Street is now a stroll through struggling small-town Americana, but things are looking up. Fresh interest in restoring Main Street to its original appearance has resulted in several antiques shops, excellent eateries, and a pocket park in the 300 block. The small cottages that line nearby First Street also offer unusual shopping. Stop too at the corner of First Street and North Houston Avenue to see the oldest artesian well in the area, drilled as a wildcat oil venture in 1912. For additional information on the area, contact the Humble Area Chamber of Commerce, 110 West Main (P.O. Box 3337), Humble, TX 77347; (281) 446-2128; www.humbleareachamber.org.

what to do

Humble Historical Museum. 219 Main Street; (281) 446-2130. A grassroots result of America's bicentennial, this small museum is bursting with a collection of interesting old things donated by local residents. Open Tuesday–Saturday. Free; donations appreciated.

Jesse H. Jones Park. 20634 Kenswick Drive; (281) 446-8588; www.hcp4.net/jones. From US 59 North go west 1.7 miles on FM 1960 and turn right on Kenswick Drive. The park is at the end of the road. This large wilderness preserve on Spring and Cypress Creeks has hiking trails, a frontier-fort-styled playground and picnic area, a pioneer homestead, a canoe launch, and a three-acre beach on the creek for fishing (no swimming). With a Texas fishing license, you can angle for white bass, crappie, catfish, and alligator gar. Nature photography is popular here, as are birding and canoeing. About 85 percent of the trails are blacktopped for wheelchair accessibility. Birders can pick up a list at the Nature Center Building, which also has wildlife exhibits, including common poisonous snakes and a cutaway look at a working beehive. One of the things that makes Jones Park among the region's best is its extensive menu of special events and programs, which range from learn-to-fish workshops for junior anglers and sunset hikes to canoe trips down Spring Creek and Sunday-morning biking adventures. Each February the park hosts Homestead Heritage Bay, and in November, Pioneer Day, programs that look at pioneer life and feature costumed reenactments of Civil War battles. Open daily.

Lake Houston. The best play places (picnicking, swimming, boating) are Dwight D. Eisenhower Park and Alexander Duessen Park, both near the dam. Take the Duessen Drive exit from the Sam Houston tollway and follow the signs.

Lake Houston Park. 22031 Baptist Encampment Road, New Caney; (281) 354-6881. Take New Caney exit from US 59, go east approximately 2 miles on FM 1485, and then turn right on Baptist Encampment Road. The park entrance will be 1.5 miles down on the left. Don't rev your boat motors or load your fishing gear; in spite of its name, this 4,913-acre park has no lake frontage. It's an outstanding spot, however, for birding, hiking and biking (12 miles of trails), and—thanks to hot showers—tent camping. A small, white-sand beach on Peach Creek offers shallow-water play for children. There also are 8 miles of separate equestrian trails, but it's BYO horse. Open daily. Fee.

Old MacDonald's Farm. 3203 FM 1960 East (2.5 miles east of Deerbrook Mall); (281) 446-4001; www.oldmacdonaldshumble.com. When the pint-size natives get restless, spend the day in this kiddie paradise. Admission includes pony and train rides, petting and feeding animals in twelve barns, playing in a mountain of sand, jigging for crawfish in a pond, swimming, milking the cow, and gathering eggs. In addition to food concessions, there's also a shady picnic area to use if you bring food from home. Open weekends November and February, daily March–October; closed December and January.

Tour 18. 3102 FM 1960 East (2 miles east of US 59); (281) 540-1818; www.tour18golf.com. There are hundreds of golf courses in the greater Houston area, but none other like this $5-million layout. In toto it re-creates eighteen of the greatest holes in the nation, a par 72, 6,807-yard challenge engineered across 200 acres. Want to test your skills against the pros on the 17th at Sawgrass? No. 14 at Pebble Beach? Nos. 11 and 12 at Augusta? Come try what may be the most difficult course in the country. Tee times can be arranged up to thirty days in advance. Open daily. Call for fees.

where to eat

Chez Nous. 217 South Avenue G; (281) 446-6717; www.cheznousfrenchrestaurants.com. In addition to a menu that features many French classics, chef-founder Gerard Brach offers outstanding daily specials such as pan-seared grouper with mangoes, tomatoes, red onion, and black bean puree, and chunks of beef tenderloin with wild mushrooms, potatoes, pearl onions, English peas, and a roasted garlic flan. French-born and trained, Gerard also has taught a wine course at the Four Seasons in New York City, expertise that shows on the wine list. This jewel of a restaurant is in an unlikely setting, a century-old church. You'll want to dress up for this dining experience. This restaurant is worth a trip to Humble if you enjoy fine food prepared with skill and care. Open Monday–Saturday for dinner; reservations strongly advised. Ask for specific directions when you call—it's hard to find. $$–$$$.

Fuel Cafe. 120 Main Street; (281) 540-3170; www.fuelcybercafe.com. This place dispels the theory that all the cool spots are located within the Interstate 610 Loop. Patrons come here to play video games and down massive quantities of caffeine. You'll find frappes and lattes of every flavor imaginable, shakes, and other specialty drinks. Feeling youthful? Try the teen-centric Peanut Butter & Jelly smoothie, a concoction of strawberries, peanut butter, strawberry yogurt, vanilla protein, and honey. Open evenings Friday–Sunday, with concerts featuring local garage bands many nights. Cover charges some nights. $.

Humble City Cafe & Bakery. 200 Main Street, at Avenue A; (281) 319-0200. What was the town's old drugstore (built in 1914) has been restored to its original porch-and-balcony appearance to house this popular cafe. Food is Texas home-style stuff, and the portions exceed generous; come hungry. Open Monday–Saturday for breakfast, lunch, and dinner; Sunday until 3:30 p.m. $–$$.

Menciu's Gourmet Hunan. 1379 Kingwood Drive, Kingwood (in the Kingwood development north of Humble via US 59); (281) 359-8489. Popular with local residents, this family-run place uses only fresh foods to prepare its tasty dishes. The menu is long, so move first to the suggestions in the New Creations section, all of which are cooked with fresh ingredients and original to this restaurant. Second tip: One of the most popular dishes on the regular menu is the Triple Delight (a dish with three meats). Budget-watchers: The Early Bird Special menu (3:00–7:00 p.m., Sunday–Thursday) offers twenty-two lower-priced combination plates, and the lunch specials are excellent values. Open Tuesday–Sunday for lunch and dinner. $–$$.

Nicole's Italian Restaurant. 22153 FM 1314, Porter; (281) 354-4242. About 8 miles north of Humble in Porter, this is a cozy place where you get to know twelve tables of fellow diners in a family atmosphere. It's Italian and it's healthy, with entrees and pizzas prepared from scratch using low-fat milk and cheeses. The menu includes Italian-style meat loaf, veal cacciatore, and chicken Marsala. *Buon appetito!* Open for lunch and dinner daily. $–$$.

The Railroad (Italian) Cafe. 105 Railroad Avenue; (281) 319-6244. This tiny, somewhat shy-looking little building is thought to be the oldest structure still standing in Humble, a concrete symbol of the town's name. You'll be tempted to pass on by, and that would be a huge mistake, because inside is one of the best Italian restaurants in the Houston area. The creative stamp of chef-owner Wayne Falgiano is everywhere—in the quiet chic of the carpeted room, the fresh flowers on the ten tables, the interesting art on the walls, and in the ravishingly fragrant scents coming from the kitchen. Between chats with customers, Falgiano turns out flawless, highly personal versions of Italian specialties such as gnocchi verdi, carciofo, and osso buco, and some surprises as well. Maiale alla Modenese, for example, is a pork loin wrapped in sage and braised in a Chianti wine sauce and cream. Then there's Anitra Frangelico—broiled duck breasts served with a Frangelico cream sauce—and a memorable fresh salmon baked with a sauce of fresh basil, pine nuts, olive oil, garlic, and Parmesan. His pastas and classic Italian desserts also are outstanding. The menu begins, as all good meals should, with an extensive list of Italian wines, including six affordable ones by the glass. Open for lunch Tuesday–Friday; dinner Tuesday–Sunday. $$–$$$.

Trigg's Cafe. 1712 First Street (at Wilson Road); (281) 540-4801. A bright spot in an otherwise undistinguished shopping center east of the business district, this family-run place offers an all-you-can-eat buffet on Sunday (11:00 a.m. to 3:00 p.m.) that draws diners from miles away. The menu also has steaks, barbecue plates, salads, sandwiches, and assorted fried fish, all in abundant portions for the price. Open for breakfast, lunch, and dinner daily. $–$$.

The Veranda. 2820 Chestnut Ridge, Kingwood; (281) 358-2820. From Kingwood Drive turn left at the first light and go 3 blocks. When cost is no object and exceptional food is your desire, try this small treasure of a restaurant. Selecting from the extensive menu is challenging, but consider two of the house specialties: Veal Veranda (stuffed with prosciutto and topped with lump crabmeat, provolone, and herbed hollandaise) or the grilled Australian lamb chops, frenched and served on a mix of caramelized tomatoes, onions, and mushrooms with mint jus. The crusty-topped crème brûlée is made daily with fresh vanilla beans. Open nightly at 6:00 p.m.; reservations strongly recommended. $$$.

continuing on

From Humble it's approximately 28 miles north via US 59 to Cleveland.

cleveland

Back in the 1880s this railroad town on US 59 north of Houston thrived with lumber shipping. Now it is better known as the main gateway to the forest and water wonderland that covers most of San Jacinto County. Entrances to the Lone Star Hiking Trail are marked on FM 1725 and FM 945 near Cleveland, and the Greater Cleveland Chamber of Commerce, 222 South Bonham Avenue, has a brochure listing activities in the area. To get one, write to Box 1733, Cleveland, TX 77328-1733 or call (281) 592-8786.

Art lovers will enjoy viewing the mural on the face of St. Mary's Church on Highway 105/FM321, immediately south of the business district. Painted by Arturo Moyers in honor of the millennium, it is entitled *Back to Our Roots; Toward the Future* and appears to be three-dimensional.

what to do

Berry picking. If you come in early summer, consider picking a year's supply of blueberries at Chain-O-Lakes Blueberry Farm (281-592-2150). You also can pick your own blueberries, peaches, plums, apples, and watermelons at Lidiak Farm (713-453-6121).

Chain-O-Lakes Resort & Conference Center. 1 Country Lane; (832) 397-4000; www .colresort.com. Although no longer open to day visitors, this woodsy retreat welcomes overnight visitors for bed-and-breakfast or camping on weekends (two-night minimum). Lodgings are in authentic log cabins with fireplaces, central air and heat, lofts, and decks with porch swings. Breakfasts are at the adjacent Hilltop Herb Farm (see "Where to Eat"), and horse-drawn carriage rides link the two seasonally. Activities include fishing (no license required), swimming in a two-and-a-half-acre spring-fed lake, hiking, and nonmotorized boating. More than 300 campsites are scattered over nearly as many acres of pine and hardwood forest, with centrally located hot-shower bathhouses, a Laundromat, and a general store. Call for rates and directions.

Cheesemakers Inc. 2266 South Walker Road; (936) 537-3570; www.cheesemakers.com. This is a family-owned and -operated business started in 1997. They produce Lone Star Goat Cheese, Mexican Jaimito Cheese, Texas Fresh Mozzarella Cheese, and others. Fresh cheeses may be purchased from the business office. But real cheese lovers are drawn to Kate the Texas Cheese Lady's two and a half hour tours, which include a history of cheese makers, films, a tour of the family dairy, and cheese tasting. Kate schedules tours by appointment only. Office hours are 8:00 a.m.–5:00 p.m. Monday–Friday. Fee.

Christmas tree farms. Call for directions to the following: D Bar D Christmas Tree Farm (936-628-3114) and Skyvara Christmas Tree Farm (936-767-4961).

Lone Star Hiking Trail. This is the gateway to the 140-mile-long trail that meanders through Sam Houston National Forest and runs roughly from Cleveland to Huntsville. Designated a National Recreation Trail, it is relatively flat with some wet sections. Bridges offer dry landing over creeks, and some of the trail runs along abandoned rail paths. The trail is well marked and is served by some camping operations. The best source for current information, including trail conditions, maps, and scheduled events, is the Lone Star Trail Hiking Club (www.lshtclub.com).

where to eat

Hilltop Herb Farm at Chain-O-Lakes Resort. 1 Victorian Place; (281) 592-5859 or (800) 397-4020; www.colresort.com. From Cleveland go 18 miles east on FM 787. After passing the Trinity River Bridge, turn right on County Road 2132 (Daniel Ranch Road) and follow signs to Chain-O-Lakes Resort and Conference Center. Delicious food based on the creative use of herbs is the rule here, along with tours of the herb garden and cooking classes. Call to get on the special-events mailing list. The gift shop sells homemade jams, jellies, chutneys, and herbal teas—you'll want to buy some mint-touched Tranquilitea mix for home. Open by reservation only for breakfast, lunch, and dinner, Monday–Saturday. Ask for directions and the day's menu when you reserve. *NOTE:* Drop-ins generally cannot be served. $–$$$.

continuing on

The drive to Coldspring is a day-tripper's delight. From Cleveland take FM 2025 north for 17 miles; turn east on Highway 150 and go another 2 miles. This takes you through a major portion of the Sam Houston National Forest. An alternate route leaves US 59 North at Shepherd and follows Highway 150 West 11 miles to Coldspring.

coldspring

This old community (population 569) was called Coonskin when it was founded in 1847. Now the San Jacinto County seat, it is showing signs of life as a budding tourist center. Most of the structures on Main Street were built between 1916 and 1923, the courthouse in 1918. Many of those vintage structures now house antiques and gift shops. There are numerous historical markers in Coldspring, including one on the United Methodist Church (1848), one of the oldest Methodist churches in Texas. Good times to come: Thursday through Saturday, when most of the shops are open, and on Trades Day (arts, crafts, antiques), the fourth Saturday of every month, March–November. For information contact the Coldspring Chamber of Commerce, P.O. Box 980, Coldspring, TX 77331; (936) 653-2184; www.cold springtexas.org.

what to do

Big Creek Scenic Area. From Cleveland continue on US 59 North 12 miles to Shepherd, then west on Highway 150 for 6 miles to Forest Service Road 217. Part of the 350,000-acre Big Thicket that spatters across vast sections of southeast Texas, this 1,130-acre preserve has numerous hiking trails, wild and varied topography, spring-fed creeks, and abundant wildlife. One segment of the 140-mile Lone Star Hiking Trail (foot traffic only) begins near Montague Church on FM 1725 and loops through the scenic area on a 25-mile jaunt to a trailhead on FM 945. Information: Sam Houston Ranger District, 394 FM 1375 West, New Waverly, TX 77358; (936) 344-6205; www.fs.fed.us.

Christmas tree farms. This is good tree-cutting country in November and December. Call the following for directions: Iron Creek Christmas Tree Farm (936-767-4541; www.ironcreek .com) or Skyvara Family Christmas Trees (936-767-4961).

Double Lake Recreation Area. On FM 2025, 15 miles north of Cleveland; (936) 344-6205; www.fs.fed.us. This twenty-five-acre lake is edged by picnic and camping areas and has boat rentals, a beach, and a bathhouse with showers. No large motorboats are allowed, but canoeing is popular. Boat rentals are available seasonally; call. Stocked with bass, bream, and catfish, this also is a great place to take kids fishing. One 5-mile path through the woods links Double Lake with the Big Creek Scenic Area and the Lone Star Hiking Trail.

Lake Livingston State Park. One mile south of Livingston on US 59; (936) 967-5032; www.tpwd.state.tx.us. This 635-acre park on the lake is a real find. It provides rental shelters, RV hookups, a swimming pool, and paddleboats. There's a 5-mile hiking trail and plenty of choice spots for mountain biking. But if you only have a little time, see the park by horseback. Trail rides (fee) take visitors on 2 miles of wooded trails. Open daily. Fee.

Old Town Heritage Center. Coldspring's original Courthouse Square is now home to a small but interesting museum in the old 1880s jail (usually open Thursday–Saturday or by appointment, 409-653-2009) and the transplanted Waverly schoolhouse, circa 1926. The latter now houses an antiques co-op. Other memorabilia are scattered around the grounds, including an old Ford fire engine and the replica of a blacksmith shop. For information call (936) 653-2009 or log on to www.oldtowncoldspring.tripod.com.

Wolf Creek Park. Located 5 miles off Highway 156 on FM 224; (936) 653-4312. This green gem, located on Lake Livingston and operated by the Trinity River Authority, offers boating, skiing, fishing, swimming, and hiking trails. There are camping sites as well as RV hookups. A marina and grocery provide all the conveniences, including boat rentals and bait, and the miniature golf course and playground make happy campers of the youngest of visitors. Fee.

where to eat

Elaine's Restaurant. P.O. Box 289, Point Blank, TX 77364-0289 (on Highway 150 West in downtown Coldspring); (936) 653-4929. One of the main nerve centers for this small town, this family-run place cuts its own steaks and also puts on a good lunch buffet and salad bar. Open daily for breakfast, lunch, and dinner. $–$$.

Sharon's Cafe. Three-quarters of a mile west of the courthouse, Coldspring; (936) 653-3777. Expect east Texas cafe basics here: oilcloth on the tables, plastic-coated menus, large servings, and a friendly staff. In addition to the expected lunch offerings, the house excels at hand-breaded shrimp and onion rings, fried catfish, and chicken-fried steak. Open for lunch and dinner Tuesday–Saturday. $–$$. No credit cards.

wandering the back roads

From Coldspring you can continue west on Highway 150 and connect with Interstate 45 at New Waverly (Northwest Day Trip 2). From there continue your travels by turning north (right) on I-45 to Huntsville (Northwest Day Trip 2). If it's time to go home, head south on I-45. From New Waverly it's 55 miles to the Houston city limits.

An alternative: If you want to visit the Lake Livingston area (Northeast Day Trip 2) from Coldspring, take Highway 156 North to its intersection with U.S. Highway 190 and turn east. From Livingston take US 59 South to home.

day trip 02

northeast

>>> **part of the tribe:**
livingston, woodville

livingston

A fire wiped out three downtown blocks around the turn of the twentieth century, so little is left of Livingston's beginnings back in 1846. Today this timber town is 76 miles north of the heart of Houston via U.S. Highway 59. The seat of Polk County, it is important to day-trippers in several ways. Shoppers come to town for Livingston's Trade Days, held monthly on the weekend preceding the third Monday of each month. For information call (936) 327-3656.

Every fall the forest around Livingston resembles the rolling hills of western Massachusetts when the frosts bring up the color in the maple, sassafras, oak, sweet gum, sumac, and hickory trees. One of the town's biggest attractions is 90,000-acre Lake Livingston, 15 miles west of downtown. The lake primarily is an impoundment of the Trinity River, and there are three short but beautiful river-float trips possible below the dam. Put-ins for canoes are at the dam, at the US 59 crossing south of Livingston, and at FM 105 near Romayor. The final takeout is at the FM 162 crossing east of Cleveland.

All of Polk County is crossed with old Indian traces, the remains of which are indicated by highway signs. For information on Lake Livingston or the general area, contact the Polk County Chamber of Commerce, 505 North Drew, Livingston, TX 77351; (936) 327-4929. You also will find useful information online at www.cityoflivingston-tx.com.

northeast day trip 02

Should you linger too long in the area, you may be interested in the Milam Home Bed and Breakfast (936-327-1173; www.milamhome.com) in Livingston. The bed-and-breakfast features an inviting wraparound porch and four antiques-filled, well-appointed rooms.

what to do

Alabama-Coushatta Indian Reservation. Route 3 (on U.S. Highway 190, 17 miles east of Livingston); (936) 563-1329; www.alabama-coushatta.com. Established by Sam Houston in 1854, this 4,600-acre reservation in the Big Thicket offers a camping/recreation/tourist complex that offers limited appeal for day-trippers. Twenty-six-acre Lake Tombigbee is a pleasant place for camping, picnicking, and swimming. RV hookups, bathhouses, and nature trails add to the appeal. There's also canoeing and fishing for bass, perch, and catfish.

More than one hundred species of trees are native to this reservation, including eight varieties of oak, the state champion water hickory and laurel oak, and a huge 200-year-old magnolia.

Tours of the reservation and the Big Thicket in open-air buses are available during a handful of weekends during the summer. Some days visitors can take in tribal dances.

If you're interested in learning about Native American culture, plan your visit for June, when the Alabama-Coushatta hosts an annual powwow featuring dance and drum competitions, an Indian arts and crafts market, and other festivities. Fee.

The tribe mans two gift shops, one located on Park Road 56 in the village. The other is in the Shell Station on US 190, just a few miles west of the village. (The Shell Station also boasts a snack bar serving Indian fry bread.) At the gift shops, you will find for sale some of the Alabama-Coushatta's beautiful baskets, woven from needles of the rare longleaf pine. Many have lids and are shaped like animals, and all are considered collector's items. Some rare, old baskets also are displayed in the Polk County Museum in Livingston.

The reservation is open daily in the summer, more sporadically in the winter. Call ahead.

Blueberry farms. You can pick a year's supply at reasonable cost at Sandy Foot Farm (936-327-2744) or at Baxter's Blueberry Farm (1835 Menard Chapel Road; 936-685-7927). Hamilton's Berry Farm (936-563-4910) has blackberries as well. *NOTE:* Blueberry season is late May through July 4.

Heritage Park. Three blocks west of the courthouse square on Church Street; (936) 327-4929. The Polk County Heritage Society maintains two pieces of the Piney Woods's past. The Jonas Davis Log Cabin was built in 1833 by one of the last members of the Pakana Muskogee Indian tribe to live in Polk County. Originally the cabin was located on a reservation on Kickapoo Creek near present-day Onalaska, but it was brought to this site in the 1980s when it was restored. Also here is the 1911 W. T. Carter Steam Locomotive #5, which for thirty years was used to carry timber from the logging camps to the mills. Guided tours are available during special events.

Johnson's Rock Shop. 5810 Indian Springs (10 miles east of Livingston off US 190 in the Indian Springs Lakes Estates; call for directions); (936) 563-4438. You'll see more than one and a half million pounds of rock, and just about that many varieties, as well as the equipment used to cut, polish, and finish same. Visitors are welcome, and there's no fee for a personal tour. Open daily; closed in February.

Lake Livingston. From Livingston take US 59 South 2.5 miles and turn west on FM 1988, then north on FM 3126 to Park Road 65. There is good public access through 640-acre Lake Livingston State Park, open daily (fee). Facilities include a swimming pool, paddle and boat rental, an activity center, hiking and biking trails, horseback riding, picnic areas, campsites, and screened shelters. Private resorts, marinas, and campgrounds along this route offer fishing guides or rent boats. Information: Route 9, Box 1300, Livingston, TX 77351 (936-365-2201); or call the Lake Livingston Area Tourism Council at (800) 766-5253.

You'll also find major fishing action on the Trinity River immediately below the Lake Livingston Dam. The lake itself has a large shad population, and those passing through the dam locks into the turbulent pool below the dam become feeder fish for incredible numbers of striped and white bass, crappie, and catfish. Fish numbers in this pool are so high that Texas Parks and Wildlife uses the pool as a source for their restocking program on other state-owned waters. In addition to bank and wade fishing, there's a cable stretched across the river for boats to use as a tie-down. *Caution:* The water force is very strong with dangerous currents. Western access is via FM 3278 East from Highway 150, south of Coldspring; eastern access from US 59 is via FM 1988.

Livingston Farmers Market. 111 US 59 Loop North. During produce seasons, this market is open Tuesday, Thursday, and Saturday from 7:00 a.m. to noon. Call the Polk County Chamber of Commerce at (936) 327-4929 for information.

Miss Effie's Cottage. 204 West Mill Street; (936) 327-7790. Maintained by the Polk County Garden Club, this historical landmark was constructed in the mid-1800s. Its lovingly landscaped grounds attract birds, butterflies, and other creatures. Gardening enthusiasts will appreciate the antique roses planted here, as well as the pear and fig fruit trees. Stop by the garden club's gift shop for a bottle of homemade preserves. Tours are by appointment only, so call ahead.

Polk County Memorial Museum. 514 West Mill Street; (936) 327-8192. Exhibits focus on the early days of Polk County, and there are some interesting Indian artifacts. Open Monday–Friday. Donation.

where to eat

Courthouse Whistle Stop Café. 318 North Washington; (936) 327-3222. This downtown cafe offers a mixed Southern and Cajun menu. Salads, soups, meat loaf plate lunches, and chicken-fried steaks make up a short list of favorites. You can browse antiques and collectibles while your meal settles. Open for breakfast and lunch daily; Friday (karaoke) and Saturday (Italian) nights until 9:00 p.m. $–$$.

Florida's Kitchen. From US 59 in Livingston, go west 1 mile on US 190, then turn left on FM 350 South for 0.7 mile; cafe will be on the right; (936) 967-4216. Hard to find but worth the hunt, this simple place serves plentiful and delicious ribs, barbecue, catfish, hamburgers, chicken-fried steak, and other standards. Thursday night is all-you-can-eat ribs; Friday night is all-you-can-eat catfish. Open for lunch and dinner Wednesday–Sunday. $–$$.

Lone Star Charlie's Family Restaurant. 4591 US 59 South; (936) 365-3017. A favorite with truckers, this clean and homey spot serves the usual road-food standards, along with homemade cobblers. Good place if you're on a budget and traveling with children. Open for breakfast, lunch, and dinner daily. $–$$.

Out to Lunch Cafe. 413 North Washington; (936) 328-8100. This cheery spot is known for its made-from-scratch sandwiches built on freshly baked bread. Try chicken salad on onion walnut bread. There are also tasty salads and daily specials. And for the road, take away a few pieces of gourmet chocolates or a local work of art from its gift shop. Open for breakfast and lunch Monday–Friday. $.

Shrimp Boat Manny's. 1324 West Church (1 block east of the US 59 bypass); (936) 327-0100. This eatery specializes in seafood prepared Cajun style. Manny and Nancy Rachal are from Lafayette in "Luziana" and serve a mean étouffée, boiled and fried shrimp, raw and fried oysters, and seafood gumbo. Open daily for lunch and dinner. $–$$$.

The Texas Pepper. 930 US 59 North Loop; (936) 327-2794. One of the most popular and pleasant eateries in the region, this spacious place serves choice steaks cut on the premises—they hand-bread the country-fried steak as it is ordered and then cook it in peanut oil. They also smoke their own barbecue meats and prepare their Mexican dishes from scratch. Open Monday–Saturday for lunch and dinner, Sunday from 11:00 a.m. to 2:00 p.m. $–$$.

continuing on

This day trip now follows US 190 due east for 33 miles through the forest to Woodville.

woodville

Although history has been relatively quiet here, the town has some surprises in store for visitors who take the time to poke around. Not only are there twenty-one historical markers in the area, but the entire town also is a bird sanctuary. So rich is the birding here that the Woodville–Angelina National Forest–Steinhagen Lake areas provide seven stops on the Big

Thicket Loop of the Great Texas Coastal Birding Trail map (upper coast). Woodville also is the northern gateway to the Big Thicket National Preserve.

Founded in 1846–47 as the county seat for the newly created Tyler County, Woodville is aptly named because it is surrounded by miles of rolling forest. The prettiest times to visit here are in late March, when the Tyler County Dogwood Festival stirs things up a bit, and again in fall, after the first cold snap coats the woods with color. Brochures, maps, and updates on the current status of spring or fall scenery are available weekdays or by mail from the Tyler County Chamber of Commerce, 717 West Bluff (US 190), Woodville, TX 75979; (409) 283-2632; www.woodvilletx.com. The courthouse in the heart of town is interesting, as are the antiques shops around the square.

what to do

Allan Shivers Library and Museum. 302 North Charlton (2 blocks north of the courthouse); (409) 283-3709. The late governor Allan Shivers had his roots in Woodville, and this restored Victorian showplace houses his papers as well as memorabilia of the Shivers family and the town. Open Monday–Saturday, Sunday by appointment. Fee.

Big Thicket information. The north district office of the Big Thicket National Preserve is at 507 Pine (409-246-2337; www.nps.gov/bith/). Open Monday–Friday, when staff is available.

Blueberry farms. June and July are prime picking months at Mott's Blueberry Farm (409-429-3196).

Boykin Springs Recreation Area. From Zavalla go southeast 11 miles on Highway 63, then south (right) 2.5 miles on FSR 313; (936) 897-1068. Some 30 miles northeast of Woodville and pushing the limits of Day Trips territory, this nine-acre lake offers swimming, canoeing, and camping (no hookups; fee). Its primary value, however, is as a richly diverse habitat for woodland birds, particularly in the spring and summer. Watch for at least three types of sparrows, painted buntings, and red-cockaded woodpecker groups. Lovely in itself, this longleaf pine forest also is extremely rich in wildlife. Hikers should investigate the 5.5-mile-long Sawmill Trail that links Boykin Springs Recreation Area with Bouton Lake Recreation Area. Adventures along the way include an old sawmill site, explorations of the Neches River bottomlands, and crossing a long swinging bridge over Big Creek. For trail information call the Texas Forestry Association at (409) 632-8733 or log on to www.texas forestry.org. Open daily. Parking fee.

Dogwood Trail. This 1.5-mile walking trail along Theuvenins Creek is maintained by Louisiana-Pacific. Watch for its sign 3 miles east of Woodville on US 190.

Heritage Village Museum. US 190 West (P.O. Box 888, Woodville, TX 75979), 1 mile west of Woodville on US 190; (409) 283-2272 or (800) 323-0389; www.heritage-village.org. Never underestimate the power of people with a mission. When it looked like Woodville's best-known tourist attraction might either close or move in 1987, the Tyler County Heritage Society turned local pockets inside out to buy the property and its restaurant.

Now what was a weathering conglomeration of early Americana is an interesting outdoor museum devoted to Texas history in general, Tyler County and Big Thicket territory in particular. Visitors wander through a replica of a small town, composed of a number of homely historic structures and some artifacts of early pioneer life (barbershop, blacksmith shop, syrup mill, whiskey still, pawnshop, apothecary, newspaper, etc.). Walking-tour maps are available at the office.

A well-done historical musical, *Whispers in the Wind,* turns the village green and surrounding buildings into an open-air stage the last two weekends in June. Costumed to the changing periods, this locally written and produced play follows three generations of a family from the time they settle in east Texas in the 1830s to the coming of the railroad in the early 1900s. Music is live, the horses and old covered wagons are real, and the audience almost becomes part of the show.

Another "don't-miss" event, the Harvest Festival and East Texas Folklife Festival on the third weekend of October, fills the village with costumed craftspeople demonstrating all the old-time skills. Although smaller in scale, the quality equals that of the Texas Folklife Festival in San Antonio.

Whenever you plan a jaunt this way, call the general information number above in advance to see if a special event is on. Heritage Village hosts several types of music festivals several times a year.

The Heritage Society also owns and operates the Pickett House restaurant (see "Where to Eat"), and the gift shop (409-283-2272 or 800-323-0389; www.heritage-village.org) specializes in east Texas handcrafts and art. Want a quilt or pine-needle basket? How about an inlaid domino set? This may be the place. Open daily except major holidays; call to confirm. *Walkers note:* Eleven and a half acres of neighboring woodlands are threaded with trails.

James Edward Wheat House. At the corner of Charlton and Wheat Streets. One portion of this house was built in 1848. It is a private residence, but you are welcome to enjoy it from the street.

Lake Tejas. Eleven miles north of Woodville via U.S. Highway 69, then east 1 mile on FM 256 in Colmesneil; (409) 837-2763 weekdays. When summer's heat hits our neck of the woods, this super swimming hole is the place to be. The sand-bottom lake has a two-level dive platform, sundecks over the water, lifeguards, bathhouse, concession stand, tubes, and paddleboats. Operated by the local school district, the lake is open on May weekends and daily from June to Labor Day. *NOTE:* Picnicking and camping are available year-round. Fee.

Martin Dies Jr. State Park. On the eastern shore of the B. A. Steinhagen Lake, 14 miles east of Woodville on US 190 (Route 4, Box 274, Jasper, TX 75951); (409) 384-5231 or (800)

792-1112; www.tpwd.state.tx.us. This 705-acre retreat offers camping (with and without hookups); screened shelters; hiking trails; swimming in two designated areas; fishing for crappie, bass, and catfish; two lighted fishing piers; five boat ramps; and numerous opportunities for wildlife observation, birding, and photography. Visitors also find an interpretive nature center and amphitheater, plus canoe/boat rentals at nearby marinas. Conservation specialists often guide canoe field trips along the Angelina-Neches River. Fee.

River floating. B. A. Steinhagen Lake, east of Woodville on US 190, also is known as Dam B, an impounding of the Neches River. If you are interested in floating on the Neches below the dam, call the U.S. Army Corps of Engineers at Steinhagen Lake at (409) 429-3491 for a report on conditions.

Tyler County Art Gallery. 210 West Bluff (US 190 West); (409) 283-2788; www.tcartleague .org. The county's fine-art center and gallery showcases original art, representing more than forty artists. These are emerging and internationally known artists working in oils, watercolors, acrylics, glass, pastels, and other media. Open Tuesday–Saturday and after hours by appointment.

where to eat

The Homestead Restaurant. On U.S. 69, Hillister; (409) 283-7324; weekdays (409) 781-8905. The owners of The Homestead, Kyle and Candace Spivey, have restored the relaxed atmosphere of the 1912 Hillister home to offer the same type of country dining and many of the same recipes made popular by restaurant founders Emily and Otho Sumner. Chicken-fried steak with homemade gravy, rib eye steak, and fried shrimp are all-time favorites. Insiders know to save room for country dessert classics such as strawberry cake or coconut pie. The Spiveys make every item possible in their kitchen, including salad dressings. The house has four dining rooms, one with a romantic fireplace recommended for couples. Other rooms have family seating or space for large groups. Reservations are not necessary but recommended, although sipping iced tea while waiting on a porch swing may add pleasure to your evening. Open 5:00 p.m.–9:00 p.m. Friday and Saturday evenings, and Sunday 11:00 a.m.–3:00 p.m.

Jarrott's Old-Fashioned Soda Fountain. 205 South Magnolia; (409) 283-2550. In business since 1952, Jarrott's takes you back to yesteryear when *drug stores* (not usually called pharmacies) sold gifts and had soda fountains. Back then, customers perched on stools at a bar-height counter and enjoyed sodas, malts, sandwiches, and chips. Today Jarrott's sells gifts and has fifteen soda-counter stools where not much has changed. Open 8:30 a.m. to 5:00 p.m. Monday–Friday. $.

Pickett House. Two miles west on US 190, behind Heritage Village; (409) 283-2272; www .heritage-village.org. This old schoolhouse has been converted into an all-you-can-stuff-in kind of place, with bright circus posters on the walls and family-style service. Authentically replicating an east Texas boardinghouse experience during the 1840–1900 period, this eatery serves huge bowls of food family style (fried chicken, chicken and dumplings, and three veggies) and your choice of fresh buttermilk or made-from-scratch iced tea, watermelon-rind preserves, corn bread, hot biscuits, fruit cobbler, and bread pudding. It's fetch your own drinks and then take your dirty dishes to the kitchen, just like home. Open for lunch Monday–Friday; lunch and dinner Saturday–Sunday. $–$$.

Texas Star. 205 North Wheeler, Colmesneil; (409) 837-4444. Stop at this big red barn for country-cafe-type food: char-grilled hamburgers, chicken-fried steak, and even surf and turf. Open for lunch and dinner daily. $–$$$.

The Tree Restaurant. On US 69, 8 miles south of Woodville in Hillister; (409) 283-8040. Sharing quarters with a Diamond Shamrock station is an unlikely venue for a good spot to eat, but that's just the case here. Owners Martin and Cindi Riley specialize in open-flame grilling over mesquite and hickory, and the resulting steaks are well worth stopping for. Their menu also runs to breaded shrimp, sandwiches, and plate lunches. The pies and cobblers are made on-site. They prepare tasty takeout, or you can be served outside under the giant oak that gives this eatery its name. Open daily for lunch and dinner. $–$$$.

wandering the back roads

If you need a swift return home from Woodville, retrace your route back to Livingston via US 190 and turn south on US 59.

From Woodville, however, you can drive northwest on U.S. Highway 287 to the small community of Chester and make a 1.6-mile jog north on FM 2097 East to see Peach Tree Village, composed of lumber tycoon John Henry Kirby's mansion (now a museum) and the community meetinghouse/chapel, built in 1912. Although drop-in visitors are welcome, advance notice helps ensure that both buildings will be open when you visit. The site is an old Alabama Indian headquarters camp called Ta Ku La, and two trails blazed by pioneers crossed here. Refurbished as a retreat and summer youth camp, Ta Ku La makes a pleasant picnic destination. For information or to arrange a tour or group retreat, call (936) 969-2455.

Another scenic drive takes you from Woodville to Saratoga and Big Thicket National Preserve (Northeast Day Trip 3). Take US 69/287 South from Woodville to Kountze, swing southwest on Highway 326, and turn right on FM 770 to Saratoga, in the heart of the Big Thicket. To continue home to Houston, follow FM 770 South to U.S. Highway 90 and turn west.

Although the wild azalea canyons near Newton are beyond the geographic scope of this book, they are well worth viewing during their pink and white blooming season, which usually comes in late March. Tip your hat to the Temple Inland for preserving these beauties, and tread carefully: Bird's-foot violets, cinnamon fern, and jack-in-the-pulpit wildflowers may be underfoot. Newton is 48 miles east-northeast from Woodville via US 190. For information contact the Newton Chamber of Commerce, Drawer 66, Newton, TX 75966; (409) 379-5527; www.newton-texas.com.

day trip 03

northeast

into the woods:
liberty and dayton; saratoga,
kountze, and silsbee; the big thicket

liberty and dayton

Although this area, east of Houston on U.S. Highway 90, is rich with history, much of what survives remains privately owned, and the towns have little to illustrate their heritages to the general public. Take away the historical markers, and the casual tourist might conclude that nothing much has happened here—which is far from the truth.

Originally this entire corner of southeast Texas was called the Atascosito District, a municipality first of Spain and then of Mexico. Now broken into ten counties, the district was built around the outpost of Atascosito, shown as a freshwater spring on maps as early as 1757. To reach the original site of Atascosito today, take Highway 146 northeast from Liberty approximately 4 miles and turn west (left) on FM 1011. A marker is just beyond the intersection, and the spring still flows nearby.

After 1821 this wilderness was controlled by Mexico, and Anglo settlers were welcome. For the most part early settlers were independent individuals who came here because they could not gain grants through Austin's colonization farther to the west. They formed settlements like Liberty and Dayton as well as many other places whose names have faded from map and memory.

The Atascosito Road crossed the district, running from Goliad and Refugio to Opelousas, Louisiana. Now its route is roughly paralleled by US 90, and the town of Dayton straddles the historic path.

northeast day trip 03

In 1831 the Villa de la Santissima Trinidad de la Libertad was established slightly south of the spring and officially laid out with six public squares. Now called Liberty, it traditionally is considered to be the third-oldest town in Texas.

Six miles west on US 90 and across the Trinity River is Dayton. It was first called West Liberty and then Day's Town in honor of an early settler, I. C. Day. Originally a lumber and agricultural community, Dayton got financial boosts with the coming of the railroad in the 1870s and oil strikes in the early 1920s. Visitors now find some vintage buildings slowly being filled with interesting shops. As you pass through, take time to read the historical marker concerning the Runaway Scrape. (In February 1836, when Antonio Lopez de Santa Anna began his conquest of Texas, small towns all over south-central and east Texas emptied as citizens attempted to outrun the Mexicans. This frantic migration is known as the Runaway Scrape.) This marker is on the eastern outskirts of Dayton on US 90 East.

Day-trippers living north or east of Houston can now access this area by taking the Sam Houston Parkway (Beltway 8) to US 90 East.

what to do

Christmas tree farms. If you are en route to Dayton or Liberty in late fall, you can pick out your Christmas tree at Hatcher's Christmas Tree Farm, near Liberty (936-389-2387), or Keith's Christmas Trees, Dayton (281-592-5032).

Cleveland-Partlow House. 2131 Grand, Liberty; (936) 336-5488. Built around 1860 and curated by the Sam Houston Regional Library and Research Center, this vintage home is open to visitors on Tuesday from 9:00 to 10:00 a.m. or by appointment. Fee.

George & Bruno Winery. 400 Messina Road, Sour Lake; (409) 898-2829 or (409) 963-8235; www.brunoandgeorge.com. This spot is a bit off the beaten path for this day trip, but as this winemaker is somewhat of a trailblazer, a detour here is fitting. Shawn Bruno had to get the help of the state legislature to get his business started. When Bruno decided to market raisin wine (a recipe developed by his late Sicilian grandfather), he discovered an old law that barred wines made with dried fruits. With some lobbying, the law was changed in 1999, and Bruno sold his first bottle of this most unusual wine in 2001. The raisin wine recalls a port-style vintage and is best served as a cordial (or, Bruno would argue, as a companion to pasta). The winery, which also bottles wines made with blueberries, peaches, and strawberries, is open for tours and tastings by appointment.

Geraldine Humphreys Cultural Center. 1710 Sam Houston Street, Liberty; (936) 336-8901 (Liberty Library). An active little theater, the Valley Players, puts on plays and musicals here. For the current playbill call (936) 336-5887. A contemporary bell tower houses an exact replica of the famous Liberty Bell, cast in 1960 by a London foundry from the original pattern and mold. The bell rings twice a year—on New Year's Day and again on the Fourth of July during an old-fashioned Independence Day celebration on the center grounds. Open Monday–Thursday and on Saturday. Free.

Historic houses. These communities are blessed with citizens who appreciate the historical value of their homes. A driving tour will take you past homes built as early as the 1840s.

In addition to the Cleveland-Partlow House in Liberty (described earlier in this chapter), you can see the G. W. Pounds Home, on FM 770 south of Daisetta, which currently is being restored by the Historical Society of East Liberty County and is not open for tours. The following homes are privately owned but can be viewed from the street (please don't bother the owners): In Liberty: Abbott-Parker Home (1841), corner of Grand and Fannin Streets; T. J. Chambers Home (1861), 624 Milam; Bailey-Chambers Home (1880), 1821 Trinity; Cameron-Norman Home (1880), 310 Fannin; Bingle-Wheat Home (1898), 2023 Cos; Lovett-Sampson Home (1902), 1723 Webster; and E. W. Pickett Home (1911), 405 Bowie. In Dayton: Judge Neel Home (1923), 1204 Main.

Huffman Horse Auction. 7903 FM 1960 East, Dayton (on FM 1960 East, 7 miles east of Lake Houston, 4 miles east of Huffman, and 7 miles west of Dayton; mail goes to P.O. Box 30164, Houston, TX 77249); (936) 258-9333. When you see a big red barn fronted by a large parking lot, you've found a piece of pure redneck Texana. It's open all day on Saturday, but the real action starts at 7:00 p.m. with the auction of tack, then used saddles, then trailers, mules, horses, and ponies. Just watching and walking through the livestock barns is worth the trip, and nonbidding visitors are very welcome.

Liberty Opry on the Square. 1816 Sam Houston Avenue, Liberty; (936) 336-1079; www.libertyopry.com. If you enjoy live country-and-western music laced with liberal servings of gospel, don't miss this family-oriented, three-hour show featuring musicians from throughout the state. The venue is Liberty's former movie theater (circa 1935), complete with plush red velvet seats, and the curtain goes up on Friday and Saturday evenings year-round. Call for reservations. Fee.

Old French Cemetery. Approximately 3 miles east of Dayton on FM 1008. Established in 1830, this is the burial place of some of the early settlers of the Atascosito District. One grave notes an 1821 death; others are enclosed inside antique iron fences.

Sam Houston Regional Library and Research Center. 650 FM 1011, Liberty; (936) 336-8821. Go 4 miles north of Liberty via Highway 146 and turn northwest (left) on FM 1011. Appropriately sited near the original settlement of Atascosito on a high knoll shaded by mature pecan trees, this massive repository is owned by the state and operated free of charge to the public by the Texas State Library. Within its fireproof vaults are valuable historical records, documents, portraits, and other artifacts of the original Atascosito District, most of which can be accessed by special request.

This also is one of the state's least-known and most interesting museums. There are three public display rooms full of goodies like Jean Lafitte's personal diary and other remnants of the days when Liberty was a major steamboat port on the Trinity River. *Genealogists note:* This library has reprints of the Atascosito census of 1826, valuable because it lists the maiden names of wives.

Several interesting structures dot the museum's grounds: the historic Gillard-Duncan Home (1848), restored and furnished to its period; the Norman House (circa 1883), with changing exhibits drawn from the library's vaults; St. Stephen's Episcopal Church (1898), used for meetings; and the Price Daniel family home, filled with antiques and mementos of former Texas governor Price Daniel's political years. Admission to the first three structures mentioned is usually free and available by request when the library is open. Group tours require two weeks' advance notice. Patterned after the original 1856 governor's mansion in Austin, the Price Daniel home is furnished with American Empire antiques. Displays also include the Sam Houston family china, furniture from one of Sam Houston's homes (no longer extant) in Liberty County, and the four-poster bed upon which Sam snoozed the night before the Battle of San Jacinto. Open Monday–Saturday. Free.

Sheldon Lake State Park and Education Center. 14320 Garrett Road, Houston (via Sam Houston Parkway/Beltway 8); (281) 456-2800; www.tpwd.state.tx.us. Only 13 miles from downtown Houston's skyscrapers and currently improving as a state park, this public preserve covers 1,200 acres of water, 400 acres of marsh and swampland, and slightly more than 600 acres of rice/milo/soybean farmland. The latter is food for an estimated 10,000 ducks and geese that winter at this refuge. Huge flocks often are easily viewed from Garrett Road. In addition, several heron/egret rookeries exist on barrier islands along the lake's western edge.

Although you can fish from the banks and five fishing piers daily year-round, the lake is open for boat and wade fishing only from March 1 through October (no motors over 10 hp) so as not to disturb the migrating birds. Catches include bass, crappie, sunfish, and three species of catfish. *NOTE:* This is alligator territory—no swimming. Park rangers are available weekdays at the above address.

A free, 600-acre Environmental Education Center at 15315 Business US 90 lies at the southern edge of the park. It offers small displays focusing on park wildlife, a gift shop filled with nature-related items, two fishing ponds for children (open Saturday and Sunday; catch-and-release), and extensive hiking and birding. The staff also conducts fishing clinics, nature hikes, and other outdoor activities for groups (fee). Open Tuesday–Sunday.

where to eat

Cedar Landing. 10614 FM 1960 East, Huffman; (281) 324-1113; www.cedarlanding.com. Overlooking Lake Houston at the east end of the FM 1960 bridge, this pleasant place has rib eye steak on the menu, but its real specialty is regional seafood fixed just about every way that's been thought up. If you love fried shrimp, come Tuesday through Thursday for all-you-can-eat. Open for dinner Tuesday–Thursday; lunch and dinner Friday–Sunday. $–$$$.

Jose's Mexican Restaurant. 901 West Clayton Street (FM 1960 East), Dayton; (936) 258-5887. A convenient stop if you're headed home from exploring Beaumont or the Liberty area, this clean and colorful place puts a few flourishes on the standard Tex-Mex menu, plus it also serves "gringo" dinners, salads, and both a half-pound hamburger and breast of chicken sandwich. Open for lunch and dinner daily. $–$$.

continuing on

This day trip moseys on to the Big Thicket via Moss Hill, Batson, Saratoga, Kountze, and Silsbee. From Liberty take Highway 146 North 15 miles to Moss Hill, turn east (right) on Highway 105 to Batson, and then northeast (left) on FM 770 to Saratoga and Kountze.

Moss Hill is a farming and ranch area, named for the Spanish moss draped in the surrounding woods. Batson was a small village called Otto prior to the discovery of the Batson Oil Field in 1903 and was the scene of the Batson Round-Up, in which all the unmarried women were gathered up and auctioned to prospective husbands. It's a bit of a racy story—ask locally or check out the faded pictures of the event at Heritage Village in Woodville (see Northeast Day Trip 2).

Other tales of the early days of the oil industry are shared at the Oil Patch Museum in Batson. In addition to pictures of roughnecks at work, there is original drilling equipment and tools. The site of the Oil Patch Festival in late June, the museum is open by appointment. Call (409) 262-8580.

saratoga, kountze, and silsbee

Saratoga was named for the famous New York spa because it had several medicinal hot springs. A hotel catering to the health-seekers burned decades ago, but some of the old foundation still can be found. No word on the fate of the hot springs. Saratoga today is one of the gateways to the Big Thicket.

Kountze got its start with the railroad's arrival in 1881 and owes its continued existence to the lumber industry. The county seat, Kountze is home to the headquarters of the Big Thicket National Preserve.

Silsbee sprang to life when lumber baron John Henry Kirby established a sawmill here in 1894. For comprehensive information on the entire Big Thicket Area, contact the Silsbee Chamber of Commerce, 835 Highway 96 South, Silsbee, TX 77656; (409) 385-5562. A reliable online source is www.bigthicketdirectory.com.

If you decide you'd like to overnight in the Big Thicket area, consider a stay in an 1840 dog-trot cabin at the Pelt Farm Bed and Breakfast (409-287-2279; www.peltfarm.com).

what to do

Big Thicket Visitor Information Center. From U.S. Highway 69/287, turn east on FM 420, 7 miles north of Kountze; (409) 246-2337. The facility will be on your left. If you don't know the Big Thicket, start with this center's slide show, and then study the exhibits detailing the plant and animal life that makes this 86,000-plus-acre national preserve so special. Ask specifically about ranger-led activities, hikes, walks, floats, and canoe routes. Open daily.

Fruit farms. You can pick a variety of things at these Hardin County patches: B & M Farms (near Silsbee; 409-385-1200) and Ethridge Farm (near Kountze; bed-and-breakfast also available; 409-246-3978; www.ethridgefarm.com).

Indian Springs Camp. 6106 Holland Cemetery Road, Kountze; (409) 246-2508; www.indian springscamp.net. From US 69 between Kountze and Woodville, turn west on Post Oak Road for 1 mile, north (right) on Holland Road for 0.8 mile, and right on Holland Cemetery Road to the first drive on the left. Watch for signs. This 200-acre bit of nature offers more than 3 miles of nature trails, a long stretch of frontage on Village Creek, and plenty of Big Thicket wilderness for city folks to experience. Day visitors are welcome (fee), and activity options include fishing, picnicking, canoeing, swimming, and walks. Additional fees apply for use of a campground with tent sites and RV hookups; cabins with bunk beds, ceiling fans, and electricity; a bathhouse with hot showers; and a lodge with kitchen that's great for reunions or group retreats. Owners Ronnie and Sundra Stockholm also offer a summer camp for children.

Kirby-Hill House Museum. 210 West Main Street, Kountze; (409) 246-8000; www.kirby-hillhouse.com. When it was constructed in 1902 by James L. Kirby, the brother of timber tycoon John Henry Kirby, this Victorian manse boasted six gables, two chimneys, a crow's nest, and 8-foot windows. Now restored, today it is a museum filled with original artifacts and furniture, including an 1884 organ. In addition to the tours, the museum also hosts bed-and-breakfast overnights and mystery dinners. Open for tours 1:00 to 3:00 p.m. Tuesday–Sunday. Fee.

Silsbee Ice House Museum. 818 Ernest Avenue (at Fourth Street), Silsbee; (409) 385-2444. Housed in the community's old icehouse, this cultural center displays the work of local artists (new shows monthly) and includes a small museum focused on Hardin County history. Open weekdays.

Village Creek State Park. On Alma Drive, off U.S. Highway 96 in Lumberton (P.O. Box 8575, Lumberton, TX 77657-0575); (409) 755-7322; www.tpwd.state.tx.us. This 942-acre facility has more than 1 mile of frontage on Village Creek and is densely forested, an excellent example of Big Thicket terrain. Facilities and activities include camping (some hookups for RVs), picnic areas, hiking, canoeing, birding, fishing, and swimming; several sandbars along the creek make ideal beaches. Floods are common here, which means there are bay-galls (small swamps) within the park boundaries. Wildlife is abundant—expect a multilevel frog chorus at night—and more than sixty species of birds have been seen in a single day. This park is a good put-in or take-out spot on a Village Creek float. If you don't have your own canoe, contact one of the outfitters listed in the Big Thicket "What to Do" section.

where to eat
Restaurant listings follow in the next section, the Big Thicket.

the big thicket
The Big Thicket National Preserve is often described as the biological crossroads of North America. It is a unique place, comprised of four major ecosystems where the flora and fauna mix from all points of the compass. Ferns, orchids, dwarf palmettos, mushrooms, several types of pine, four types of insect-eating plants—the abundance and variety of this particular mix is unequaled anywhere else on our globe.

Unfortunately, many folks visit what they think is the Big Thicket and go home wondering what all the shouting is about. The problem is that there are twelve Big Thicket areas in all, and you have to know where to look to find them. The preserve is composed of eight land sections and four river/stream corridors and spreads out over 86,000 acres and seven counties. The beautiful, biologically unique portions lie well away from the highways. Just driving through won't do.

The above statistics refer to acreage already within the national preserve. In general terms, the Big Thicket covers three and a half million acres of southeast Texas, including portions of Harris County.

All Texans love a tall tale, and the Big Thicket has its share. One concerns the Kaiser Burnout near Honey Island near Kountze. Local residents called Jayhawkers who had no sympathy for the Confederate side of the Civil War hid out in the woods to escape conscription. Charged with capturing them, Confederate captain James Kaiser set a fire to flush them out. Two were killed in a later skirmish, and the rest vanished once again. Some claim the descendants of those Jayhawkers still live in the depths of the Big Thicket. As more people explore this wilderness, there may be an update on the story.

Then there's the mysterious light that spooks travelers on the Bragg Road, a pencil-straight graded lane that follows the old railroad right-of-way between Saratoga and Bragg. Sometimes called a ghost or the "Saratoga light," it appears as a pulsating phenomenon and has been seen by enough people to warrant serious investigation. Some say it is the ghost lantern of a railway worker killed on the old line. Other less imaginative types claim it's swamp gas or the reflected lights of cars on a nearby highway. Whatever, it adds to the Big Thicket mystique. Now protected as the Ghost Road Scenic Drive County Park, this spooky drive begins at a bend in FM 787 that is 1 mile north of the FM 787/FM 770 intersection in Saratoga and runs almost due north for approximately 10 miles to FM 1293.

In addition to the back-roads route to the Saratoga area listed in the preceding day trip, Houstonians have several other ways of getting to the Big Thicket. The most direct route follows US 90 East to a left turn onto FM 770 North at Raywood, continuing to Saratoga. An alternative is to take Interstate 10 East to Hankamer, go north on Highway 61 to US 90, turn west and go 4 miles to FM 770, and then go north to Saratoga.

Depending on what unit of the Big Thicket you want to visit, there also is access from Woodville, Kountze, Cleveland, and Beaumont. A good state map is indispensable, as are maps and guides of the area itself. Pick up the latter at the Big Thicket Information Center (previously mentioned) north of Kountze or request in advance by contacting Big Thicket National Preserve, 3785 Milam Street, Beaumont, TX 77701; (409) 951-6700; www.nps .gov/bith/. Do remember that this is a young park, developing slowly on limited funds, and that many of the areas are recovering still from people's earlier abuse. *NOTE:* There are no accommodations within the preserve.

where to go

The National Park Service operates twelve units within the national preserve's sprawling boundaries: Turkey Creek, Beech Creek, Hickory Creek Savannah, Big Sandy Creek, Lance Rosier, Neches (River) Bottom/Jack Gore Baygall, Beaumont, Upper and Lower Neches Rivers, Pine Island/Little Pine Island Bayou, Loblolly, and Menard Creek. For information, maps, and trails listing, stop at the Big Thicket National Preserve Visitor Information Center on FM 420, immediately east of US 69/287 between Warren and Kountze (open daily, except Christmas and New Year's Day; 409-246-2337).

The Nature Conservancy operates the Roy E. Larsen Sandylands Sanctuary near Kountze. Guided hikes for groups can be arranged by writing P.O. Box 909, Silsbee, TX 77656; calling (409) 385-0445; or logging on to www.nature.org.

The following units are the most easily accessed:

Beech Creek, off FM 2992 southeast of Woodville, is a 4,856-acre plant community composed of beeches, magnolias, and loblolly pines. Unfortunately, a 1975 beetle epidemic killed almost all the loblolly pines, so the forest is not as pretty as it once was. The Beech Woods Trail, a 1-mile loop, passes through a mature stand of hardwoods.

The **Big Sandy Creek** unit includes a rich diversity of plant and animal life. The 5.4-mile Woodland Trail, at the northwestern edge of the unit (near the Alabama-Coushatta Indian reservation), covers a floodplain, dense mature mixed forest, and upland pine stands. The trail entrance is not well marked, 3.3 miles south of U.S. Highway 190 on FM 1276. The trail also offers two shorter loops and is one of the closest to Houston. *Equestrians and all-terrain bikers, take note:* This unit also has an 18-mile trail designed specifically for horseback riding, hiking, and mountain biking. This trail often is closed during the November–January hunting season, however; call (409) 246-2337 to check.

The **Hickory Creek Savannah** unit, 0.5 mile west of US 69/287 via FM 2827 and a dirt road, combines the longleaf pine forest and wetlands with the dry, sandy soil found in the uplands. This is great wildflower territory in spring. The Sundew Trail (1 mile) is open to the public, and there also is a 0.25-mile wheelchair-accessible loop that is also appropriate for the elderly and those pushing strollers.

Roy E. Larsen Sandylands Sanctuary is on Highway 327, 3 miles east of Kountze. Although it is considered an excellent example of the arid sandylands, it has 9 miles of frontage along Village Creek. The canoe float from FM 418 to Highway 327 has some good swimming holes and white sandbars; about three hours long in paddling time, it is one of the most popular outings in the park (see the Boating section under "What to Do" for canoe livery services). If you prefer to walk, a 6-mile trail is open daily, and interpretive brochures are available at the trailhead. Guided tours for groups can be arranged by writing to P.O. Box 909, Silsbee, TX 77656; calling (409) 385-0445; or logging on to www.nature.org.

Turkey Creek is noted for changing habitats and carnivorous plants and is best accessed from the visitor information center on FM 420, mentioned above. The Kirby Nature Trail loops out nearby, primarily a 1.7- or 2.4-mile walk to Village Creek. Persons interested in insect-devouring carnivorous plants should ask directions to the Pitcher Plant Trail, and those seeking a longer hike should ask how to connect with the 15-mile Turkey Creek Trail, which rambles the length of the unit.

what to do

Biking. Mountain bikes are permitted only on the 18-mile-long Big Sandy Trail.

Birding. Excellent, particularly from late March through early May, when hundreds of species pass on their way north up the Mississippi flyway. The Big Thicket is one of the first stops on the upper Texas coast section of the Great Texas Coastal Birding Trail.

Boating. Guided fishing and sightseeing trips on the Neches River can be arranged through Eastex Canoe Trails (409-385-4700; www.eastexcanoes.com). Small watercraft can be launched at several places on the Trinity River, Neches River, Pine Island Bayou, and both Village and Turkey Creeks. Road crossings generally provide access. Water levels fluctuate, so check before you make firm plans. The national preserve often organizes free trips with a naturalist guide—you must bring your own canoe, life jacket, paddles, and the like. The preserve provides shuttle service at the end of the trip back to the starting point. Reservations are required; call (409) 246-2337 or (409) 839-2689.

Although there are two established canoe trails, exploring the Big Thicket's waterways on your own can be difficult. There are few takeouts as much of the land bordering the creeks is privately owned, which makes visitors subject to trespass charges. Seek advice and equipment from one of the following canoe livery services: Sharp's Canoe and Kayak in Silsbee (409-385-6241 or 409-656-2590; http://sharpcanoerental.com), Eastex Canoe Trails (409-385-4700; www.eastexcanoes.com), Piney Woods Canoe Co. in Kountze (409-751-0911; www.canoetexas.com), or Whitewater Experience in Houston (713-774-1028; www.whitewaterexperience.com).

Ask about Cook's Lake Canoe Trail and Franklin Lake Canoe Trail. An easy trip through bald cypress and water tupelo, the Cook's Lake trail is bounded by Pine Island Bayou and the Neches River. The twisting Franklin Lake trail takes paddlers through a bald cypress slough on Black Creek and along an old bluff line on the Neches. Get detailed maps of the routes before putting in.

Camping. Primitive backpacking is allowed by free permit from the National Park Service in the Turkey Creek, Beaumont, Jack Gore Baygall/Neches Bottom, Beech Creek, Big Sandy, and Lance Rosier units, as well as the Upper and Lower Neches River corridors. For information call (409) 246-2337. *NOTE:* All primitive camps must be at least 200 feet from trails. There are no developed campgrounds within preserve boundaries.

Fishing. Allowed in all waters. A license is required, and state regulations apply.

Hiking. There are eight established trails covering nearly 45 miles in the Big Thicket. The longest is 18 miles. Wear sturdy, water-repellent boots. This is rain country at certain times of the year, and the shady trails often have standing water. Mosquito repellent is an absolute necessity. Unleashed pets and motorized vehicles are not permitted on any of the trails, and please register your hike at the trailhead. Be aware that cougars and wild boars may be in the park. Request in advance a list of hiking trails from the visitor center listed previously.

Hunting and trapping. Allowed in specific areas. Permit required. For information and season details, write to the National Park Service, 3785 Milam, Beaumont, TX 77701, or call (409) 246-2337.

Naturalist activities. National park rangers offer an extensive program that includes talks, guided hikes, and canoe trips. Reservations are required; call (409) 246-2337.

Photography. There is a great range of natural subjects, particularly if you use macro or long lenses. Most of the beautiful things are found in deep shade, so bring a tripod and high ISO film. Several outstanding photographic books on the Big Thicket are available at Houston libraries and bookstores to start your creative juices flowing.

Picnicking. Many sites throughout the park, some with fire grates; all are shown on the park map available at the visitor center. Open fires, tree or brush cutting, and wood collecting are prohibited, and bringing your own water is strongly advised.

Swimming. Although there are no designated swimming areas within the Big Thicket, many people enjoy a dip from the Lakeview sandbar area of the Neches River in the Beaumont unit and from numerous sandbars along the Neches River and Village Creek.

where to eat

Catfish Cabin. 192 SLHS Drive, Lumberton; (409) 755-6800; www.catfishcabin.com. Arguably this city's most popular restaurant, it charms locals and visitors with its country kitsch decor, well-stocked salad bar, and the novelty of tossing the shells of your complimentary peanuts right on the floor. Luckily the catfish is as good as it is. The James family has been frying up catfish, shrimp, and other seafood for about three decades. And to all you Northern transplants, that condiment on the table is pickled green tomatoes. Give 'em a try, and you'll probably want to buy a jar for the road. Open Tuesday–Saturday for lunch and dinner. $.

The Cottage. 5125 Old Evadale Highway (1 block north of US 96), Silsbee; (409) 385-9057. This small, ten-table eatery has been serving more than 1,000 folks every week for as long as anyone can remember. Serving "most everything folks are hungry for," they peel more than fifty pounds of potatoes every morning just for the french fries. Menu choices include catfish, steaks, shrimp, burgers, sandwiches, and salads. Open Monday–Saturday 8:30 a.m. to 9:00 p.m. $–$$.

The Homestead Restaurant. Hillister (see Northeast Day Trip 2).

Katfish Kitchen. 835 North Main, Lumberton; (409) 751-5378. With no fewer than three seafood restaurants serving this tiny town, the locals love to debate which is the best. Our vote goes to the Katfish Kitchen. This former burger shack is nothing to look at, but ignore the decor and dig into some of the freshest, tastiest catfish served in east Texas. You're served a crisp slaw and perfectly moist hush puppies before the main event, which is crispy planks of firm-fleshed catfish without a hint of greasiness. The shrimp in the gumbo are a little small for big-city tastes, but the spicy sausage gives it some kick. Open daily for lunch and dinner. $.

Mama Jack's Restaurant. 215 Pine Street (US 69), Kountze; (409) 246-3450. Owned and watched over by Barbara and Jerry Jackson, this popular eatery specializes in full buffets of home-cooked-style foods, as well as hamburgers and sandwiches. Open daily for breakfast and lunch until 3:00 p.m. $.

Munchie's Olé. 1198 North Fifth Street, Silsbee; (409) 385-5003. Mexican-food lovers will find lots of house specials here, including shrimp fajitas and owner Chris Urbena's Christo Dinner. Open daily for lunch and dinner. $–$$.

Novrozsky's. 441 South Main, Lumberton; (409) 755-1224. Hamburgers, chicken-fried steaks, and other hearty fare served in a super-casual setting. (See details in East Day Trip 1.) Open for lunch and dinner daily. $.

Pickett House. Woodville (see Northeast Day Trip 2).

Red Onion Restaurant. 120 Candlestick, Lumberton; (409) 755-7422. Tucked away behind Wal-Mart, this popular eatery dishes up home-cooked specialties such as chicken and dumplings, grilled pork chops, pot roast, veggie soup, and so on. There's a huge daily all-you-can-eat buffet, with many fish entrees featured on Friday. On a low-fat diet? Look for the green spoons on the buffet. Tiny appetite? Check out the chef specials (smaller portions). No surprise that local folks voted this the best restaurant in the area in 1992. Open daily for lunch and dinner. $–$$.

The Tree Restaurant. Hillister (see Northeast Day Trip 2).

West Texas Bar-B-Que. 3078 US 96 North, Silsbee; (409) 385-0957. (Send mail to 8603 Bussey Road, Silsbee, TX 77656.) It takes four cords of mesquite every month to fuel the smoke pits at this family-run spot. A favorite with the Big Thicket's NPS rangers, the flavorful meat's so tender it often falls off the fork. Locals also love the homemade pies—they buy more than 150 every Thanksgiving. Open for lunch and dinner Monday–Saturday. $. No credit cards.

east

day trip 01

east

spindletop's legacy:
beaumont

beaumont

From Houston Interstate 10 East takes you straight to Beaumont and its surrounding Golden Triangle area—Orange and Port Arthur. The world first heard about Beaumont when it brought in the world's greatest oil well in 1901, but its history is much older. The riverfront downtown today is part of the first land grant Mexico issued to an Anglo. By 1825 there was a trading post on the Neches River, and Jefferson County, of which Beaumont is the county seat, is one of the original counties formed by the Texas Republic in 1836. Since that time Beaumont has made its own brand of history in several ways.

That historic oil well—the Lucas gusher at the Spindletop oil field in January 1901—was the most vivid and important to modern America. Almost overnight Beaumont grew from 8,500 souls to 30,000 folks with advanced cases of oil fever, and a wooden shanty-town called Gladys City was hammered into instant life on Spindletop Hill. By the end of that decade the oil was gone, and Gladys City was a ghost town of wooden shacks. Those glory days live again in the re-creation of Gladys City, 0.5 mile north of its actual site, at Beaumont's successful bicentennial project.

Economically linked with the volatile oil and petrochemical industry, Beaumont has had its ups and downs in recent years. By the late 1960s shifting financial fortunes had created another ghost town of sorts in the downtown area. But that scene has changed dramatically to a downtown alive with new venues offering activities for all ages. The dining and

east day trip 01

entertainment district keeps the atmosphere lively and festive in all seasons, day and night. Brick-paved walkways with old-time streetlights and benches take you to the Neches River, four quality museums, a rich genealogical library, and a renovated, grand palace-style theater listed on the National Register of Historic Places.

Four self-guided trails outlined in the *Beaumont Visitor's Guide* (available from the Beaumont Convention and Visitors Bureau) will help you target your personal exploring. The Black Gold Trail begins with the Lucas gusher and ends inside the mansion of an oil-rich family. The Faith Trail leads you to Beaumont's historic Minor Basilica and finishes at a Buddhist temple and lotus gardens in Port Arthur. On the Nature Trail you visit botanical gardens; Big Al, the largest known alligator in Texas; and the Big Thicket National Preserve, a rare and extensive World Biosphere. Lastly, the Pioneer Trail shows you the people, places, and events that made history in the Golden Triangle region.

For free maps, brochures, and advice, stop at the Visitor Information Center in the Babe Didrikson Zaharias Memorial (MLK exit 854 from I-10; open daily; 409-833-4622). Another good source is the Beaumont Convention and Visitors Bureau, 505 Willow, Beaumont, TX 77701; (409) 880-3749 or (800) 392-4401; www.beaumontcvb.com. You can also stop in at the Ben J. Rogers Regional Visitors Center, 5055 I-10 South (it's actually west), at Ford Park; (409) 842-0500. Pick up a visitors guide here, along with information on the Bolivar Peninsula and eight Texas counties: Jefferson, Chambers, Liberty, Orange, Hardin, Tyler, Jasper, and Newton. Open daily.

what to do

Art Museum of Southeast Texas. 500 Main Street; (409) 832-3432; www.amset.org. This handsome, $5-million museum showcases a wide variety of nineteenth- and twentieth-century American art. Exhibits change every six weeks. Open daily. Free.

The Art Studio. 720 Franklin Street; (409) 838-5393; www.artstudio.org. This refreshing mix of working studio and gallery is at the pulse of Beaumont's thriving bohemian scene. It provides cheap space for artists working in ceramics, metal, photography, wood, and paint. Its gallery space hosts art exhibits, poetry readings the third Thursday of each month, and performances by artists performing original compositions. A sales gallery features some unique artwork at great prices. Open Tuesday–Saturday or by appointment.

Babe Didrikson Zaharias Museum and Visitor Center. P.O. Box 1310, Beaumont, TX 77704 (MLK exit 854 from I-10); (409) 833-4622; www.babedidriksonzaharias.org. In her time this outstanding woman athlete put Beaumont on the map, and the town repaid her with a love and admiration that live on beyond her death from cancer in 1956. This memorial museum chronicles a life and career that saw her six times named Woman Athlete of the Year by the Associated Press. Open daily. Free.

Beaumont Art League. 2675 Gulf Street; (409) 833-4179; www.beaumontartleague.org. For more than sixty years, this arts organization has been dedicated to exhibits spotlighting homegrown talent. Its Brown and Scurlock Galleries present several shows each year. Open Tuesday–Saturday.

Beaumont Botanical Gardens and the Warren Loose Conservatory. 6088 Babe Zaharias Drive (in Tyrrell Park off Fannett Road [Highway 124] on western outskirts of Beaumont); (409) 842-3135; www.beaumontbotanicalgardens.com. Whether you love flowers or just want to stretch your legs, this ten-acre demonstration garden (free) and its adjacent conservatory (fee) are worth a stop. Opened in late 1997, the conservatory is the second-largest such facility in Texas. Among its tropical collection are rare palm trees and extraordinary bromeliads. The gardens are open daily from dawn to dusk, but the conservatory is open only on weekends and by advance arrangement. Tyrrell Park also includes a 900-acre constructed wetlands known as Cattail Marsh. Although not always accessible, it generally provides extensive refuge for numerous aquatic animals, reptiles, and more than 350 varieties of birds. This park also provides camping, playgrounds, picnic areas, an eighteen-hole golf course, and riding stables with boarding and daily trail rides. Call the latter at (409) 842-1515 for hours and fees.

Blueberry farms. Call the following for directions to pick-your-own berry patches: Dishman Brothers Berry Farm (409-860-1700), Griffin's Farm (409-753-2247), and Lazy D Berry Farm (409-296-2882).

Canoeing. Why not take a paddle on the Neches or Sabine Rivers? These rental and livery services provide paddles, life jackets, maps, and basic instruction: Eastex Canoes in Silsbee (409-385-4700; www.eastexcanoes.com) and Piney Woods Outfitters in Kountze (409-751-0911; www.canoetexas.com).

Christmas tree farms. Places to cut your own tree in Chambers, Jasper, and Jefferson Counties include: Beavers Christmas Tree Farm (409-253-2372), K & K Evergreen Farms (409-746-2412), Reaves Christmas Tree Farm (409-746-2522), and Spell's Golden Triangle Trees (409-746-3615).

Clifton Steamboat Museum. P.O. Box 20115, Beaumont, TX 77720 (south of Beaumont on Highway 124; call for directions); (409) 842-3162. Opened in 1995, this attraction honors military and civilian heroes with exhibits relating to the Republic of Texas, the Civil War in southeast Texas and southwest Louisiana, the steamboat era, and World War II. Visitors also tour a 1938 tugboat, the *Hercules,* and a replica of the Sabine Pass lighthouse and keeper's dwelling. The latter includes a restaurant. Call for information and hours of operation. Fee.

Collier's Ferry Recreation Area & Natural Preserve. 5390 Pine Street. This riverside park attracts boaters and picnickers. There are four boat ramps, a playground, tree-sheltered picnic tables, and a pier for fishing and crabbing. A 1.8-mile walking trail will let you work that picnic off.

Crockett Street Entertainment District. Beaumont's beleaguered downtown got a much needed boost in 2002 with the opening of this $13-million-plus complex spread across five historical buildings. The complex, with its brick-paved walkways and ornate details, features a winning mix of nightclubs and restaurants. Within the complex, you'll find the casually elegant steak house, Spindletop; Rio Rita's, a Tex-Mex Cantina (see "Where to Eat"); Ten, a sophisticated lounge; and Dixie Dance Hall, where you'll find real cowboys kickin' it. Antone's, named to honor Austin's famous club, brings in national acts, as well as local up-and-comers. If you're day-tripping on a weekend, grab a table on the sidewalk and enjoy the parade of cyclists on vintage bikes that seems to just find its way here regularly. Open daily. For more information call (409) 832-2944 or log on to www.crockettstreet.com.

Dishman Art Gallery. Martin Luther King Parkway at Lavaca Street on the Lamar University campus; (409) 880-8141. If you're a fan of porcelain, you'll want to check out this showplace tied to the university. In addition to special exhibits, the gallery displays the Dr. Heinz and Ruth Eisenstadt Collection, which comprises 140 nineteenth-century European and American paintings and more than 200 porcelain and decorative objects. Open weekdays. Call for directions and parking instructions.

The Edison Museum. 350 Pine Street; (409) 981-3089; www.edisonmuseum.org. What was once the old Travis Street substation of Gulf State Utilities now houses various adventures in electricity, including films, recorded music, and other inventions of Thomas A. Edison. Open 9:00 a.m.–5:00 p.m. weekdays.

The Fire Museum of Texas. 400 Walnut (at Mulberry); (409) 880-3927; www.firemuseum oftexas.org. This 1927 fire hall now contains a good collection of old fire equipment and memorabilia, including seven major fire-fighting units used from 1779 to the present. A Learn-by-Doing exhibit teaches thirty fire and home safety facts to children ages six to twelve. There's also a child-size safety house, a fire safety theater, displays of toy fire trucks, and a life-size Smokey Bear. The world's largest fire hydrant also is here—a 24-foot black-and-white-spotted fiberglass replica that spouts water. Created by Walt Disney Studios as part of the *101 Dalmatians* craze, it anchors a memorial plaza that honors firefighters from 1881 to our time. Open weekdays and by appointment.

Ford Park. 5115 I-10 South; (409) 951-5400; www.fordparktx.com. This 221-acre complex features an 18,000-seat amphitheater; a 9,500-seat arena, home to the Texas Wildcatters ECHL-Premier AA Hockey League and the Beaumont Drillers National Indoor Football League; a 48,000-square-foot exhibition area; a dozen championship baseball and slow-pitch ball fields; and the Gulf Coast RV Resort, with 121 RV sites and four family cabins (I-10 at Brooks Road; 409-842-2285; www.gulfcoastrvresort.com). The complex also stages numerous regional concerts and events. There's almost always something going on here. Call for a schedule of events.

Jefferson Theater. 345 George Jones Place; (409) 835-5483. Listed on the National Register of Historic Places, this property reopened in the spring of 2003 after $6.5 million in renovations and was recently named "Best Restoration in Texas." It was built in 1927 and features one of seven existing Robert Morton Wonder organs—and this one is still in working condition.

John Jay French Museum. 2985 French Road (Delaware exit from U.S. Highway 69/96/287 North; turn west and watch for signs); (409) 898-0348; www.jjfrench.com. This substantial museum was John J. French's trading post and home back in 1845, now restored and operated by the Beaumont Heritage Society in a beautiful wooded setting north of town. Open Tuesday–Saturday. Fee.

McFaddin-Ward House. 1906 McFaddin Avenue; (409) 832-2134; www.mcfaddin-ward .org. Don't leave Beaumont without touring this impressive home. It is one of the few restored Beaux Arts–colonial houses in the United States. Built in 1906 on land granted by the Mexican government to earlier generations of the McFaddin family, it was occupied by that oil-wealthy and socially prominent family until 1982. Tours begin every thirty minutes with an excellent slide show and continue through numerous rooms, a kaleidoscope of family life and American decor styles from the 1907 period on. Most of the furniture is American, most of the accessories are European, and the 1908 Pink Parlor is particularly grand. Open Tuesday–Saturday and on Sunday afternoon; no children under eight are allowed. The last tours begin at 3:00 p.m. Fee.

Old Time Trade Days. 14902 FM 1663, Winnie; (409) 296-3300. From I-10 take exit 829 and follow signs. This buy-and-sell trade market has more than 700 exhibitors on the weekend that follows the first Monday of each month. Parking fee.

Old Town. East of Calder and Eleventh Streets. When the first Gladys City was in its heyday, this portion of Beaumont was a highly desirable, tree-lined residential neighborhood. It still is. Some of the homes remain impressive, and many now house galleries, restaurants, and specialty shops. A free map helps you find out what's what in this 30-block area. Pick up one at the Tourist Information Center or order it in advance from the Beaumont Convention and Visitors Bureau.

Port of Beaumont. 1255 Main Street. In Texas's early days, clipper ships sailed from here to ports around the world. Today, the port is not only the fourth largest in the nation in domestic and foreign tonnage, but it also serves as the number one military port for Operation Iraqi Freedom in the United States and number two worldwide. (Kuwait is number one.) In the last few years the port has doubled its land-property with a master plan to develop the other side of the river. Since the tragedies of 9/11, tours and use of the observation tower had to be stopped, but you can still marvel at the visible reminder of Beaumont's maritime heritage. The 21-foot-diameter propeller at the port's entrance weighs 80,000 pounds. It began service in 1957 on the tanker *Gulf Prince,* commissioned by Gulf Oil, and it is on loan from the U.S. Maritime Administration.

Riverfront Park. 1255 Main Street. A miniature amphitheater seats fifty, and there is a fully equipped play area for children, an observation deck, plus a small covered pavilion. The park has accessible boat docks for pleasure craft and a scenic view of the Neches River. You can bring your family and picnic baskets to the park and enjoy a serene afternoon by the river.

Spindletop/Gladys City Boomtown Museum. P.O. Box 10070, Lamar University, Beaumont (at the intersection of University Drive and US 69/96/287); (409) 835-0823; www.spindletop.org. Although it lacks the grime of the original, this reconstruction is a good look at 1910 America as well as life in an oil field boomtown. A rickety boardwalk connects most of the structures, just as it did nine decades ago.

The furnished replicas include a surveying and engineering office, the pharmacy and doctor's office, a photographer's studio, a general store, and more. Vintage oil field equipment is scattered around, and the Lucas Gusher Monument is out back on its own site. From I-10 take the US 69/96/287 turnoff to Port Arthur and then the Highland Avenue/Sulphur Drive exit. Signs guide you from there. Open Tuesday–Sunday afternoons. Fee.

Texas Energy Museum. 600 Main at Forsyth (across from the civic center complex); (409) 833-5100; www.texasenergymuseum.org. Exhibits about Beaumont before and after Spindletop are featured in this $5-million showcase, along with the entire collection of oil patch artifacts of the Western Company Museum of Fort Worth. Exhibits animated with cine-robots show how oil is created, found, pumped, and refined. A remodeled section of the museum including the Unlocking the Energy of Oil exhibit took seven years to build. The exhibit shows a real-time video of an oil tanker sailing up the Sabine Waterway to the Exxon-Mobil docks in Beaumont. A complete model of an oil refinery takes you through the steps to refine gasoline and other petroleum products. Another must-see is the theater that takes you—as an animated molecule of petroleum—on a processing ride through pipelines and converters to become gasoline. Open Tuesday–Sunday. Fee.

Tyrrell Historical Library. 695 Pearl; (409) 833-2759. People come from all parts of the world to research their roots at this genealogical library. The building was constructed in 1906 as a Baptist church. Open Tuesday–Saturday.

where to eat

Al-T's Seafood & Steakhouse. 244 Spur 5 (Highway 124), Winnie; (409) 296-9818; www.al-ts.com. Take exit 829 from I-10 and go 1 block south; the restaurant will be on the left.

A welcome stopping spot between Houston and Beaumont, this is where the locals go when they want great regional and Cajun food. House specialties include chicken and sausage gumbo, fried gator balls, alligator appetizers, and a rib eye steak topped with a spicy crawfish étouffée. The breakfasts also win raves; try a boudin (sausage) omelet. Open daily for breakfast, lunch, and dinner. $–$$.

Bistro LeMonde. 3199 Dowlen Road; (409) 860-5800; www.bistrolemonde.com. When you crave fine food in a casual setting, try this spacious modern sister to Bryan's 797. The Bistro offers casual dining but full service, with menu items such as bluefin tuna burgers, a 100 percent sirloin burger, étouffée, pizza, and other global fare. Open for lunch daily; dinner Monday–Saturday. $–$$.

Broussard's Links Plus Ribs. 2930 South Eleventh (at Washington); (409) 842-1221. All-beef, homemade links bring locals here, along with ribs so tender the meat nearly falls off the bone. All is pit cooked over oak out back. Open for lunch and dinner Monday–Saturday. $–$$.

Bryan's 797. 797 North Fifth Street (at Hazel); (409) 832-3900; www.bryans797.com. Housed in a 1905 home in Beaumont's historic district, this chef-owned restaurant consistently offers some of the finest continental food in town. *Oenophiles, note:* Their list of California and French wines has won a *Wine Spectator* award of excellence. Chef Bryan Lee trained at Four Seasons Hotel in Taiwan, and it shows. Your best bet is to just ask what's great today and go with your server's suggestions. Do ask the price of the specials, however; they are not offered voluntarily by the waiter and could lead to sticker shock when you get your bill. Menu choices include a marvelous stacked crab appetizer, numerous entrees featuring Angus beef, and assorted variations on quail and lamb. Open for lunch Monday–Friday; dinner Monday–Saturday. There are only fourteen tables, so reservations are strongly advised. $$–$$$+.

Carlito's. 2610 College Street; (409) 839-8011. If Mexican food appeals to you, give this place a try. Open for lunch and dinner Monday–Saturday; breakfast and lunch on Sunday. $.

Carlo's. 2570 Calder; (409) 833-0108. If you want Italian and your spouse wants Greek, this is the place—it specializes in both. Paintings by local artists and live entertainment provide a pleasant ambience. Open for lunch and dinner Tuesday–Friday; dinner only on Saturday. $$–$$$.

Elena's. 1801 College, downtown; (409) 832-1203. In addition to the Mexican standards, this place also serves menudo and chorizo. Open daily for lunch and dinner. $–$$.

Frankie's Italian Grill. 105 I-10 North; (409) 835-9200. Located in a former Cajun seafood restaurant, Frankie's has quickly become a local favorite among Italian-food aficionados. Dress is casual, and they serve a plate-size fresh salad with entrees. Lasagna and cannoli are among the most-ordered dishes. Expect crowds at lunch. Open for lunch and dinner Tuesday–Sunday. $–$$.

The Green Beanery Cafe. 2121 McFaddin (at Sixth Street in Old Town); (409) 833-5913. This chef-owned restaurant offers tasty, unusual twists on sandwiches, soups, salads, and quiche. Expect a more continental flair at dinner. Open Tuesday–Saturday for lunch and dinner; closed midafternoon. $–$$.

Log-on Cafe. 3805 Calder; (409) 832-1529; www.logoncafe.net. Need to check your e-mail? This clever cafe at the rear of the Gyedco Technology store is set up with numerous individual computer terminals, each with direct Internet service (fee). While you work or play online, you can be served unusual snacks, sandwiches, and soups, plus there's espresso, cappuccino, beer, and wine. Open Monday–Saturday. $–$$.

Lone Star Steakhouse Seafood & Grill. 6685 Eastex Freeway; (409) 898-0801. The former J&J Steakhouse, a Beaumont landmark, has given way to the Lone Star Steakhouse, and there's no reason to mourn J&J's passing. Lone Star is serving up terrific takes on east Texas favorites, such as chicken-fried steak, blackened catfish, and crawfish étouffée. Fans of fried seafood have a friend in the kitchen: Try the fried shrimp, which are large, fried golden, and piled high on the plate. Best news for longtime J&J patrons: The new management has retained the Eye of the World Museum, which features the folk art carvings of "Poppa" John Gavrelos. Open for lunch and dinner daily. $–$$.

Novrozsky's. 4320 Calder, 4438 Dowlen, and five other locations; (409) 898-8688; http://novrozskys.com. The owners of this small Beaumont chain took their inspiration from a Houston institution and then ran with it. The burgers are hand-shaped, grilled to order, and served "all the way." An extensive appetizer menu features nachos, stuffed jalapeños, and tasty boudin balls. Really hungry? Try the chicken-fried steak and a basket of sweet potato fries. Open daily for lunch and dinner. $.

Pine Tree Lodge. 3296 Pine Tree Road (on the east side of LaBelle Road, 2.5 miles north of Highway 73; watch for a drive opposite the volunteer fire station); (409) 796-1600; ww.pinetreelodgerestaurant.com. Opened in the 1940s, this low-key family restaurant and bar is a good stop if you're roaming the country roads northwest of Port Arthur en route to or from Beaumont, I-10, or Winnie. While there are plenty of burgers and sandwiches on the menu, locals come here for the seafood platter, chicken-fried steak, pork chops, or rib eyes. On Sunday from 2:00 to 6:00 p.m., April–November, there are live bands with hot fiddles and lots of dancing on the big covered porch along the bayou. If the kids get antsy, there's fishing for white perch, brim, and catfish in the picnic area. Open for lunch and dinner Thursday–Tuesday. $–$$.

Rao's Bakery. 2596 Calder (also at 4440 Dowlen Road); (409) 832-4342; www.raos bakery.com. Grab a seat on the outdoor patio and enjoy the best baked goods in

Beaumont. The chocolate éclairs are inspiring (and not a little messy), and no one south of the Mason-Dixon Line does cannoli better. That should be no surprise, because Rao's has been baking since 1941. Reliable soups, salads, and sandwiches for lunch. Open Monday–Saturday for breakfast and lunch. $.

Rio Rita's Cantina. 230 Crockett Street; (409) 833-0750; www.crockettstreet.org. Anchoring one end of the Crockett Street eatertainment district, this brightly painted Mexican restaurant pulls in the crowds, most looking for a spot on the see-and-be-seen patios. The fare is fairly standard—fajitas, beef tacos, chicken-filled chimichangas, and chili-topped tamales—but the staff is attentive, the portions generous, and the margaritas big and strong. If you've room, try the skillet apple pie, which comes out sizzling and topped with cinnamon sugar and vanilla ice cream. It's decadent. $–$$.

Spindletop. 290 Crockett Street; (409) 833-9688; www.crockettstreet.com. Anchoring another end of the Crockett Street dining and entertainment district, this lively place is a renovated building where about a century ago, stocks were bought and sold for the great Spindletop oil field. Historical photos bring oil field scenes to life. The menu is a triumph of regional salads, shrimp, and steak favorites. Open daily for lunch and dinner. $–$$$.

Suga's Deep South Cuisine and Jazz Bar. 461 Bowie at Park; (409) 813-1808; www .sugasdeepsouth.com. Dedicated foodies may consider this place reason enough to make the trip to Beaumont. It's a big hit in downtown with specialties such as tilapia stuffed with shrimp and crab, and smothered in a seasoned crab sauce. Other menu items offer the best in Deep South cuisine, with live music from the upstairs jazz bar Friday and Saturday nights. Billed as "Food for the Soul," on Sunday, Suga's has a jazz brunch. Open Monday–Friday for lunch and dinner, Saturday for dinner, and Sunday for brunch. $–$$$.

Taste of Orleans. 672 Orleans Street in Beaumont; (409) 833-9460; second location in Port Arthur's Central Mall food court; (409) 722-3113; www.tasteoforleansonline.com. Diners find authentic Cajun beans and rice, sausage, and seafood gumbo, all slow-cooked in the New Orleans style. The mall location is open daily for lunch and dinner, but the downtown spot was open only for weekday lunch at this writing. That may change, so call to check. $–$$.

Willy Ray's Bar-B-Q. 145 I-10 North; (409) 832-7770; www.willyraysbbq.com. Seven meats come two ways here, either light on the sauce and smoke-flavored, or hot, sweet, and saucy. Add to that your triple choice from their thirteen fresh vegetable sides (all made from scratch), and you'll have a down-home feast that has garnered favorable national attention. Want a picnic? Use the drive-through. Open daily for lunch and dinner. $–$$.

day trip 02

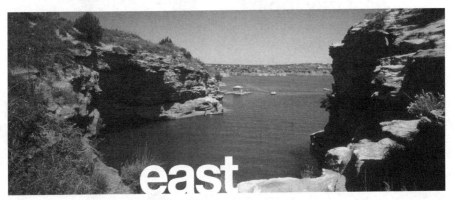

east

>>> **airboat adventures:**
orange

orange

Some 25 miles east of Beaumont and the last gasp of Texas on Interstate 10 before you find yourself in Louisiana, Orange has some interesting places to visit.

Officially founded in 1836, Orange has a traceable history that begins about 1600, when the Attacapas Indians settled here. French fur traders came a century later, followed by the Spanish, and the city's name comes from this latter period—early French and Spanish boatmen looked for the wild oranges that grew along the banks of the Sabine River. Anglo settlers ventured west across the Sabine in the early 1800s, but little is left in Orange to mark those times. Most of the city's tourist attractions date from the prosperous lumber and ranching days of 1880 to 1920.

Local information, including a list of antiques stores, can be had from the Orange Convention and Visitors Bureau, 803 West Green Avenue, Orange, TX 77630; (409) 883-1011 or (800) 528-4906; www.orangetexas.org. Do cross the Sabine when you come on this day trip; the Louisiana State Information Center combined with the Sabine National Wildlife Refuge is on the right immediately beyond the bridge. It has an outstanding picnic area and boardwalk through the marshes where you may see numerous water birds, nutria, and so on. Bring your camera, preferably one with a long lens. You also may want to play the ponies at Delta Downs racetrack, just over the bridge in Vinton, Louisiana.

east day trip 02

Anyone who thinks chili is the definitive Texas dish hasn't been with the 20,000 folks in Orange for gumbo at the International Gumbo Cook-off. Please note, so you don't show up with your big spoon at the wrong time—the huge gumbo event, usually in May, has been combined with Mardi Gras and changed to February.

what to do

Adventures 2000 Plus Swamp and River Tours. 813 East Lutcher Drive, (409) 988-9342; www.swampandrivertours.com. Trained as a biologist and oceanographer, local resident Eli Tate offers ninety-minute narrated boat tours throughout the Sabine River estuary that borders Orange on the east and south. His deep-V aluminum outboard boats (22 and 26 feet long, respectively) have half-convertible tops, so you will be exposed to weather; dress appropriately. On nature and birding trips through a variety of coastal habitats and ecosystems, you'll get close-up photos of gators and eagles, and pass old Indian sites and ship graveyards. Call for fees and directions.

Christmas tree farms. Orange County may be the Virginia pine capital of Texas. Call any of the following for directions: K&K Evergreen Christmas Tree Farm (409-746-2412), Reaves Christmas Tree Farm (409-746-2522), or Spell's Golden Triangle Trees (409-746-3615).

Delta Downs. Twelve miles east via I-10, then north on Louisiana Highway 109. Slightly beyond the two-hour/110-mile limit of this book, this horse racing track is still a good reason to visit the Beaumont/Orange/Port Arthur area, especially since the opening of its all-slot casino. September–March is the racing season for thoroughbreds, and April–Labor Day is reserved for quarter horses. Meanwhile, the casino, with its 1,500 state-of-the-art slot machines, is open twenty-four/seven. For information write P.O. Box 175, Vinton, LA 70668; call (800) 589-7441; or log on to www.deltadowns.com.

Farmer's Mercantile. 702 Division (at the corner of Sixth and Division Streets, where it has been since 1928); (409) 883-2941. Saddles rest next to bins of nuts and bolts, onion sets are offered just below packets of bluebonnet seeds, and horse collars line the high walls. Whatever you might need, it's here—somewhere. People have been known to dawdle here for hours, remarking on the old woodstoves, bottle cappers, and such. You can't miss the place—just look for hay bales on the sidewalk. Open business hours on weekdays; until 2:00 p.m. on Saturday.

First Presbyterian Church. 902 West Green Avenue; (409) 883-2097 or (409) 883-4116. One wonders what there would be to see or do in Orange without the Lutcher and Stark families (see entries on W. H. Stark House and Stark Museum that follow). This impressive domed building is a Lutcher/Stark contribution to the city and is thought to be the first public building to be air-conditioned east of the Mississippi. The power plant with the air-conditioning unit was installed during the church's construction in 1908. The handmade stained-glass windows are impressive, as is the entire interior of the church. Tours are available for six or more by advance reservation. If you can't fit those tour requirements, stop in for Sunday services.

Fishing. Fed by a huge coastal marsh ecosystem, Lake Sabine and its twisting bayous offer excellent seasonal fishing for redfish, speckled trout, and flounder. Additionally, fly fishermen cast for bass and bream in the cypress-tupelo zone of Blue Elbow Swamp, and both the Neches and Sabine Rivers function almost as fish sanctuaries. Brochures available from the Orange Convention & Visitors Bureau detail numerous marinas, fishing camps, guide services, and boat launches. As an alternative, call one of the following: Fishing, the Sabine Connection (409-883-0723); Fish-on Guide Service (409-735-8761); Skip's Guide Service (409-886-5341); or Chuck's Guide Service (409-886-5222). For additional information contact the local Texas Parks and Wildlife office, 5550-L Eastex Freeway, Beaumont, TX 77708; (409) 892-8666 or (800) 792-1112. *Tip:* September through December are prime fishing months.

Heritage House. 905 West Division Street; (409) 886-5385; www.heritagehouseof orange.com. While not as elegant as the Stark House (below), this early-twentieth-century home is worth a stop. Not only is it furnished as an upper-middle-class home would have been in those times, there are several "see-and-touch" exhibits for children, as well as historical items of interest. Open Tuesday–Friday. Fee.

Lutcher Theater for the Performing Arts. 707 West Main (in the Orange Civic Plaza); (409) 886-5535 or (800) 828-5535; www.lutcher.org. If you are coming over for the weekend anytime during the September–May season, call to see who and what is playing. Recent offerings have included *100 Years Broadway* and *Lost in Yonkers* and performances by Ballet Folklorico. Tours available weekdays; advance reservations required.

Piney Woods Country Wines. 3408 Willow Drive; (409) 883-5408. This small vineyard produces some tasty fruit wines—drop in for a sample of Texas-grown sunset muscadine or peach. The tasting room is open daily, except for some weekends and vacation periods. Call ahead.

Shangri La Botanical Gardens and Nature Center. At the junction of Sixteenth Street (Highway 87) and Park Avenue; (409) 670-9113; www.shangrilagardens.org. Lutcher Stark had a deep appreciation for plants, as well as the wealth to build his personal Shangri-la and almost hide it in this small community. In 2002, the Stark Foundation began building a new Shangri La on the original site of his gardens, overgrown and battered by hurricanes. The one you see displays various plants from around the world. Its nine garden rooms and four sculpture rooms show visitors more than 300 species of plants. A boardwalk lets you explore a swamp with its own classroom. Call for information.

Stark Museum of Art. 712 Green Avenue (across from the Stark House); (409) 883-6661; www.starkmuseum.org. William H. Stark was a prominent financial and industrial leader in Orange, who married Miriam Lutcher in 1881. She began collecting European art in the 1890s, and her son Lutcher and daughter-in-law Nelda continued the family tradition with further emphasis on art of the American West and the Taos school of New Mexico. The Audubon print and Steuben glass collections also are particularly worth seeing. This contemporary museum was completed by the Starks in 1976 and houses the varied and impressive collections. Open Tuesday–Saturday. Free.

Texas Travel Information Center and Blue Elbow Swamp. Exit 880 (Sabine River Turnaround) on I-10. Built with ecological sensitivity on the southern edge of the Blue Elbow Swamp, this travel facility includes a picnic area and the Tony Houseman State Park and Wildlife Management Area. The latter is the first stop on the Great Texas Coastal Birding Trail and includes a boardwalk with informational exhibits regarding the swamp and the flood-plain forest. Ask for an upper coast birding map, a state map, and the latest *Texas State Travel Guide;* all three are basic field equipment for exploring the greater Houston region and beyond. Open daily, year-round.

W. H. Stark House. P.O. Box 909, Orange, TX 77630 (in the Stark Civic Center complex at Green Avenue and Sixth Street); (409) 883-0871; www.whstarkhouse.org. Built in 1894, this massive Victorian home with its gables and turrets is a visual delight, inside and out. A ten-year restoration project and now on the National Register of Historic Places, this fifteen-room structure can be toured only by advance reservation. No children under twelve are allowed. Tours start in the carriage house, where an excellent glass collection is on display. Open Tuesday–Saturday. Fee.

where to eat

Old Orange Cafe. 914 West Division; (409) 883-2233; www.oldorangecafe.com. In addition to savory lunch plates daily, these inventive folks serve some super salads, sandwiches, spuds, soups, and desserts. They also have special pretheater dinners prior to certain performances at the Lutcher Theater for the Performing Arts; call for schedule and reservations. Open from 8:00 a.m. to 2:00 p.m. weekdays. $–$$.

The Original Cajun Cookery. 2308 I-10; (409) 670-1000. Although the regular menu is good, nearly everyone comes here for the Cajun seafood buffet. Open daily for lunch and dinner. $–$$.

Richard's Cafeteria. 4040 I-10 West; (409) 886-4002. Located in a former Luby's, Richard's offers you a choice of thirty to forty cafeteria-style items, or you can be seated and choose from a full menu of popular fare such as steaks, chicken, shrimp, or Richard's popular liver 'n onions. Open daily for lunch and dinner. $–$$.

Southern Magnolia Tea Room. 1627 Strickland Drive; (409) 883-4144; www.southern magnolia.net. It's hard to choose between the tomato bisque or the creamy potato soup at this old-fashioned tearoom, one of the few places you'll still find a Jell-O salad on the menu. Here it is—the Cherry Fling, cherry Jell-O filled with pineapple and cherries and topped with cream cheese and pecans. There also are New Orleans–style muffulettas and hot ham and cheese sandwiches on grilled Texas toast. The tearoom also serves very good desserts, such as the mandarin orange cake and the fudge pecan cake. This is not the place to count calories. Open for lunch weekdays and dinner when the Lutcher Theater is offering a performance. $.

Tuffy's Eatery. Highway 12 at Highway 62, Mauriceville (8 miles north of I-10 via Highway 62); (409) 745-3170; www.tuffyseatery.com. Expect Southern and Cajun-style cooking here, along with excellent pastries and biscuits. A full menu, plus all-you-can-eat specials (Monday and Friday, catfish; Tuesday, shrimp; Wednesday, chicken and dumplings; Thursday, prime rib), pack in the local folks. Open for lunch and dinner daily. $–$$.

day trip 03

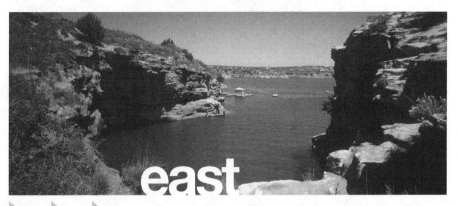

east
windmills and gulf breezes:
nederland, port arthur

nederland

When you want to fish or hunt in southeast Texas, you well could be headed for the Port Arthur area. From Houston the most direct route is Interstate 10 East to Beaumont, followed by a swing southeast on U.S. Highway 69/96/287. For the day-tripper there are several activity options in the area, but first let's take a look at one of the smaller towns you will pass on the way—Nederland.

You'll think you are in Cajun country when you first drive up the main street of this small community—the local market usually is advertising fresh boudin (sausage). Confusion may set in when you see Dutch names on some stores and a windmill at the end of the street. Established as a railroad town in 1897, Nederland first was settled by Dutch immigrants, who were soon followed by French settlers from the Acadiana area of southwestern Louisiana, and both ethnic groups make Nederland what it is today. For information contact the Nederland Chamber of Commerce, 1515 Boston Avenue, Nederland, TX 77627; (409) 722-0279; www.nederlandtx.com.

what to do

La Maison Beausoleil. 701 Rue Beausoleil Avenue, Port Neches (off Grigsby Avenue, in Port Neches Park); (409) 832-6733. This fully furnished 1810 Acadian home was barged in from Vermilion Parish, Louisiana. Notable for its mud-and-moss walls that are mortised and

east day trip 03

pegged with square nails, this "House of Beautiful Sunshine" is fully furnished and open weekend afternoons; weekdays by appointment.

Windmill Museum and La Maison des Acadiens Museum. 1500 Boston Avenue in Tex Ritter Park; (409) 722-0279. These adjacent museums keep the dual heritage of Nederland alive. The first floor of the authentic Dutch windmill is devoted to mementos of a local boy who made the big time in country-and-western music—Tex Ritter. The remaining two floors have a sparse but interesting collection of assorted cultural treasures. Best is the old pirogue, hollowed out of a cypress log prior to 1845 and in use until bought and donated to the museum in 1969.

La Maison des Acadiens Museum honors the French Cajun culture. A bicentennial project by local volunteers, this authentic replica of a French Acadian cottage has furniture to match. Both museums are open Tuesday–Sunday afternoon March through Labor Day, and Thursday–Sunday afternoon thereafter through February.

where to eat

Cowboy Red's BBQ. 1920 Nederland Avenue, (409) 721-5774; second location is on Highway 124 in Stowell. Word of mouth spread the news about this small-town barbecue place, and it has expanded with popularity. Cowboy's makes breakfasts, barbecue sandwiches, and plate dinners with all the fixin's. It's a favorite with locals. Open for breakfast, lunch, and dinner daily. $–$$.

Sanderson's Restaurant and Bar. 2095 US 69 North; (409) 722-8900; www.sandersons restaurant.com. This handsome dining room is a local favorite thanks to a "something-for-everyone" menu and a friendly bar. The steaks are thick-cut and smartly grilled, the pasta bowls brim with grilled shrimp (or chicken), and the burgers are monsters. Ribs are a specialty, and you've a choice of barbecued, glazed, citrus glazed, or jalapeño glazed. Open for lunch and dinner daily. $–$$.

The Schooner. US 69/96/287 at FM 365; (409) 722-2323. Famous for stuffed flounder and stuffed red snapper steak, this restaurant goes all the way with a few stuffed fish and game trophies for decor as well. Open daily for lunch and dinner. $$.

port arthur

From Nederland continue southeast on US 69/96/287 to Port Arthur. The Sabine and Neches Rivers form Sabine Lake, which empties into the Gulf of Mexico 8 miles south of Port Arthur. The town sits on the lake's northwest edge.

Settled as Aurora about 1840, the town became Port Arthur in 1898 as the terminus of the Kansas City–Pittsburgh and Gulf Railroad, and the ensuing oil strike in nearby Beaumont ushered in Port Arthur's golden age of growth. At present the city is primarily a large industrial and refining center with a growing number of things of interest to visitors. The Port Arthur Convention and Visitors Bureau is a good source of specific information, maps, and so on: 3401 Cultural Center Drive, Port Arthur, TX 77642; (409) 985-7822 or (800) 235-7822; www.portarthurtexas.com.

Planning to drive to Port Arthur from Galveston via Highway 87? Be aware that, at this writing, that road remains washed out immediately south of Sea Rim State Park. From High Island (on Bolivar Peninsula), go north 29 miles on Highway 124 to Winnie, then east 30 miles on Highway 73 to Port Arthur.

what to do

Airboat rides. This activity comes and goes in Port Arthur. Sea Rim State Park operates airboat and outboard marsh tours (see park entry below), but check either with the park (409-971-2559) or with the visitor bureau (800-235-7822) for an update before you come.

Birding. This is a growing sport here, particularly at Sabine Woods, an Audubon Society–owned preserve on Highway 87 south of Port Arthur and 5 miles west of Sabine Pass. Like High Island on the Bolivar Peninsula (see East Day Trip 4), this is a major "fallout" zone for migratory birds in spring and fall. A complete list of birding sites and maps are available from the Port Arthur Convention and Visitors Bureau (previously mentioned). Birding hot spots can be downloaded at www.portarthurtexas.com.

Fishing. You can fish in the lake, the freshwater bayous that feed it, or the Gulf of Mexico via Sabine Pass. Top game fish are speckled trout, red snapper, mackerel, billfish, and tarpon. A license is required. For information on marinas, guides, and so forth, contact the visitor bureau, above. Fishing charters currently are available; contact the visitor bureau.

Hunting. To see vast flocks of birds on the wing in sunrise light is unforgettable. Even seasoned hunters have been known to put down their guns in awe, though you rarely find one who will admit it. You can have that experience in the Port Arthur area, prime territory for duck and goose hunting, with four areas open to the public at various times during the November–January season. For overall information contact Sea Rim State Park (P.O. Box 1066, Sabine Pass, TX 77655; 409-971-2559) or the J. D. Murphree Wildlife Management Area (409-736-2551). Other areas open for public hunting include the Texas Point and McFaddin Beach national wildlife refuges (409-971-2909).

La Rue des Soldats. This one-way drive tops Port Arthur's $89-million hurricane protection system, which forms a dike around the city. Open weekdays to vehicular traffic and accessed via the first drive to the left just past Gates Library on Lakeshore Drive.

Museum of the Gulf Coast. 700 Procter (on the ship channel in downtown Port Arthur); (409) 982-7000; www.museumofthegulfcoast.org. Before the construction of the Intracoastal Canal, there were beautiful sand beaches on Lake Sabine. Several sprouted luxury hotels that live on only in the photographs displayed with other area memorabilia in this interesting museum. The Port Arthur area also has spawned a number of noted musical artists, among them Janis Joplin, Harry James, Aubrey "Moon" Mullican, J. P. Richardson ("The Big Bopper"), Johnny Preston, and Ivory Joe Hunter. Their legacies, complete with gold records and a replica of Janis Joplin's wildly painted convertible, are celebrated in the museum's outstanding Southeast Musical Heritage exhibit and Music Hall of Fame. *Also here:* extensive works depicting Gulf coast life over the centuries, the Robert Rauschenberg Art Gallery, the Snell Decorative Arts Collection, a maritime and petroleum hall, and a mammoth mural by Kerrville artist Travis Keese. Open daily. Fee.

Oriental Village. 801 Ninth Avenue; (409) 983-7676. More than 8,000 Vietnamese settled in the Port Arthur area in the early 1970s, 95 percent of whom were Roman Catholics and 5 percent of whom were Buddhists. Their culture and expressions of religion have changed the face of this town. Hoa-Binh (Area of Peace) shrine has a triple life-size statue of the Virgin Mary, surrounded by ornamental gardens. A block of Vietnamese shops is adjacent. The Buddhists bought an old Baptist church at 2701 Proctor Street and turned it into Buu Mon Buddhist Temple, complete with a lighted, four-tiered pagoda tower. Call for tours. There are dragon dances for Buddha's birthday, and the Lotus Festival offers exotic plants and unusual bamboo. All are public events, including the Tet (New Year's) celebration every year at the Buu Mon Buddhist Temple (409-960-1462; www.buumon.com).

Our Lady of Guadalupe Shrine. 3648 Staff Sgt. Lucian Adams Drive. Amid the cattle fields, golf courses, and senior-citizen centers that clump this stretch of Port Arthur is a 17-foot-high statue depicting Juan Diego's encounter with the Virgin. Sculpted by Miguel Angel Macias of Mexico City and local artist Douglas Clark from Port Arthur, this eye-popping and popular work was commissioned by a local parish.

Pleasure Island. In Sabine Lake, across the Sabine-Neches ship channel and south from metro Port Arthur; (409) 982-4675 or (800) 235-7822; www.pleasureislandtx.com. Follow signs to the Martin Luther King Bridge and Pleasure Island. This multimillion-dollar development, an 18.5-mile-long man-made body of land, offers numerous activities and amenities, including fishing and crabbing; lighted fishing piers; a marina, restaurant, golf course, and disc golf course; spots for picnicking, tent camping, and RV camping; boat ramps; private homes and condos; and birding. Part of the lake around the island is reserved exclusively for sailboarders.

Pompeiian Villa. 1953 Lakeshore Drive; (409) 983-5977. Believe it or not, this is a multimillion-dollar house. Built in 1900 by Isaac Ellwood, the "Barbed Wire King," it later was sold to the president of Diamond Match Co. He in turn traded it for $10,000 worth of Texaco stock worth millions on today's market—or so the story goes in Port Arthur. Whichever, this pink stucco villa is listed on the National Register of Historic Places and is now owned by the Port Arthur Historical Society. Open Monday–Friday. Fee.

Rose Hill Manor. 101 Woodworth Boulevard; (409) 985-7292. Built in 1906 as the family home of Rome Woodworth, a Port Arthur banker and mayor, this gracious home sits next to the Sabine-Neches Waterway. Docent-led tours can be arranged by calling in advance.

Sabine Pass Battleground State Historic Site. Fifteen miles south of Port Arthur via Highway 87 to Sabine Pass, then 1.5 miles southeast on Dowlen Road; (512) 463-6323; www.thc.state.tx.us. Now a small settlement on the outflow channel from Sabine Lake, Sabine Pass (then known as Sabine City) was a major center for the shipment and trading of cotton as well as a supply center for Confederate forces during the Civil War. To protect this strategic entry into Texas from Union invasion, the Confederate forces began construction of Fort Griffin in 1863.

On August 29 of that year, 5,000 Union soldiers on twenty-two ships of various types sailed from New Orleans, accompanied by four heavily armed gunboats and one command vessel. Their goal was to capture Fort Griffin, invade Texas in the vicinity of Sabine City, advance to Beaumont, seize the railroad, and then take Houston and Galveston from the north. An additional 10,000 troops would then be brought in from New Orleans to overcome all resistance.

But they didn't figure on Confederate lieutenant Richard W. "Dick" Dowling and the forty-seven men he commanded at the not-yet-completed Fort Griffin. On September 8 the Union fleet arrived offshore of Sabine City. After the Union's initial shelling of the fort elicited no response, it was decided that the fort was deserted. When the gunboats got close to the fort, however, Dowling's forces opened fire. With extreme cunning and only six cannons, Dowling and his men destroyed two Union gunboats and took between 300 and 350 prisoners, with no Confederate casualties. The remainder of the Union fleet then panicked and fled back to New Orleans, the Federal invasion of Texas a total failure. A monument to Dowling's act of heroism now stands on what may have been the site of Fort Griffin.

This fifty-six-acre park also has four concrete ammunition bunkers (no guns) constructed during World War II. All this has given rise to a small forest of historical markers.

Visitors will find exhibits about the Civil War battle, backdropped by huge oil rigs stacked offshore, awaiting deployment in the Gulf. Other activities include picnicking, camping, and fishing along the 0.25 mile of waterfront. *NOTE:* The park is being rebuilt after damage from Hurricane Rita. It is expected to reopen in 2008. Call ahead to check before driving there.

Sea Rim State Park. About 23 miles south of metropolitan Port Arthur on Highway 87 (P.O. Box 1066, Sabine Pass, TX 77655); (409) 971-2559; www.tpwd.state.tx.us. Thanks to enlightened management, the sea rim marshlands between Port Arthur and Galveston are treated as the fragile natural resource they are. Important to the seafood industry as nursery grounds for shrimp and fish, they also provide a unique experience for visitors.

Sea Rim State Park is a perfect example; it is far more than the usual seaside camping and sunning spot. With more than 15,000 acres, this is the third-largest state park in

Texas. Also the only marshland park, it is divided into two distinct areas. The beach unit has camping with and without hookups along 3 miles of sand; a main headquarters with restrooms, hot showers, and concessions; an outstanding interpretive center; and the Gambusia Trail, a 3,640-foot boardwalk through the wetlands behind the dunes.

The second unit is a pristine marsh, easily explored on your own via a small powerboat or canoe. Be aware, however, that you must file a float plan with the rangers and that marsh maps are essential to safely navigate this wilderness. Inquire also about the airboat tours operated by park rangers at various times March through October (fee). You may surprise a flock of herons or egrets or see an alligator or two—unless they see you first. There are four camping platforms and observation blinds within the marsh; reservations required. Fee.

NOTE: Hurricane Rita damaged the park, and it is currently closed. It should reopen in 2008. Call ahead to check before driving there.

Snooper's Paradise. 5509 East Parkway, Groves (at the northwest corner of Thirty-ninth Street and Highway 73); (409) 962-8427; www.snoopersparadise.com. These folks have been importing antiques from Europe since 1952, and their 30,000-plus-square-foot facility bulges with beautiful things, primarily from the 1860–1900 period. Delivery to Houston is all in a day's work. Open Monday–Saturday.

Veterans Memorial Park. On Highway 87, in the shadow of the impressive Neches River bridges, this park pays tribute to veterans of all branches of the military. Visitors will find the names of more than 10,000 servicemen and women, spanning World War I to Operation Desert Storm. Kids and military buffs will marvel at all the hardware here, including an F4-D Phantom Jet, a Huey helicopter, and an M60A3 tank.

Vuylsteke Dutch Home. 1831 Lakeshore; (409) 984-6101. This home was built in 1905 for the first Dutch consul to Port Arthur and contains its original furniture. Tours by appointment.

Walter Umphrey State Park. Located at the south end of Pleasure Island on Mesquite Point; (337) 802-4320 or (409) 982-4675. This state park, named for a local attorney, boasts a lighted fishing pier, boat launch, and RV park. Open daily.

White Haven. 2545 Lakeshore; (409) 984-6101. Now owned by Lamar University–Port Arthur, this 1915 Greek Revival mansion is open for tours on Monday, Wednesday, and Friday or by appointment.

where to eat

Esther's Seafood and Oyster Bar. 9902½ Gulfway Drive, Groves; (409) 962-6268. If you're hungry for spicy Cajun seafood and steaks, search out this barge eatery at the foot of the Rainbow Bridge. Open for lunch and dinner daily. $$–$$$.

La Hacienda Mexican Restaurant. 7700 Ninth Avenue; (409) 724-1477. Known for sizzling and spicy Mexican food, La Hacienda packs in a crowd. Most choose from the large buffet, while others just reorder their favorites again and again from the extensive menu. Open for lunch and dinner daily. $–$$.

Larry's French Market & Cajun Restaurant. 3701 Pure Atlantic Road; (409) 962-3381. Cajun-style shrimp, crab, and fish are favorites here, along with locally made sausages, and on weekends the live music keeps folks dancing. This is Louisiana border country, where a hot fiddle makes it hard for couples born on either side of the river to sit still. Another plus: All that moving and shaking helps work off some of your big dinner. Open for lunch Tuesday–Friday; dinner Thursday–Saturday. $–$$.

Tammie's Old Tyme Diner. 5404 South Gulfway Drive, Sabine Pass; (409) 971-2573. Salads are good here, along with the burgers, chicken-fried steak, shrimp, and catfish. This is a good place to bring the kids. Open for breakfast and lunch Monday–Saturday; dinner Thursday–Saturday. $–$$.

Tropical Grill. 4751 Gulfway Drive; (409) 982-3357. Caribbean and Mexican specialties headline here. For something different, try the pineapple stuffed with fish, shrimp, scallops, and crabmeat and then topped with mozzarella. Open for lunch and dinner daily. $–$$.

wandering the back roads

The most logical and the swiftest access from Houston to the entire Golden Triangle area is via I-10 East. But if time is no problem and you prefer quiet country roads, detour south from the interstate just past the Trinity River Bridge and explore Wallisville and Anahuac (see East Day Trip 4).

Interested in rice farming? Plan a stop at the East Chambers Agricultural and Historical Museum in Winnie (409-296-2231), open weekdays or by appointment. Exhibits here include early farm equipment and an old crop-duster airplane. From I-10 take exit 829, turn south on Highway 124, and turn east on LeBlanc; the museum will be 1 block down on the left. If you have children with you, take note of the very nice playground across the street. Winnie also hosts Old Time Trade Days on the first Friday–Sunday after the first Monday of the month. This event draws many of the dealers from First Monday at Canton and is of major interest to hunters of antiques and general junk (see East Day Trip 1).

day trip 04

east

the wild life:
wallisville, anahuac,
high island, bolivar peninsula

wallisville

One of the oldest towns in Chambers County, Wallisville was torn down in 1966 by the U.S. Army Corps of Engineers in preparation for a large flood-control dam that then remained stalled in controversy for many years. The project's scope subsequently was scaled back to being a barrier and navigation locks between the saline waters of the Gulf and the fresh water and marshes of the Trinity River. In the process a major new recreation area has been created (see "What to Do"). The original Wallisville town site, however, remains green, rolling, and open. What once was a handsome, Victorian-era town is now just a fading memory.

what to do

Cedar Hill Park. From Interstate 10 take FM 563 north 2.8 miles and turn left on Lake Charlotte Road (watch for HATCHER'S CHRISTMAS TREE FARM sign); the park will be 1.1 miles down on the left. Although some will come here for the camping and pleasant picnic area by the lake, this park is of interest primarily as a birding and wilderness exploration site. A boardwalk and observation deck, lined with cypress trees, extends into Lake Charlotte. Nonmotorized boats can be launched here, so come with a kayak or canoe. Bring a camera as well—this is a favored habitat for eagles and roseate spoonbills. For camping reservations call the Chambers County Courthouse at (281) 576-2243.

east day trip 04

The J. J. Mayes Wildlife Trace. South of I-10 on the west bank of the Trinity River; (409) 389-2285. This complex of roads, trails, and boardwalks allows easy viewing of the wildlife and vegetation that makes its home on the Trinity River. Visitors may glimpse raccoons, river otters, bobcats, and coyotes, as well as alligators and dozens of species of birdlife. The complex, maintained by the U.S. Army Corps of Engineers, includes a 4-mile nature trail along the river levee, a 2.5-mile trail that follows the river's bank, and a small wheelchair-accessible loop. Restrooms, picnic tables, and nature-viewing platforms enhance the experience. Open sunrise to sunset daily.

Lake Wallisville Ranger Station and Visitor Center. P.O. Box 293, Wallisville, TX 77957; (409) 389-2285. From I-10 East take exit 807 and turn south on the first levee road. Operated by the Army Corps of Engineers (ACOE), this well-designed nature center has educational exhibits well worth a stop.

In addition to a visual history and maps of old Wallisville, visitors also are captivated by the large topographical map that explains the extensive and complicated Wallisville project. This also is where you file a float plan if you want to boat these waters. The locks operate hourly as needed during the day, plus their high walls are popular perches for pelicans. Birding trails follow several of the levees (apply at the visitor center for access).

The watery maze that makes up this recreational area tantalizes boaters, but all must file a float plan with the ACOE. The best put-in is via the Turnaround exit from I-10 on the west side of the Trinity River Bridge. Many water routes flow from there, one of which—the Cypress Swamp Canoe Trail—accesses Lake Charlotte when water levels permit. That I-10 exit also leads to a major birding trail that includes two boardwalks over the marsh. No motorized vehicles are allowed beyond the parking area. If the gate is closed, request a key at the visitor center. Open daily.

Wallisville Heritage Museum. 20136 I-10 East (P.O. Box 16, Wallisville, TX 77597-0016); (409) 389-2252. Take the Wallisville exit (807) and continue on the eastbound frontage road. Created in 1979 as a nonprofit foundation to restore the old town of Wallisville and preserve the adjacent El Orcoquisac Archaeological District, this small museum has three of Wallisville's old buildings on-site. Only one—an 1869 school—can be toured; a lack of funds delays restoration of the others. Ancestor hunters also find an extensive genealogical library focused on America's eastern coast, the ancestral home of many Chambers County pioneers. Open Monday–Saturday.

continuing on

From Wallisville take the Old Wallisville Road to its intersection with FM 563 and continue south to Anahuac. The road itself is a delight—no center stripe or traffic—and it's easy to imagine how things were when this was a horse-and-buggy route.

anahuac

Founded as a Spanish fortress in 1821, Anahuac (pronounced Ana-whack) was the site of a fort and customs house constructed in 1831 by prisoners of the Mexican government. Built where the Trinity River empties into Galveston Bay, the fort was captured the following year by Texian forces under the command of William B. Travis, who subsequently met his doom at the Alamo. The site now is a large city park south of town (see below). Today Anahuac is both the Chambers County seat and the official alligator capital of Texas, a fact the town celebrates with Gatorfest every September.

what to see

Anahuac National Wildlife Refuge. On East Galveston Bay, 18 miles southeast of town via FM 562, FM 563, and FM 1985 (follow the signs). This 35,000-acre wildlife refuge hosts more than 270 species of birds (fifty-two of which nest here), twenty-four species of mammals, an extensive number of reptiles, and uncountable mosquitoes (wear industrial-strength repellent). When weather conditions permit, approximately 12 miles of graveled roads offer excellent opportunities to observe wildlife. A major stop on the Great Texas Coastal Birding Trail, this refuge offers birders an observation platform along Shoveler Pond and a footpath to the Willows, a major "fallout" area during the spring and fall tropical migrations. The rare palm warbler often is sighted here during spring migration. There also are two boat ramps if you want to explore on your own by shallow-draft boat. Hunting is allowed on three tracts in season; request information on times, restrictions, and required permits. Other activities include photography, fishing, and crabbing. Apart from restrooms, there are no amenities, concessions, or picnic facilities; bring drinking water. All visitors must register at the Visitor Information Center. Refuge brochures and bird checklists are available here, and a small bookstore sells natural-history books related to the general area. For advance information and a birding list, write P.O. Box 278, Anahuac, TX 77514; call (409) 267-3337; or log on to www.southwest.fws.gov/refuges.

Anahuac National Wildlife Refuge also includes the East Bay Bayou Tract on FM 1985, 7 miles east of the refuge's main entrance. Opened in 1998, this birding and fishing area has a 1.5-mile wooded trail along East Bay Bayou, a good spot for viewing migratory songbirds in the spring. Other activities include freshwater fishing from the bank or from three fishing piers. Nonmotorized boats also are allowed. Open during daylight hours, with twenty-four/seven access to the bay.

Candy Abshier Wildlife Management Area. At Smith Point on east Galveston Bay, 23 miles south of Anahuac via FM 562; (409) 736-2551, ext. 25. Also a major "fallout" area for migrating birds in spring and fall, these 207 acres of oak-studded coastal prairie provide welcome roosts and cover for orioles, buntings, warblers, swallows, pelicans, storks, frigates, and raptors. Some twenty species of the latter have been sighted here during the fall migration (late August to early October; third week of September is prime). These Hawk Watches are sponsored by the Gulf Coast Bird Observatory (979-480-0999; www.gcbo.org). Apart from a 30-foot-tall viewing tower on the shore of East Bay, there are no other public facilities or water. Insect repellent strongly advised. Open daily.

Chambers County Library. 202 Cummings Street; (409) 267-8261. The library is open Monday–Friday, and until 1:00 p.m. on Saturday. Outside you'll find two very old buildings on the library's lawn. The first, Chambersea, was built in 1845 and is one of the prettiest and most unusual homes remaining from that early statehood era. The other, a frontier doctor's office, was floated into Anahuac from its original home in Cedar Bayou. For access to either call the local historical commission at (409) 267-8363.

Fort Anahuac Park. Main Street at Trinity Bay. Diligent researchers here find traces of Fort Anahuac (circa 1831), built as a combination fort and customhouse by prisoners of the Mexican government. This also was the site of a skirmish between Texian and Mexican forces prior to the Texas Revolution. This is another major stop on the upper coast birding trail. There is a lighted fishing pier on the Anahuac Barge Channel below the bluff. It is free and open around the clock. A paved, 1.9-mile-long levee road offers excellent wade fishing and wildlife observation, and the Judge Oscar Nelson Boardwalk starts at the boat ramp and continues along the Trinity River.

Frascone Winery. 377 Bayside Drive, Oak Island; (409) 252-4506; www.frasconewinery.com. This winery, which had its grand opening in April 2005, is located in a tiny fishing village, a bit off the beaten path even for visitors to Anahuac. In addition to making traditional grape-based wines, they also produce other fruit wines, including blackberry, raspberry, strawberry, and peach. Open Friday–Sunday, or by appointment. Call for directions.

Picnic and play places. Two parks make good leg-stretching stops in the Anahuac area. Double Bayou Park, on Eagle Ferry Road between FM 563 and FM 562, offers day-use areas, a covered pavilion, boat ramps, and other amenities. White's Park, on Highway 61 south of I-10, has a rodeo area, bayou access for fishing and crabbing, a picnic area, and camping. Insect repellent is advised at both parks.

Upper Texas Coast Waterborne Education Center. P.O. Box 9, Anahuac, TX 77514. This facility's goal is to provide on-the-water educational experiences to enhance the general public's understanding of coastal resources in general, the Trinity River delta in the specific. To that end they operate boat explorations within the Trinity River watershed (fee). Aimed primarily at groups, these trips last up to four hours. Activities aboard may include water testing, seining, specimen collecting, and so on. These are not pleasure trips in the general sense of the term; rather they are educational experiences. Nor do they use pleasure craft. Their fleet consists of two 45-foot-long retired Coast Guard buoy tenders configured with teaching facilities, tools, galley, air-conditioning, and overnight bunks. For additional information call (409) 267-3547.

where to eat

DJ's. At the intersection of I-10 and Highway 61; (409) 374-2144. This unfancy grocery store serves some of the best barbecue in the region, which you can eat at picnic tables under the trees. Open daily for lunch and dinner. $.

continuing on

To continue this day trip from Anahuac to High Island and the Bolivar Peninsula, follow FM 562 south to FM 1985, then turn east (left) and go 15 miles to a south (right) turn on Highway 124 to High Island. From that tiny community continue south on Highway 124 to its intersection with Highway 87 at the coast. *Warning:* The washed-out sections of Highway 87 to the left of that last intersection are no longer passable, even with four-wheel drive.

After touring Bolivar, you have two options for returning to Houston. The first is to ride the free car ferry that connects Bolivar's southwestern tip with Galveston and then take Broadway down-island to Interstate 45 North. Or just park your car at the Bolivar ferry dock, walk aboard (no waiting) for a round-trip ferry ride, and then return home the way you came: Highway 87 east up the Bolivar Peninsula to Highway 124 and High Island, then 20 miles north on Highway 124 to I-10 west at Winnie. From there it's 63 freeway miles west to Houston.

high island

Author's note: High Island's fabulous birding areas were severely damaged by Hurricane Humberto in September 2007. Please check with the Houston Area Audubon Society (see below) before making this trip.

Another major stop on the Great Texas Coastal Birding Trail, this tiny community, just 1 mile inland from the Gulf of Mexico, is particularly rewarding to birders from mid-March through mid-May. Following instinctive migration patterns, as many as 25,000 exhausted songbirds (wood warblers, tanagers, orioles, catbirds, buntings) make their first landfall here after flying 600 to 700 miles across the Gulf from winter homes in Mexico and Central America. Many carry colorful plumage in preparation for breeding and nesting farther north. Their favored landing trees are the one-hundred-year-old live oaks that shade numerous High Island sites. Four of those areas—Boy Scout Woods, Smith Oaks, Eubanks Woods, and the S. E. Gast Red Bay Sanctuary—are owned and operated by the Houston Area Audubon Society (713-932-1639; www.houstonaudubon.org). Bring binoculars, insect repellent, and your best manners; the birds must not be disturbed. Donations requested. For accommodations contact the Birder's Haven Resort, 2081 Winnie, High Island, TX 77623; (409) 286-5362.

As you approach High Island on Highway 124, stop at the High Island Roadside Park to locate the above sites and to check out the birds in that rest stop's sheltering oaks.

bolivar peninsula

In contrast to Galveston's burgeoning commercial development, this 32-mile stretch of unrestricted sand flexes with the whims of Mother Nature, changing with every storm. As a laid-back, low-cost, somewhat funky getaway, however, Bolivar can't be beat.

Once on Bolivar you won't find much, which is its biggest attraction—just some fishing camps and stilt-legged residential developments, RV resort camping, a seemingly endless beach, a few small communities, and an abandoned lighthouse built in 1872 and currently closed to the public. The latter was used some years ago as the set for the film *My Sweet Charlie.*

The beaches are open—you can drive, ride horses, or just walk for miles. There are waves to play in, sand to loll in, and enormous numbers of shorebirds to keep you entertained.

Two warnings: Apart from portable toilets, there are no public facilities on Bolivar's beaches, and the strand opposite the blinking light in Crystal Beach is locally known as "the Zoo," a mecca for unsupervised teenagers during spring break.

Love seashells? Time your visit to catch either an outgoing high tide or a minus tide. The beaches around High Island usually have the most abundant shells as well as an occasional fossil liberated from the prehistoric clay deposits that line much of the Gulf bottom. The flats at the southwestern tip of the peninsula also are good for shelling; wear insect repellent.

Bed-and-breakfast also is possible here, at Out by the Sea (409-684-1555 or 888-522-5926; www.outbythesea.com).

Tip to oyster lovers: Locals consider oysters harvested from beds in Bolivar's East Bay to be among the best in the world. Local oysters are big deals on Bolivar menus; they're also sold by the pint and quart at several local markets.

For a vacation packet, birding list, and tourist information, contact the Bolivar Peninsula Chamber of Commerce, P.O. Box 1170, Crystal Beach, TX 77650; (409) 684-5940; www.bolivarchamber.org.

what to do

Birding. Bolivar Flats, a 550-acre stretch of coastal beach near the southwestern tip of the peninsula, is considered one of the prime birding areas on the upper Texas Gulf coast. From Highway 87 watch for Rettilon Road (reverse spelling of "no litter"), 3.7 miles east of the Bolivar ferry terminal. Turn south on Rettilon to a right turn at the beach and drive to the vehicular barricade. *NOTE:* Please stay on the beach and keep your animals on a leash. Entering the vegetated dunes and marshes is discouraged because of fragile nesting sites and poisonous snakes.

Fishing. Rollover Pass is the favored spot because strong currents bring large numbers of flounder, redfish, croaker, speckled trout, sand trout, and other game fish close to shore. This narrowest part of the peninsula got its name during Prohibition, when bootleggers would take delivery of barrels of hooch from ships on the Gulf side of the peninsula and then roll those barrels overland to local boats waiting in East Bay.

Fort Travis Seashore Park. South end of the peninsula, near the ferry. Noted as the spot where Jane Long, "the Mother of Texas," gave birth to the first Anglo child on Texas soil, it also has the remains of a fort built before the turn of the twentieth century. Now partially renovated, the fortifications provide stairs to a long beach and rocks for fishing. For information call (409) 934-8100.

where to eat

Bob's Sports Bar and Famous Grill. 1755 Highway 87, Crystal Beach; (409) 684-4929. Locals favor this place for its hamburgers, shrimp, and barbecue. The 9-inch muffuletta is big enough for four. Open for lunch and dinner daily. $–$$.

De Coux's Pub & Restaurant. 3150 Highway 87, Crystal Beach; (409) 684-0177. A good Sunday-drive destination in itself, this clean and classy eatery offers the chef's creations on a blackboard menu in addition to burgers, sandwiches, crabmeat nachos, crawfish in season, and so on. If the weather turns chilly, come enjoy their fireplace. Open for dinner daily year-round, lunch also on weekends. $–$$.

Mama Teresa's Flying Pizza & Italian Restaurant. 2770 Highway 87, Crystal Beach; (409) 684-3507. Nearly an icon for the area, this busy place serves highly praised, hand-tossed pizza and numerous other Italian entrees. The fettuccine shrimp Alfredo is one of their top sellers. In winter this spot is open for dinner only on Thursday and Friday, lunch and dinner on the weekends. Dinner also is served Tuesday and Wednesday in the summer. $–$$.

Outrigger Grill. 1035 Highway 87, Crystal Beach; (409) 684-6212. This family-oriented restaurant even has toys to keep the kiddies happy while you wait for a delicious oyster po'boy, giant burrito, Mexican plate, burger, steak, or whatever else strikes your fancy on their long menu. Owner Skip Rohacek buys her fish fresh off local boats and guarantees that no one leaves her place hungry. Open Thursday–Tuesday for breakfast, lunch, and dinner. $–$$.

Steve's Landing. 1290 Bay Vue Road, Crystal Beach; (409) 684-1999. You can come by car or boat to this attractive place that overlooks the Intracoastal Canal, and then dine either indoors or on the screened-in patio. *Attention oyster lovers:* On Thursday and Sunday during the winter, this lively spot offers all-you-can-eat oysters fixed seven different ways, in addition to the regular menu (seafood straight off their own boats, chicken, and steaks). From May 1 to October 1, they serve lunch and dinner Wednesday–Sunday, dinner only on

Monday and Tuesday. From October through April they serve dinner only Wednesday–Friday, lunch and dinner on the weekends. $–$$$.

Stingaree. 1295 Stingaree Road, Crystal Beach; (409) 684-2731. Considered by many people to be Bolivar's premier eatery, this spot's specialties include barbecued crab, charbroiled snapper, honey jalapeño shrimp, and snapper throats (when available). Save room for the bread pudding with bourbon sauce. For drinks and appetizers, the second-floor deck, with its view of East Bay and the Intracoastal Canal, is the place to be on Bolivar. Open for lunch and dinner Wednesday–Sunday in winter; Tuesday–Sunday during spring break; daily during summer. $–$$$.

southeast

day trip 01

southeast

history lessons:
pasadena, la porte,
baytown, morgan's point

pasadena

As you drive southeast from Houston on Interstate 45 and look east to the vast industrial-chemical complex that is Pasadena today, it's hard to believe that this once was projected to be Houston's garden. Its bucolic future was altered permanently by two events: the completion of the Houston Ship Channel as a deepwater port in 1915 and the discovery of oil in nearby Baytown the following year.

Slightly off the usual Sunday drive itinerary, this upper bay region has several things to see and do. Start with a tour of the Port of Houston and the ship channel, and then head east on Highway 225 to digest some history at San Jacinto Battleground State Historical Park in La Porte. From there ride the free Lynchburg Ferry to Baytown and return to the Morgan's Point/La Porte area via the Fred Hartman Bridge. En route you'll find crabbing, swimming, and bird-watching—all at a laid-back pace. For area information call the Pasadena Chamber of Commerce, (281) 487-7871.

what to do

Heritage Park and Museum. 205 Main at Eagle Street (1 block south of Highway 225; use the Shaver Street exit); (713) 472-0565. This new park features three historic houses. The first two, Anna's House (1928) and the Pomeroy House (1906), are in their original locations. The third, Strawberry House, originally stood on a nearby Mexican land grant and is fur-

southeast day trip 01

Aldine Westfield Rd.

Jesse Jones Park

Humble

Houston Dayton

Huffman

Liberty

Hull

Daisetta

Raywood

San Jacinto Historical Park

Sheldon Res.

Beltway 8

Houston

Lynchburg Ferry

Wallisville

Harka

Anahuac

Port of Houston

Baytown

Pasadena

Spencer Highway   La Porte

Atkinson Island
Sylvan Beach

Morgan's Point

Trinity Bay

Candy Abshier Wildlife Management Area–Smith Point

Seabrook

Kemah

Clear Lake

League City

Dickinson

Alvin

Texas City

Galveston Bay

Bolivar Peninsula

La Marque

Texas City Dike

Free Ferry

Galveston

Danbury

Angleton

Brazoria National Wildlife Refuge

Gulf of Mexico

0   15 miles

nished to illustrate three periods: the early 1880s when it was new, the 1920s, and the 1940s. The homes are open only by advance request, and groups are welcome. The museum showcases local history from early settlement days to recent times. Museum open Tuesday–Saturday; call for hours.

Port of Houston. 7300 Clinton Drive, Houston (Clinton exit from Loop 610 East); (713) 670-2416; www.portofhouston.com. Due to heightened security, a boat tour is now the only way to tour the port. The free ninety-minute trip aboard the MV *Sam Houston* takes you close to huge ships from around the world, grain elevators, refineries, docks—the heart of the second-largest port in America. This is an official inspection vessel, and reservations are required. Make them two to three months in advance, although you often can get reservations at the last minute due to cancellations. Closed on Monday, holidays, and for the month of September.

la porte

Founded by French settlers in 1889, this modest community now stretches north to include one of the state's most significant historic sites. See that portion of La Porte now, en route to the Lynchburg Ferry, and the Sylvan Beach area on the final leg of this trip.

what to do

Little Cedar Bayou Park. 1322 South Broadway; (281) 470-7275. From Highway 146 in La Porte, turn east onto Fairmont Parkway, right on Eighth Street, and left on M Street. This pleasant city park has play and picnic areas, a mile-long nature trail that ends at Galveston Bay, and a WaterWorld–type wave pool (fee) that operates during summer.

Lynchburg Ferry. From the cemetery and picnic area of the battleground park (see below), continue northeast on Highway 134 to this free ferry, a relic from prefreeway days. You are welcome to park your car and take the fifteen-minute round-trip as a passenger, or you can drive aboard and then continue to Baytown. The ferry operates twenty-four hours a day, year-round. For more information call (281) 424-3521.

San Jacinto Battleground State Historical Park. 3800 Park Road; (281) 479-2431; www.tpwd.state.tx.us. From Pasadena continue east on Highway 225 to Highway 134, and turn north to Park Road 1836. Here, in just eighteen minutes, Sam Houston and his ragged Texian Army defeated the Mexican Army in 1836. This event changed not only the future of Texas but that of the western half of continental America. The dramatic story is chiseled in granite and unfolds as you walk around the base of the 570-foot-tall San Jacinto Monument. There is no better capsule lesson in Texas history.

Inside, the interesting San Jacinto Museum of History (281-479-2421) has artifacts from the Spanish-Mexican period (1519–1835) and the Anglo-American settlement years

(1835–81). A multi-image documentary presentation, *Texas Forever! The Battle of San Jacinto,* brings history to life in the museum's Jesse H. Jones Theatre for Texas Studies. The museum is free, but there are charges to see the film and to ride the elevator to the top of the monument. Open daily.

The battlefield flanks the monument, and a free map available at the museum will guide you to markers and various positions of the Texas and Mexican armies. This oak-studded parkland also has numerous picnic sites along one arm of the bay and on the ship channel, so bring your lunch and crabbing gear.

The battleship *Texas* is nearby. Moored here since 1948, and now with a restored hull, it is billed as the only surviving heavily armed dreadnought-class battleship, a relic of both world wars. Open daily. Fee.

Sylvan Beach. From Highway 146 in La Porte, turn east on Fairmont Parkway to where it ends at this park. This pleasant, thirty-two-acre county park has a playground, picnic areas, a bait and tackle shop, restrooms, and a free boat launch but no swimming. There also is good crabbing here. The old train depot at the park's entrance now serves as a historical museum for La Porte and is open by appointment. For information call (281) 326-6539.

where to eat

Monument Inn Restaurant. 4406 Battleground Road; (281) 479-1521. This long-standing favorite place still serves up whopping portions of seafood, chicken, and steak. House specialties include the "Monumental" salad and Key lime pie for dessert. A scrumptious cinnamon roll comes in your bread basket, just right for breakfast the next day. Open for lunch and dinner daily. $–$$$.

continuing on

From the San Jacinto Monument area and La Porte, the Lynchburg Ferry takes you across the ship channel to Baytown, where you continue on Highway 134 to Decker Drive (Highway 330). Turn southeast (left) and drive into Baytown. At the intersection with Highway 146, a turn southwest (right) will take you back to La Porte via the Fred Hartman Bridge.

baytown

Both Lynchburg and Baytown were early Anglo settlements, the former an important trading post and the latter originally a sawmill and a store on Goose Creek near the junction of the San Jacinto River and Buffalo Bayou. What was then known as Bay Town boomed after the Civil War and again with the discovery of oil nearby in 1916. When Humble Oil and Refining Co. bought 2,200 acres for a refinery in 1919, present-day Baytown began to evolve. Antiques hounds may enjoy a stroll through the Goose Creek historic district (Texas Avenue and Defee Street between Pruett and Commerce).

what to do

Baytown Historical Museum. 220 West Defee; (281) 427-8768. This interesting look at the area's past is housed in a 1936 post office. Note the fresco on the lobby wall, painted by noted artist Barse Miller as part of a WPA project during the Great Depression. Other major exhibits include replicas of an Indian hut and midden; the poetry of the Sage of Cedar Bayou, John P. Sjolander; and Humble/Exxon memorabilia from the early days in the oil patch. The Texas Room has artifacts relevant to David Burnet, Sam Houston, and Lorenzo de Zavalla, all of whom lived in the area. Open Tuesday–Saturday; call for hours. Donation.

Eddie V. Gray Wetlands Education and Recreation Center. 1724 Market Street; (281) 420-7128. Opened in January 1998 and the activity hub for the Goose Creek Greenbelt, this 14,000-square-foot facility has much of interest to the traveling public. Aimed at teaching environmental education, the Wetlands Center includes a large display area and a Living Lab as well as numerous classrooms used by Lee College and the Goose Creek school district. For visitors the primary focus is the Living Lab, where indoor education blends with outdoor recreation, even in bad weather. In addition to taxidermist displays and touch tanks, it features the (indoor) Exxon Learning Trail, which simulates an outdoor nature trail experience. An aboveground pool replicates a cypress swamp, complete with fish, turtles, and two baby alligators. Call for current program and fees.

Fred Hartman Bridge. Glorious double diamond-shaped towers mark this soaring structure over the waters between La Porte and Baytown. Total length of this portion of Highway 146 equals eight football fields. Drive slowly and enjoy the views.

Goose Creek Stream Greenbelt. An ongoing project begun in 1990, this ambitious development currently is three-quarters complete, with a final phase scheduled to be finished soon. Visitors now find 3.5 miles of hike-and-bike trail between Bayland Park Marina and Goose Creek Park, a pavilion, extensive playgrounds, fishing and boating piers, and other facilities at Goose Creek Park. The final phase will add about another half mile to the greenbelt when completed.

Houston Raceway Park. 2525 FM 565 South; (281) 383-2666; www.houstonraceway .com. Take exit 798 from I-10 east of downtown, go south to Highway 146, then right to FM 565. Billed as the world's fastest drag-racing track, this 0.25-mile strip hosts the NHRA O'Reilly Spring Nationals annually in February/March and the 4-Wheel Jamboree Nationals in April. Want to test your wheels in pro territory? Come on a Friday night and bring $20. Some type of racing or special event is always going on, year-round. Fee.

where to eat

Going's Barbeque Company. 1007 North Main; (281) 422-4600. The name says it all at this locally popular spot. In addition to the usual meats/plates/sandwiches, there's an all-you-can-eat evening buffet on Thursday. Open daily for lunch and dinner. $–$$.

Rooster's. 6 West Texas Avenue (at Main Street); (281) 428-8222. This extremely popular locals' hangout specializes in steaks and burgers. Open for lunch and dinner Monday–Saturday. $–$$$.

morgan's point

Back in the good old days, Morgan's Point combined with La Porte to provide a beach and bay playground for Houstonians. Big-name bands brought crowds to the dance pavilion at Sylvan Beach, and folks drove around Morgan's Point just to see the handsome homes on the "Gold Coast."

A drive along Bayridge Road still takes you past some of those places, among them a grand replica of the White House, built by former Texas governor Ross Sterling. It has been a landmark on the Houston Ship Channel for around three generations. At the end of Morgan's Point is an undeveloped beach area well known to birders. With binoculars you can watch roseate spoonbills and other species on Atkinson Island, a sanctuary in this upper portion of Galveston Bay.

wandering the back roads

From the San Jacinto Monument, you easily can skip tours of Baytown, La Porte, and Morgan's Point in favor of a jaunt to Clear Lake and Kemah (see Southeast Day Trip 2). Just retrace your route to Highway 225 and turn east (left) to its intersection with Highway 146. Turn south (right) and go approximately 10 miles to Clear Lake and Kemah.

day trip 02

southeast

boardwalk:
clear lake, seabrook and kemah,
league city

clear lake

A drive south from Houston on Interstate 45 brings you to NASA Road 1. Turn east to explore Clear Lake and the laid-back towns of Seabrook and Kemah.

The launching of *Sputnik* also launched America's space program and triggered the construction of the NASA/Lyndon B. Johnson Space Center. Visitors now access some portions of that facility via Space Center Houston, a neighboring $70-million educational/entertainment project (see "What to Do" section) that's become one of the most popular visitor attractions in the state.

After investigating the exploration of space, you can challenge some new frontiers on your own. A few miles away is nature at its most primitive, a wilderness bayou seemingly untouched by civilization, and almost across the road you'll find the boating and water fun capital of Texas, Clear Lake. That 2,418-acre water playground sports more marinas, boat slips, and boats than any other Lone Star lake. Less adventurous folk enjoy the shops and docks in Seabrook and Kemah, a day's outing in themselves. Toss a cooler in the car to haul home some fresh fish. You'll also enjoy exploring the oak-shaded shops and tearooms in League City.

For information contact the NASA–Clear Lake Convention and Visitors Bureau, 1601 NASA Road 1, Houston, TX 77058; (281) 338-0333 or (800) 844-5253; www.nasaclearlake texas.com.

southeast day trip 02

Houston

Sheldon Resv.

Lynchburg Ferry

San Jacinto Historical Park

Baytown

Port of Houston

Pasadena

La Porte

Morgan's Point

Sylvan Beach

Atkinson Island

Armand Bayou Nature Center

Bay Area Blvd.

NASA Road 1

Seabrook

Candy Abshier Wild Management Area Smith Point

Space Center Houston

Clear Lake

Kemah

Bacliff

San Leon

Webster

League City

Dickinson

Galveston Bay

Alvin

Texas City

Texas City Dike

La Marque

Danbury

0   30 miles

what to do

Armand Bayou Nature Center. 8500 Bay Area Boulevard, Houston; (281) 474-2551; www.abnc.org. One of the largest urban wilderness and wildlife refuges in America, this 2,500-acre haven is home to more than 370 species of wildlife. This refuge hits its birding peak during March and April as a major stopover for migrating flocks. A covered bird blind with interpretive materials allows an educated look.

A 600-foot-long teaching boardwalk leads from the parking lot to the nature center, and additional walking trails thread woods, prairie, and the bayou's edge. Also on the grounds are a restored prairie with an observation platform, a raptor house, and a three-acre exhibit farm focused on the 1890s–1900s. The latter includes a restored and furnished farmhouse (live demonstrations on weekends), a barn, outbuildings, and a vegetable garden. There's also a children's day camp program here in June, July, and August.

The water portions of this wilderness park are best explored by canoe. You can either bring your own and put in at adjacent Bay Area Park, or you can participate (fee) in the canoe trips sponsored by the nature center (reservations required). Groups of ten to twelve also can reserve naturalist-led trips via pontoon boat (fee). Consider buying a family membership while you're at the nature center to help preserve this wilderness. Open Tuesday–Sunday. Fee.

Boating and other water sports on Clear Lake and Galveston Bay. Numerous sources provide charters, rentals, lessons, or excursions. The following are of particular interest to casual day visitors.

Several companies offer brief water trips on Clear Lake and/or Galveston Bay at various times and seasons. Here is one to consider: Tropical Express (281-538-0773; www.tropical express.com/).

Clear Lake Charter Boats and Clear Lake Powerboat Rentals (281-334-4858; www .clearlakecharterboats.com), based at South Shore Harbour Resort in League City and at the Nassau Bay Hilton, offer sailboat and powerboat rentals, bay and Gulf fishing trips, and parasailing.

South Coast Sailing Adventures and Gateway Charters (281-334-4606; www.south coastsailing.com) at the Kemah Boardwalk Marina (formerly Lafayette Landing Marina) in Kemah offers private sailing lessons, boat and breakfast, sunset and moonlight cruises (minimum eight people), and boat charters (with captain and crew, or without).

The following offer sailing lessons, boat charters, and/or fishing trips: At the Helm (281-334-4101), based at Kemah Boardwalk Marina in Kemah, offers sailing and rowing lessons.

Windward Seaventure Charters (281-334-5295 or 281-467-2279; www.windwardsea venture.com), based at Waterford Harbor in Kemah, offers sailing lessons as well as sailboat and powerboat rentals (with or without a captain).

The following offer charters: Majestic Ventures (281-333-3080), Sackett's Sailing Center (281-334-4179), Star Fleet (281-334-4692), and Ultra Sailing Charters (281-333-2011). Star Fleet offers a few public cruises at various times of the year; call for details.

Canoeing the bayous. There is canoe access at Bay Area Park and at the NASA Road 1 bridge at Clear Lake Park, 5001 NASA Road 1. Canoes can be rented by the hour or day at Cecil's Red Lantern Restaurant, 2908 Red Bluff Road (at the bridge on Taylor Lake; 817-301-6617). If you don't want to canoe at those specific sites, inquire whether the proprietors provide or rent car-top carriers or racks to transport canoes. You may need to bring your own.

You'll also find pleasant canoeing in Dickinson Bayou, which roughly parallels FM 517, both west and east from I-45. There is a good put-in and parking at Paul Hopkins Park in Dickinson, and then you have your choice of takeouts: a carry either at the FM 646 crossing (3.5 miles) or at Cemetery Road. This last section is the most beautiful and undisturbed. *NOTE:* Canoeing here is best on weekdays.

Galveston Bay Foundation. 17330 Highway 3, Webster; (281) 332-3381; www.galvbay .org. There's no need to go to Galveston to explore and enjoy bay waters. This volunteer nonprofit organization sponsors numerous activities and workshops annually, all focused on the natural ecology of Galveston Bay. Past trips have included canoe tours of Armand Bayou, Cedar Bayou, and Double Bayou; inspection by boat of the Houston Ship Channel; and a guided look at Anahuac National Wildlife Refuge. Emphasis always is on responsible ecotourism. Trips fill fast, and preference goes to members. Membership fees start at $25.

Space Center Houston. 1601 NASA Road 1, Houston; (281) 244-2100 or (800) 972-0369; www.spacecenter.org. From I-45 South take the NASA Road 1 exit and go 3 miles east. Billed as "A Magical Place to Discover Space," this focal point for America's manned space flight program has interactive exhibits that are easy to understand and fun to operate. Care to try your hand at landing the shuttle? Intercepting an errant satellite in space? Performing space chores at zero gravity? You can do all three and more, courtesy of a large bank of computer stations in the "Feel of Space" section, on the left as you enter.

An ideal outing regardless of the season or weather, Space Center Houston has an IMAX theater, a full-size mock-up of portions of the space shuttle, a super display of moon rocks (you can touch one), and tram tours that scoot you around limited portions of Johnson Space Center, next door. Got children under twelve in tow? A $1.2-million Kids' Space Place offers numerous out-of-this-world activities designed specifically for that age group. Kids can create a mock shuttle flight at Mission Kidtrol, experience what it feels like to walk on the moon, and so on. New to the center is Amazon Voyage, a 5,000-square-foot exhibit geared to families with children. On a tour of seven ports of call along the Amazon River, visitors will encounter creatures such as stingrays, anacondas, and piranhas. The exhibit also includes computer interactives, multimedia presentations, and hands-on activities. Plan to spend at least four to six hours here, more if you eat at the Zero G Diner, a cafeteria-style food court. *Nice to know:* If you just want to visit the gift shop, you have a forty-five-minute free period during which you can get your entrance fee back. There's also a day camp program for children in summer. *Also note:* The NASA–Lyndon B. Johnson Space Center, including Rocket Park, is no longer open to the public except through Space Center Houston. Open daily. Fee.

where to eat

Chabuca's Steaks and Rotisserie. 316 West NASA Road 1, Webster; (281) 554-8000; www.chabucas.com. This handsome restaurant, owned by brothers Charles and William White, serves a sumptuous buffet for both lunch and dinner. In the evening, your choices may include St. Louis–style ribs, Cajun redfish, six-pepper sirloin, duck confit, coconut shrimp, rosemary lamb chops, or flamed turkey. Best of all, you can try them all, along with a delectable selection of salads and sides. Open for lunch and dinner daily, except Monday. $$–$$$.

Frenchie's. 1041 East NASA Road 1, at El Camino Real, Webster; (281) 486-7144. This small, friendly place has been a local favorite since it was opened almost two decades ago by the Camera family, formerly of the Isle of Capri in Italy. You'll find scads of photographs on the walls, as well as a menu that ranges from family-style Italian to seafood and steaks. Although casual for lunch, it's a bit dressier for dinner. Open for lunch and dinner Monday–Saturday. $$–$$$.

continuing on

From Clear Lake this day trip follows NASA Road 1 east to its intersection with Highway 146 in Seabrook, and then turns south. The area on the north side of the bridge is Seabrook. On the south side is Kemah.

seabrook and kemah

Each of these small communities makes an ideal day trip destination in itself. The number of things to do in the general area keeps growing, however, so consider reserving overnight accommodations at the Boardwalk Inn on the Kemah Boardwalk (281-334-9980 or 877-285-3624; www.kemah.com). Or check out and into one of the area's very interesting bed-and-breakfasts: the Back Bay Inn (281-474-3869; www.backbaybnb.com) or Beacon Hill Guest House (281-326-7643; www.visitbeaconhill.com).

Both Seabrook and Kemah are heaven for seafood lovers and boat watchers, but each has its own distinct personality. Their common boundary, the Clear Creek Channel under the Kemah-Seabrook (Highway 146) bridge, is the only passage from Clear Lake into Galveston

Bay, and views of the constant boat parade are great from the outside decks of Kemah Boardwalk's waterfront restaurants. If you want to buy shrimp and other Galveston Bay catches fresh and relatively cheap, check out the numerous fish markets that line the channel on the Seabrook side of the bridge. Seabrook's channelfront also sports several eateries.

Away from the water, the quaint buildings of "Old" Seabrook now house assorted antiques stores, tearooms, and specialty shops. To find them, follow NASA Road 1 east through the signal at Highway 146 (it becomes Second Street) and turn right. Keep your eye out for the 6- to 8-foot-tall fiberglass pelicans, embellished by different artists, that appear in front of various businesses around town. They are the result of the Pelican Path Project (www.pelicanpathproject.com), a movement begun to promote community pride and tourism.

Always vulnerable to intermittent change by storms, Kemah's somewhat funky but charming fishing village character finally has been forever vanquished. Long loved by Houstonians as an unpretentious spot to sit, sup, and sip while enjoying the channel boat parade and the breezes off Galveston Bay, all of Kemah's channelfront now functions as a fourteen-acre entertainment theme park called the Kemah Boardwalk, courtesy of Landry's Seafood Restaurant, Inc., which bought out the entire strip in early 1997. Successful in the extreme, the Kemah Boardwalk now attracts more than three million visitors annually and provides an economic stability the region truly needed.

Visitors now find a slickly designed, upscale complex composed of several themed restaurants (most of them names you know from other locations; see "Where to Eat"), retail shops, hotel, water park, and amusement zone, all connected by a wide and lighted boardwalk along the channel. The latter's a plus, something that the old Kemah lacked. You also can get around via a gas-powered choo-choo, the *C. P. Huntington,* which replicates an 1863 Central Pacific Railroad train. For information regarding ongoing events, call (281) 334-9880 or (877) 285-3624, or log on to www.kemahboardwalk.com.

Kemah also has a delightful old-fashioned carousel, an enormous slide, and a 65-foot Ferris wheel on the edge of the bay. Thrill seekers gather at the Inventer, the Aviator, and the new wooden rollercoaster. Also bring waterwear, the better to play in the "dancing fountains" in the hotel's courtyard. Pinwheel in shape, the fountains intermittently shoot water up to 12 feet through seventy-five jets, a handsome sight when lit by colored lights at night.

To reach all of Kemah's fresh splendor, turn east at the Sixth Street stoplight at the southern end of the Highway 146 bridge, and then go north on Bradford. You'll also find interesting shopping, several eateries, and the Kemah Boardwalk Marina (formerly Lafayette Landing Marina) on the streets immediately behind the channel area and bayfront.

where to eat

Of the restaurants on the Kemah side of the channel, six are major chain eateries travelers usually know well from other locations: Cadillac Bar, Joe's Crab Shack, Landry's, and Babin's Seafood House, Saltgrass Steak House, and the Chart House. There's also a pizza parlor, a coffeehouse, and a Starbucks. Another popular chain, Pappadeaux, is across the channel on the Seabrook waterfront. If you're interested in other dining experiences, try one of the following.

in kemah:

The Aquarium. No. 11, Kemah Waterfront; (281) 334-9010. Top-notch in every respect, this very fishy place delights as a sensory experience. Its two-story heart is a huge cylindrical aquarium filled with major saltwater fish. If you're there at feeding time, you'll see a scuba diver hand-delivering dinner to some of the aquarium's more reclusive denizens. The human food is equally spectacular. The multipage menu offers numerous entrees, and each will arrive at your table properly cooked and presented. You can economize a bit on the desserts; each easily serves two. Don't miss doing some time on the outside decks—that's what Kemah's really all about. Open for dinner daily; lunch and dinner Friday–Sunday. $–$$$.

The Flying Dutchman Restaurant and Oyster Bar. No. 9, Kemah Waterfront; (281) 334-7575. Ask local residents where they take visitors for good and inventive seafood, and this place wins by a landslide. It's dressy duds upstairs, cutoffs and casual boating wear down. Unless the weather's at one of its uncomfortable extremes, try for a table on the deck, the better to watch the boat traffic. Open daily for lunch and dinner. $–$$$.

T-Bone Tom's Meat Market and Steakhouse Restaurant. 707 Highway 146; (281) 334-2133; www.tbonetoms.com. Why anyone would want a great steak, spicy sausage, ribs, chicken, or barbecue in the midst of fresh fish territory is beyond understanding, but if that's your pleasure, this is the place. Open Monday–Saturday for lunch and dinner. $–$$.

in seabrook:

Frenchie's Villa Capri. 3713 NASA Road 1; (281) 326-2373. Dress up here. This "Cucina d'Italia" is one of the prettiest places on Clear Lake, complete with an outdoor patio and Italian-style gardens stretching to the water's edge. Italian dishes get top billing, along with grilled seafood and steaks. Open for lunch and dinner Tuesday–Sunday. $$–$$$.

Pier du Lac. 3329 NASA Road 1; (281) 326-7437; www.pierdulac.com. The Italian and Indian backgrounds of the owners show in the menu, although there are plenty of standards and fresh fish dishes as well. Some folks never get past the appetizers, from the jumbo lump meat crab cake to oysters served five ways. Lunches are light and very affordable. Open for lunch and dinner Tuesday–Saturday, from noon on Sunday. $$–$$$.

Riviera Waterfront Restaurant and Bar. 2513 NASA Parkway (on Highway 146, 1 mile west of the Kemah bridge at the corner of NASA Parkway and Lakeside Drive); (281) 326-0900. Whether you come by boat or car, the deck of this casual, two-story waterfront spot is a good place to sample some memorable seafood gumbo (bouillabaisse). Not in the mood for fish? There's much more on the menu, all at good prices. Open for lunch and dinner daily, brunch on Sunday. $–$$$.

Seabrook Classic Cafe. 2511-A NASA Road 1; (281) 326-1512. This is a great place for weekend breakfasts, particularly if you have a fondness for those nifty little New Orleans doughnuts called beignets. Everything is fresh here and made from scratch. Open for lunch and dinner daily, breakfast on weekends. $–$$.

Tequila Boom's Mexican Restaurant. 3138 NASA Road 1; (281) 326-3999; www.tequila booms.com. Serves some of the area's best fajitas, piled high on a platter. Open for breakfast, lunch, and dinner daily. $–$$.

Tookie's. 1202 Highway 146; (281) 474-3444. When you are hankering for a hamburger, thick and sweet onion rings, and real iced tea (huge and made with freshly brewed hot tea), come here. Open daily for lunch and dinner. $.

in the area:

Clifton by the Sea. 10 Grand Avenue, Bacliff (at bay end of FM 646); (281) 339-3474; www.cliftonbythesea.com. This spiffy eatery has a diner atmosphere, great outdoor decks, and a patio that overlooks Galveston Bay. Nearly everything edible that swims in the Gulf dominates the menu, but they also offer steaks and one or two versions of chicken. Try the stuffed jalapeños. Open for lunch and dinner daily. $–$$$.

Gilhooley's Restaurant & Oyster Bar. 222 Ninth Street, San Leon; (281) 339-3813. The most popular menu item here is the Shrimphooleys—oysters grilled with shrimp on top. Try them and you'll be back for more. Open daily for breakfast, lunch, and dinner. $–$$.

Joe Lee's Seafood Kitchen. 1108 FM 2094, Clear Lake Shores; (281) 535-0148. The specialties of the kitchen revolve around succulent, lightly breaded seafood of all kinds. The creamy shrimp salad is delightful and worth coming back for. Open for lunch and dinner daily. $–$$.

Market Seafood. 16512 El Camino Real, Clear Lake; (281) 488-2722. The relaxed and friendly atmosphere at the market encompasses inexpensive fried shrimp or catfish. If you're looking for something a little more gourmet, try the grilled garlic shrimp, snapper Ponchartrain, or Caribbean grouper in a sherry cream sauce with crabmeat. Open lunch and dinner daily. $–$$$

Noah's Ark. 4438 Boulevard Street, Bacliff; (281) 339-2895. This casual joint has all you need: terrific food, a view of the water, a friendly staff, and good happy-hour prices. Start with the grilled oysters. The three-alarm version is topped with picante sauce and jalapeños. There's every version of the burger, including a well-executed patty melt, and plenty of fried seafood offerings. Breakfast also is a treat here. Try the shrimp and Colby Jack omelet. It's a reason to get out of bed. Open for breakfast, lunch, and dinner daily. $–$$.

The Reef Seafood House. 1301 31½ Street at Palmer Highway, Texas City (behind the Raceway); (409) 945-6151; www.thereefseafood.cc. The inventive menu here includes such casual fare as bun-wiches of seafood and regular beef burgers and ranges to more sophisticated choices like orange roughy smothered in a creamy shrimp sauce and Red Snapper Cancun. Or, the undecided can create their own platter with any combination of four seafood choices. Open daily for lunch and dinner. $–$$$.

Top Water Grill. 815 Avenue O, San Leon; (281) 339-1232. Enjoy the sea breeze on the pier and watch the boats bring in shrimp and oysters in season. The seafood is some of the best—it comes fresh right off the boats here, which belong to the family of the grill's owner. Try the crab-stuffed jalapeños appetizer. Open for lunch and dinner daily. $–$$$.

continuing on

From Kemah drive south on Highway 146 to the signal at FM 2094 and turn west (right) to the FM 518 West intersection. That latter road becomes Main Street in this day trip's next stop: League City.

league city

This community, at the conjunction of Clear Creek and Sugar Bayou—the site of a Karankawa Indian village in pre-Anglo settlement times—was known as Butler's Ranch and/or Clear Creek when it was first settled by ranchers around 1854.

Two decades later, J. C. League acquired a large amount of local land and laid out his namesake town site along the right-of-way for the Galveston, Houston & Henderson Railroad. League City melds its Victorian past with current tourism in several pleasant ways. Walking-tour maps, available in several shops and cafes, lead you to more than two dozen historic sites, and both tearooms and antiques shops seem to be growth industries. For advance information contact the League City Historical Society, P.O. Box 1642, League City, TX 77574, or the League City Chamber of Commerce and Business Association, 621 Park Avenue, League City, TX 77573; (281) 338-7339; www.leaguecitychamber.com.

what to see

West Bay Common School Children's Museum Complex. 210 North Kansas Street (at Second Street); (281) 554-2994 or (281) 332-1644; www.oneroomschoolhouse.org. This award-winning, hands-on history experience captivates everyone regardless of age. A costumed "school marm" brings alive the rural education experience typical of Texas at the turn of the twentieth century; there's even a forty-five-star American flag. Sitting at old-fashioned desks in a real one-room school, youngsters use slates to learn the three R's from late-nineteenth-century textbooks, practice Spencerian penmanship in old-time pen and ink, and so on. The building itself was built in 1898 in west Chambers County and moved to the site of League City's original school in 1992. League City's 1927 icehouse and barber shop (1936) also have been moved here and restored as exhibits, and an old barn serves as a regional museum. Open Monday–Thursday and on Friday mornings. Classes are conducted only for groups with advance reservations.

where to eat

Esteban's Cafe and Cantina. 402 West Main; (281) 332-4195. One of the most appealing Mexican eateries in the greater Houston region, this family-owned spot makes its own sauces and tortillas from scratch daily. Don't miss either the spinach or crab enchiladas, just two of the house specialties. Open daily for lunch and dinner. $–$$.

Sudie's Catfish & Seafood House. 352 Gulf Freeway; (281) 338-5100; www.sudies.com. A tractor-trailer-length catfish dangling from a line announces you've arrived at Sudie's. This family-owned restaurant has been serving up delicious fried catfish for more than twenty years. Dominated by a stone fireplace, the dining room is family-friendly and warm despite its oversize dimensions. All manner of fried and grilled seafood can be found on the menu, but you won't go wrong with the fried catfish. And bring an appetite or a teenager—the all-you-can-eat catfish is a good deal at $14.99. Try an order of fried dill pickles—it's much better than it sounds. And save room for a bowl of banana pudding, which will make you feel ten years old again. $–$$.

wandering the back roads

To return to Houston, swing west on FM 518 to its intersection with I-45 North. If you want to extend this day trip, however, consider heading east on FM 518 to Highway 146, and then turning south for a short drive to the Texas City Dike (signs). A 5-mile-long strip of road and breakwater jutting into Galveston Bay, the dike is popular with sailboarders and folks with small sailboats and catamarans because the winds are relatively dependable. Fishing and crabbing are wherever you find a spot. There also are boat-launching facilities and plenty of beach/auto access at the Texas City Dike Beach Park. Due to a major cleanup effort, the dike now is reasonably clean, with adequate parking available along the sides of the road. The numerous fish-camp shanties and ramshackle cafes that lined much of its distance for some years have been removed, and visitors now find open vistas of Galveston Bay, portable toilets, and even a few potted palms for atmosphere. There are no rentals or concessions, however, so bring everything you might need (water, shade, chair, sunscreen, food, bait, and tackle) with you. Also bring binoculars; the birding's often excellent.

As an alternate to the dike, sailboarders and wade fishers may prefer to turn left at the entrance to the dike onto Skyline Drive. Great kite-flying territory, it also offers a 6-mile view and water playground along the bay. Along the way you'll find an interesting hike-and-bike path, a lighthouse-styled pavilion with information panels, a rifle range (open Wednesday–

Sunday), a small beach with rustic changing room and toilets, and the Thomas S. Mackey Nature Center. The latter is a thirty-five-acre wildlife habitat within the northern section of Bay Street Park, developed with the aid of local Boy Scouts and opened in 1998.

A third site in this same general area, the Texas City Prairie Preserve on Moses Lake, will be of interest to birders. Operated by the Nature Conservancy and usually open to the public on weekdays, the visitor center is primarily an educational facility for groups. Day-trippers with binoculars get good looks at shorebirds, but the surrounding land is a sensitive habitat for the endangered Attwater prairie chicken; please observe signs. *NOTE:* Neither dogs nor picnics are allowed here, and fire ants can be fierce. For information contact this preserve at 4702 Highway 146 North, Texas City, TX 77590; (409) 941-9114.

Birders note: This Texas City area has a total of five sites on the upper Texas coast version of the Great Texas Coastal Birding Trail. Instructions for ordering that map are in the "Additional Resources" listing in the front of this book.

day trip 03

beach party:
galveston

galveston

Cabeza de Vaca found it first. Later a pirate named Jean Lafitte made this sliver of island his base of shady operations in 1817. Legend says his treasure still lies buried in the shifting sands, and hunting for it with metal detectors is a favorite Galveston pastime.

To Houstonians this small city, one hour's drive south via Interstate 45, traditionally has been a relief valve, a place to escape from big-city life for a lazy day or weekend at the beach. But Galveston is far more than surf and sand.

Long before Houston was much more than a landing on Buffalo Bayou, Galveston was a major port and the threshold to Texas for thousands of immigrants. By the 1870s it was the wealthy and thriving "Queen City of the Southwest," and during the golden era of 1875–1900 some of the most remarkable architecture in America lined its streets.

A devastating hurricane in 1900 killed some 6,000 people and swept much of the city out to sea. Vulnerable to every passing storm, Galveston seemed doomed to follow the earlier Texas coast ports of Indianola and Lavaca into oblivion. To save the city and ensure its future security, two major engineering projects were undertaken, both remarkable for their times. The first was the building of a massive seawall, 17 feet tall and 10 miles long. The second was the raising of all the land behind that seawall from 4 to 17 feet.

These projects took seven years and were followed by another economic blow in 1915, when the successful completion of the Houston Ship Channel began to draw off the cream

southeast day trip 03

of the port trade. Galveston never recovered its prehurricane commercial importance, and gradually it degenerated into one of the wildest gambling towns in the state. The Texas Rangers finally brought down the law in the 1950s, and after that Galveston slumbered along as a rather seedy seaside city for a time.

But all is changing and on the upswing once again. The renovation and restoration of many historic buildings and a growth in the hotel/convention sector has sparked fresh capital investment, and Galveston now is thriving. Don't miss a ride on the $10-million rail trolley system that connects, in 1890s–1920s style, the Strand Historic District with the seawall. Additionally, electric bus shuttles ($1 per ride) operate approximately every twenty-five minutes Thursday–Sunday on a route that includes several stops in the Strand Historic District, on the Seawall, and at the Moody Gardens Hotel/Entertainment complex. Information: www.islandtransit.net.

Bed-and-breakfast also is strong in Galveston. For booking information contact the Galveston Island Visitors Center noted below.

Information on Galveston is available from the Heritage Visitors Center, operated by the Galveston Historical Foundation (GHF) (2328 Broadway, Galveston, TX 77550; 409-762-3933), the Moody Gardens Visitors Center (1 Hope Boulevard, Galveston, TX 77554; 800-582-4673), and the Galveston Island Visitors Center (2027 Sixty-first Street, Galveston, TX 77551; satellite location at 2215 Strand; 409-763-4311 or 888-425-4753).

exploring the beaches

There are 32 miles of beachfront on the island and a variety of options. The decisions start after you cross the causeway from the mainland on I-45 and see the directional signs for East and West Beaches. If you continue east (left lanes), I-45 becomes Broadway Boulevard and runs in an easterly direction the length of the island. If you follow the signs to West Beach from I-45, you will cross the island on Sixty-first Street, which ends at Seawall Boulevard, the island's second east-west main drag. Turn right; West Beach starts where the seawall ends. The road becomes FM 3005 at this point and continues down-island to San Luis Pass. Do note that cars are not allowed on Galveston's beaches at any time of the year and that alcohol is banned both along the seawall and at Stewart Beach.

Seafood tip: Want to buy fresh from the boats? Bring a cooler and check out the fish markets in the 1700–1900 blocks of Sixty-first Street.

There is one beach pocket-park on FM 3005, at Eleven Mile Road. Operated by Galveston County, it has changing rooms, showers, food concessions, and picnic areas and is backed by protected natural dunes. Horseback riding, parasailing, sailboarding, and other commercial beach activities often are available nearby during warm-weather months. West Beach offers the best jogging and shelling, particularly near San Luis Pass.

In town you'll find numerous small beaches tucked between the rock jetties along Seawall Boulevard. Stop and watch the dolphins roll in the offshore swells, and then walk out onto the jetties and chat with the fishermen. There are several places to rent roller skates, bicycles, and pedal surreys, and the wide sidewalk along the top of the seawall is a favorite promenade. The boulevard curves at the east end of the island and intersects Broadway at Stewart Beach. This city-run stretch of sand is popular with families because of its lifeguards, bathhouse, lockers, parking, and concessions.

A short drive farther east brings you to R. A. Apffel Park, a $2-million, 1980s development at the extreme end of East Beach. A favorite with fisherfolk and families as well as teenagers looking for like kind, it has excellent boating and fishing facilities and an 11,000-square-foot recreation center that includes a bathhouse and concessions. *Also here:* the Big Reef Nature Park with observation platforms for birding.

Galveston Island State Park. West of downtown Galveston on FM 3005 at the intersection with Thirteen Mile Road; (409) 737-1222 or (800) 792-1222; www.tpwd.state.tx.us. Another beach facility with picnicking and camping, this 2,000-acre state park also offers bird-watching from observation platforms and nature trails along its north boundary. The latter faces the protected waters of West Galveston Bay. Some seven acres of freshwater ponds within the park often are stocked with trout during the winter months; call (409) 737-1744 or (800) 547-4697 for information. The park's Mary Moody Northen Amphitheatre features major musical productions during the summer.

Palm Beach. West of town in Moody Gardens, 1 Hope Boulevard off Eighty-first Street; (409) 744-7256; www.moodygardens.com. This three-acre freshwater swimming complex faces the bay. Facilities include whirlpools, lockers, a boardwalk, concessions, and lifeguards. This is the only beach in Texas with Caribbean-style white sand and palms. Fee.

exploring historic galveston

Start at the Strand, once called the "Wall Street of the Southwest" and now the heart of one of the island's three historic districts. In itself the Strand is considered one of the largest and best collections of nineteenth-century iron-front commercial buildings remaining in America.

To reach the Strand area from the I-45 South causeway, take the Harborside Drive exit and turn east (left). To get to the Strand from Broadway, turn north on Twenty-fourth Street and continue 8 blocks. Most of the buildings along the Strand now house shops, galleries, businesses, and restaurants—more than ninety-five in all. Dickens-on-the Strand, a Victorian-themed Christmas festival on the first weekend in December, often draws crowds in excess of 70,000 and is covered by the national press.

The following major historic sites are either within the Strand Historic District or nearby:

The 1882 H. M. Trueheart–Adriance Building. 210 Kempner. This Nicholas Clayton–designed building is one of the most ornate and distinctive structures in the area. Its restoration in 1970 sparked the Strand's renaissance.

The 1871 League Building. Strand at Tremont. One of the nicest restorations in the city and home to several interesting shops.

The *Elissa*/Texas Seaport Museum. Harborside Drive at Pier 21 (1 block north of the Strand); (409) 763-1877; www.tsm-elissa.org. An 1877 square-rigged barque called *Elissa* rides at anchor here. One of the oldest vessels in Lloyd's Register of Shipping, she also represents Texas in assorted "tall ship" parades and is open daily for tours. Visitors roam (self-guided) through restored after-cabins, the hold, and the decks. In addition to a film detailing *Elissa*'s acquisition and restoration, the museum chronicles Galveston's rich maritime heritage through interactive exhibits and a wide-screen multimedia presentation on the age of sail. Open daily. Fee.

Galveston Arts Center. 2127 Strand; (409) 763-2403; www.galvestonartscenter.org. If you like mixing art with history, drop in at this eclectic gallery, housed in the old First National Bank Building. Closed Monday from Labor Day to Memorial Day.

Galveston Railroad Museum and Terminal. Strand at Twenty-fifth Street; (409) 765-5700; www.galvestonrrmuseum.com. The top draw here is the original waiting room of Galveston's old train depot, where life-size sculptures of travelers are frozen in a moment of 1932; unusual "hear" phones allow visitors to eavesdrop on their conversations. Two exhibits of particular interest: an O-scale railroad layout, complete with four tracks, a snow-covered winter scene, and twinkling fluorescent "stars"; and displays of passenger timetables, dining car menus, and china from famous trains. Out back are numerous steam locomotives and assorted railroad cars, a picnic gazebo, and exhibits of steam-powered machines. A mini train offers rides for children on select weekends. Open daily; closed Monday in January and February. Fee.

The Marx and Kempner Building. 2100 block of the Strand. Can you spot the clever trompe l'oeil mural? The original window detailing of this building was removed decades ago, and what looks like several vintage facades actually is hand-painted artwork.

The Tremont House. 2300 Ship's Mechanic Row; (409) 763-0300, (713) 480-8201, or (800) 874-2300 (reservations only). This superbly restored 1879 building now houses one of the most elegant small hotels in Texas.

Driving (or renting a bike) is recommended to cover these more distant historic sites:

The Bishop's Palace. 1402 Broadway; (409) 762-2475. The only East End Historic District home open to the public, this massive place was built between 1886 and 1892 for the Walter Gresham family. Designed by noted Galveston architect Nicholas Clayton, it is considered one of the one hundred most outstanding residential structures in America. Even more interesting than its turreted, rococo exterior are the details and furnishings inside. Guided tours are given daily, year-round. Fee.

The East End Historical District. This special area covers 40 blocks of Victoriana bounded by Broadway, Market, Nineteenth, and Eleventh Streets. It can be driven or walked, but the best way to see the most is by bicycle or on the historical foundation's Homes Tour in early May.

1859 Ashton Villa. 2328 Broadway; (409) 762-3933; www.galvestonhistory.org. This Italianate beauty was built in 1859 of bricks made on the island and survived both a disastrous island-wide fire in 1885 and the 1900 storm. It now is restored as the showplace of the Galveston Historical Foundation and home to the Heritage Visitors Center. An interesting urban archaeological dig exposes a small portion of the home's original raised basement, which was filled in when the level of the island was raised after the 1900 storm. Open daily. Fee.

1839 Samuel May Williams Home. 3601 Bernardo de Galvez (Avenue P); (409) 765-1839; www.galvestonhistory.org. One of the two oldest structures in Galveston, this charming restoration now looks as it did in 1839. Open weekends. Fee.

Galveston County Historical Museum. 2219 Market Street; (409) 766-2340; www.galveston history.org. The handsome City National Bank Building, circa 1919, houses more of Galveston's glorious past. Open daily, except major holidays.

Galveston Island Trolley. Styled to resemble the trolleys operating in early-twentieth-century Galveston, this streetcar system has seven routes. Fee. For more information call (409) 797-3900 or log on to www.islandtransit.net.

Garten Verein Dancing Pavilion. Avenue O and Twenty-seventh Street, in Kempner Park; www.galvestonhistory.org. Built in 1880 and now restored, this is a delightful, "very Galveston" spot to have a picnic or let children spend some energy.

The Grand 1894 Opera House. 2020 Postoffice Street; (409) 765-1894 or (800) 821-1894; www.thegrand.com. The interior of this interesting building has been restored to its early-twentieth-century grandeur, and the stage once again hosts a variety of performing arts throughout the year.

The Hotel Galvez. 2024 Seawall Boulevard; (409) 765-7721. Constructed in 1911 at a cost in excess of $1 million, this six-story Spanish Colonial Revival building was named after Bernardo de Galvez, the Spanish colonial governor who first charted the Texas Gulf Coast and for whom the island is named. The Galvez was the island's showplace and a celebrity playground during the 1920s and 1930s, and its registers held the names of presidents and movie stars until it became U.S. Coast Guard housing during World War II. A multimillion-dollar renovation completed in 1998 has returned the hotel's public rooms to their original appearance, refurbished guest rooms to luxury status, and created seven over-the-moon suites. Day visitors are welcome to explore the lobby level. There's also an outstanding Sunday brunch.

John Sydnor's 1847 Powhatan House. 3427 Avenue O; (409) 763-0077. Home to the Galveston Garden Club, this handsome mansion with its oak-filled gardens is on the National Register of Historic Places. No high heels, please; they damage the beautiful pine floors. Public tours on Saturday afternoon. Fee.

The Michel Menard Home. 1605 Thirty-third Street; (409) 762-3933; www.galveston history.org. Galveston's oldest home has been restored and contains an outstanding collection of nineteenth-century furniture. Open Friday–Sunday. Fee.

The Moody Mansion & Museum. 2618 Broadway; (409) 762-7668; www.moodymansion .org. This marvelous old home is the Smithsonian of Galveston. The city's grande dame, the late Mary Moody Northen never threw anything away—archivists even found Christmas presents in their original wrappings, with full notation as to year and giver—and her lifelong home has been restored to the way it looked at her debut in 1911. Open daily. Fee.

Postoffice Street. Four blocks south of the Strand between Twentieth and Twenty-third Streets, this once-busy thoroughfare again bustles with life as the main artery of Galveston's evolving art and entertainment district. A stroll here reveals shops, galleries, coffeehouses, antiques stores, and the Grand 1894 Opera House (see above).

The Silk Stocking Historical District. Biking or windshield tours of this 9-block area, loosely bounded by Rosenberg, J and N Avenues, and Tremont Street, are visual fun. The Silk Stocking National Historic District Neighborhood Association has produced a brochure mapping a walking tour that takes in nearly seventy-five historic homes and buildings. The Galveston Island Visitors Center can provide one.

today's galveston

If you've had it with history or are burned out with beaches, there is still plenty to do.

Bicycle rentals. Numerous shops along Seawall Boulevard rent almost anything that rolls.

Birding. An ideal location for either novice or expert, Galveston Island has more than a dozen prime birding sites on the Great Texas Coastal Birding Trail map for the upper coast. For a list of guided birding tours, call Galveston Island Visitors Center at (409) 763-4311 or (888) 425-4753, or log on to www.galveston.com.

Boat launching. Free facilities on Teichman Road, Sportsman Road, and at Washington Park on Sixty-first Street.

Carriage rides. Horse-drawn surreys leave daily from the vicinity of Twenty-first Street and the Strand on thirty- and sixty-minute tours of the various historic districts. Fee.

Fishing. In addition to the rock jetties along the seawall, there are commercial fishing piers at Twenty-fifth, Sixty-first, and Ninetieth Streets and at Seawolf Park on Pelican Island. Surf fishing is allowed along most of the open beaches, and common catches are speckled trout, flounder, catfish, and redfish.

Party boats for fishing in either the bay or the Gulf leave early in the morning from Piers 18 and 19 and from the yacht basin. A Texas fishing license is required for everyone between the ages of seventeen and sixty-five unless you are fishing at least 10.5 miles off-shore. Check to see if a license is required when you make your reservations. Common Gulf catches include red snapper, sailfish, pompano, warsaw, marlin, ling, king mackerel, bonito, and dolphin. Take precautions against seasickness before you go—the Gulf can get rough. For specific charter information contact Galveston Party Boats, Inc. (409-763-5423; www.galvestonpartyboatsinc.com), Williams Party Boats (409-762-8808; www.galveston.com/captjohn), or Captain Max Harris (281-334-0138; www.fishgalvestontexas.com).

Galveston duck tours. Twenty-fifth and Seawall; (409) 621-4771; www.galvestonducks.com. These amphibious transports scoot you around the city's tourist spots and then enter the water to cruise Offats Bayou, a ninety-minute excursion that shows off the island in an unusual way. Reservations advised during peak tourism months. Fee.

Harbor tours. Galveston Harbor Tours (409-765-1700), based at Pier 22 on Fisherman's Wharf, runs daily one-hour narrated boat tours of Texas's oldest seaport. Dolphin sightings are frequent, so keep your eyes peeled. Call the day before to check on weather and scheduling. Fee.

Moored at Moody Gardens, *The Colonel* (409-740-7797; www.moodygardens.com) churns its way around Galveston's harbor and inner bay with old-fashioned, stern-wheeler style. There is one narrated cruise Monday–Friday, two on Saturday and Sunday, weather permitting, as well as dinner-dance and jazz options. Fee.

Horseback riding. Weather permitting, you can rent a steed at Gulf Stream Stables, Eight Mile Road (409-744-1004).

Loggerhead Sea Turtle Head Start Project. 5000 Avenue U; (409) 766-3670. Operated by the National Oceanic and Atmospheric Administration of the U.S. Department of Commerce and by the Galveston laboratories of the National Marine Fisheries Service, this research facility offers free tours three times a week, on Tuesday, Thursday, and Saturday.

Lone Star Flight Museum and **Texas Aviation Hall of Fame.** 2002 Terminal Drive (next to Moody Gardens and Galveston International Airport); (409) 740-7722; www.lsfm.org. Aircraft from the 1930s to the 1960s—all restored and in flying condition—fill this immaculate facility. In all, this is considered the world's finest (and possibly largest) collection of mint-condition "war birds." Situated on what was a military airfield during World War II, this growing collection includes fighters, bombers, a rare F-7-F Tigercat, and one of only two P-47-G Thunderbolts remaining in the world. In 1999 this museum was expanded to include the $2.2-million Texas Aviation Hall of Fame, a series of exhibits and artifacts that document the careers and contributions of Texans to various military efforts. The gift shop carries World War II memorabilia, aircraft engines are on display, and the research library is a find for historians. Don't miss the remarkable essay on what World War II was all about, particularly if you have teens in tow. You can also reserve a flight on one of their World War II–era bombers (fee). Open daily. Fee.

Mardi Gras Museum. 2309 Ship's Mechanic Row; (409) 765-5930. If you can't participate in the island's annual festival, a visit here is the next best thing. Open daily. (Hours may be seasonal, so call ahead.) Free.

Mary Moody Northen Amphitheatre. Galveston Island Outdoor Musicals, P.O. Box 5253, Galveston, TX 77554; (409) 737-1744 or (800) 547-4697. This outdoor theater is in Galveston Island State Park, west on FM 3005 at the intersection with Thirteen Mile Road. Broadway favorites light up this stage Monday–Saturday from Memorial Day through Labor Day. Tickets are available at Houston ticket outlets, at the box office (409-737-3440), and at the gate. Insect repellent advised. Fee.

Moody Gardens. 1 Hope Boulevard (near the Galveston International Airport); (409) 744-4673 or (800) 582-4673; www.moodygardens.com. Don't come here in a hurry—this is a daylong experience that's well worth its somewhat hefty admission fee. In addition to a hotel/convention center, restaurant, ice-skating rink, and gardens, this $18-million, nonprofit project features three huge glass pyramids, each devoted to super family-learning experiences.

Start at the Rainforest Pyramid, one of the largest single structures under glass in the country. Beneath a 55-foot-high canopy of tropical vegetation, this conservatory's more than 170 animal and 1,700 plant species flourish amid waterfalls, cliffs, and caverns. Beautiful birds and butterflies are everywhere; some even perch briefly on visitors.

Nearby, the Discovery Pyramid features more than forty interactive, futuristic exhibits developed with the assistance of NASA's Johnson Space Center. Downstairs, America's first 3-D IMAX theater presents images that seem to leap from the six-story-tall screen. *Also here:* the nation's first IMAX Ridefilm Theater with three separate screening rooms, each with an eighteen-seat motion base and a 180-degree wraparound screen. Folks over 45 inches high can fasten their seatbelts and "rocket" off into an asteroid adventure, a swim with dolphins, or an exploration of cyberspace. Whichever experience is selected, you'll feel as though you are "in" the film, not just watching it.

The Aquarium Pyramid uses viewing tanks filled with more than two million gallons of water to showcase habitats common to the oceans of the North and South Pacific, the tropical Pacific, and the Caribbean. Two viewing levels provide both shoreline and underwater looks, and the Antarctic Exhibit showcases three species of live, tuxedo-clad penguins. Diver-to-guest communications answer questions, while touch tanks make other aquatic exhibits extremely personal.

There is also a 4D Special FX Theater, where you will hear, see, feel, and smell the action. A short-film experience is intensified by the addition of special effects such as seat buzzers, smoke, leg ticklers, and wind. No matter what the current film is, it will be an experience to remember.

The Moody Gardens complex also is home to *The Colonel* harbor cruises and the Palm Beach swimming area, both of which have separate listings. Fee.

Ocean Star at the Offshore Energy Center. Pier 19; (409) 766-7827; www.oceanstar oec.com. This $3.2-million combination museum and educational attraction puts you inside a full-size offshore drilling rig. Three decks of videos, equipment exhibits, and interactive displays bring alive the day-to-day world of offshore drilling and production. Open daily. Fee.

Pier 21. This lodging/restaurant/marina/shopping complex adjacent to the Texas Seaport Museum also houses the Great Storm Theater, a multimedia presentation on Galveston's devastating 1900 hurricane. Fee. For information call the theater at (409) 763-8808.

Postoffice Street Arts and Entertainment District. Slowly assuming a distinct personality, this area is anchored by the historic Grand 1894 Opera House and includes art galleries, antiques shops, eateries, and taverns. Boundaries extend from Market to Winnie Streets and from Nineteenth to Twenty-fifth Streets. A ghost town of sorts not long ago, Postoffice Street's more than twenty historical buildings are taking on new life. Shopping guides are available at many of the businesses.

Sailing, surfing, and waterskiing. These scenes are ever changing. For a list of operators contact the Galveston Island Visitors Center, 2428 Seawall Boulevard, Galveston, TX 77550; (409) 763-4311 or (888) 425-4753.

Seawolf Park on Pelican Island. Accessible from either Broadway or Harborside Drive via a turn north on Fifty-first Street. Adults enjoy watching Galveston's busy harbor from this unusual vantage point, and children love scrambling over a series of naval exhibits (fee) that include an airplane, a destroyer escort, and a submarine. There is no swimming at Seawolf Park, but there are good facilities for fishing (fee) and picnics. Open daily. Parking fee.

Tennis and golf. Information on specific locations is available from the Galveston Island Visitors Center. If you are a hotel guest, ask about membership privileges at private facilities on the island.

Treasure Isle Tour Train. The tram with the fringe on top takes you all over town on a ninety-minute narrated tour. Daily trips, March–December. Fee. For information call (409) 765-9564.

where to eat

Benno's on the Beach. 1200 Seawall; (409) 762-4621; www.bennosofgalveston. Don't let the converted Taco Bell building discourage you from trying this super-casual diner. The menu provides a primer in fine fried fare, but it's the Cajun dishes, including superior gumbo, jambalaya, and crawfish étouffée, that will make you yearn for your next visit. $–$$.

Clary's. 8509 Teichman Road (across from the *Galveston Daily News*); (409) 740-0771; www.galveston.com/claryssseafood. Don't judge this place by its low-key exterior. Locals think it serves some of the best seafood on the island, often with a Creole touch. An off-menu item, spiced shrimp, is a house specialty. Other memorable choices include the crab balls and the grilled seafood plate. Slightly dressy crowd here, so no beach clothes, please. Open Tuesday–Friday and on Sunday for lunch and dinner, Saturday for dinner only. $–$$$.

Fisherman's Wharf Seafood Grill. Pier 22 and Harborside Drive; (409) 765-5708; www .landrysrestaurants.com. You'll find indoor and outdoor dining here, with great views of the port. The fresh seafood menu ranges from shrimp and oyster po'boys to full-course meals, and there's also a fresh seafood market with a tank where children can fish for perch. Don't pass up their signature Shrimp Kisses appetizer—Gulf shrimp stuffed with jalapeño Jack cheese, wrapped in bacon, and fried. Formerly a shrimp unloading and cold storage facility until its reincarnation as a restaurant in mid-1995, this eatery's hardwood floors came from some of Galveston's old cotton warehouses, and the vintage photographs that line the walls are either family memorabilia or reproductions from the Rosenberg Library collection. Open daily for lunch and dinner. $–$$$.

Fish Tales. Twenty-fifth and Seawall; (409) 762-8545; www.landrysrestaurants.com. If you have only one casual meal to eat in Galveston, this lively spot's upstairs deck is a good choice. You'll be able to see out over the Gulf while filling up on seafood in all sizes and guises. The menu also has some nonfishy selections, along with a long list of appetizers, several of which are large enough to make a meal. Open for lunch and dinner daily. $–$$$.

Gaido's. 3900 Seawall; (409) 762-9625; www.gaidosofgalveston.com. Whether it's fried, broiled, or boiled, the fresh seafood here is excellent, partly because the dressings and sauces are made from scratch. The menu changes daily to reflect the best from the sea, but you can't go wrong with the grilled red snapper. Open daily for lunch and dinner. $$–$$$. *Tip:* If Gaido's is crowded, try Casey's casual family dining next door; they share a kitchen.

Landry's. Fifty-third and Seawall; (409) 744-1010; www.landryssseafoodhouse.com. Excellent steaks and seafood, often with Cajun touches, bring crowds to this eatery. Open daily for lunch and dinner. $$–$$$.

Leo's Cajun Corner. 3201 Broadway; (409) 765-5151. Want to picnic? Stop by Leo's, where everything must be taken to go. While this joint is not much more than a portable building on an ugly corner of a once-glorious boulevard, it is what is inside Leo's that counts. And "it" is barbecue and Cajun boudain, a spicy mixture of rice and ground meats that resembles sausage. The barbecue ribs is a favorite. If you're feeling adventurous, try the crawfish boudain. $. No credit cards.

Luigi's Ristorante Italiano. 2328 Strand; (409) 763-6500; www.galveston.com/luigis. This outstanding restaurant brings a warming touch of Tuscany to its surroundings, the 1895 Hutchings-Sealy Bank Building. The wine bar is in the old bank vault, and the Piccola Tavola (chef's table; reservations required one week in advance) gives ten to twelve diners a close-up look at Chef Luigi Ferre creating culinary masterpieces in the kitchen. Open Monday–Saturday for lunch and dinner. $–$$$.

The Merchant Prince. 2300 Ship's Mechanic Row (inside the Tremont House hotel); (409) 763-0300; www.galveston.com/thetremonthouse/. This quiet retreat really takes the edges off a hectic day, particularly when your psyche begins to respond to the piano music coming from the Tremont's lobby. Inventive food beautifully served is the rule here, but ultrafancy dress is not. Open for breakfast, lunch, and dinner daily. $–$$$.

Mosquito Cafe. 628 Fourteenth Street; (409) 763-1010; www.mosquitocafe.com. Basically a neighborhood cafe, this clean and trendy eatery is a good place to explore what's happening on the Galveston casual-food scene. Just how unusual are this cafe's choices? First-timers might try a Mosquito Benedict breakfast (a scone topped with portabello mushrooms, shrimp, sun-dried tomatoes, artichoke hearts, asparagus, and poached eggs, finished with a serrano hollandaise) or the Napa Salad for lunch. The latter takes grilled breast of chicken, adds walnuts, blue cheese, apples, red grapefruit, and grapes, and then tosses all with greens and a champagne vinaigrette. Worry not—if neither of those appeals, there's much, much more. Open for breakfast and lunch daily; dinner Thursday–Saturday. $–$$.

Rainforest Cafe. 5300 Seawall; (409) 744-6000; www.rainforestcafe.com. This mighty chain restaurant is worthy of inclusion here for a number of reasons. One, because of its prime real estate, adjacent to the luxurious San Luis Resort on the Seawall. Two, because of its unusual exterior (its dramatic volcano spouts and spews every half hour from the otherwise flat island). And third (and perhaps most important), because the chain is owned by Galveston native (B.O.I.—born on the island, as they call it here) Tillman Fertitta, the entrepreneur also responsible for Kemah's Boardwalk and the entire Landry's Restaurants family. The food ranges from inspired to indigestible. Stick with the basics and enjoy the show. Open daily. $–$$.

Rudy & Paco. 2028 Postoffice Street (adjacent to the Grand 1894 Opera House); (409) 762-3696; www.galveston.com/rudypaco. Another top entry in Galveston's fine-dining competition, this extremely popular and interesting eatery specializes in Central and South

American cuisine. Born and raised in Nicaragua, owner Francisco Paco Vargas has a management resume that reads like a list of Galveston's top restaurants, and his chef hails from Argentina. As a result, the empañadas and steaks with chimichurri sauce are outstanding, and you'll also want to try the *vuelva la vida* (back to life) appetizer, a combination of crab claws, shrimp, and calamari sautéed in a lightly spicy lemon-butter sauce. *Nice to know:* They serve both pre- and post-show dinners and also open on Sunday whenever there's something playing at the Grand Opera House. Open for lunch and dinner Monday–Friday (closes between lunch and dinner); dinner Saturday. $–$$$.

Saltwater Grill. 2017 Postoffice Street; (409) 762-3474; www.galveston.com/saltwatergrill. Perhaps the most inventive restaurant on the island, this handsome dining spot is also one of the quietest—a nice contrast to the tourist eateries on the Seawall. A great favorite with Galveston's business community, it's also very well regarded by those who relish fresh fish, chicken, and beef properly prepared and efficiently served. Nothing has been frozen—there isn't even a freezer on the premises—and nothing is fried. Instead your selection will be pan-seared, grilled, or steamed to your specifications. Menus change weekly to capitalize on what's fresh in the markets, and the affordable lunch specials are a good place to start selecting your meal. Consider the barbecued spiced oysters on a baguette or the lobster and shrimp tacos. If those don't interest you, it may be a good day for the Gulf blue-crab cakes or the veal chop with a wild-mushroom risotto. Whatever appeals, you'll definitely remember to come here again. Open for lunch and dinner weekdays; dinner only on Saturday and Sunday. Reservations are required. $–$$$.

Shearn's. 7 Hope Boulevard (on the top floor of the Moody Gardens Hotel); (409) 741-8484; www.moodygardenshotels.com. You'll want to dress up for this dining experience. The surroundings are lovely, the service exceptional, and the quality of the continental food extremely high. Open only for dinner Tuesday–Saturday, and reservations and appropriate attire (no jeans, shorts, or tank tops) are required. $$$.

Shrimp & Stuff. 3901 Avenue O; (409) 763-2805; www.galveston.com/shrimpnstuff. Beach-weary folks love this simple place for its tasty shrimp and oyster po'boys, homemade gumbo, and ample fish dinners. Open daily for lunch and dinner. $–$$.

The Waterman Restaurant. 14302 Stewart Road at Pirate's Cove; (409) 632-0203; www.watermansatpiratescove.com. Grilled seafood is the specialty at this elegantly casual restaurant overlooking Galveston Bay. Its handsome dining room is filled with architectural treasures rescued from a one-hundred-year-old cotton warehouse. Start with the confetti crab balls, a tasty mixture of crab, shrimp, and crawfish. Then have the tequila shrimp, sautéed in oil and garlic and then grilled with tequila, cilantro, tomatoes, and lime juice. There's also pasta dishes. On fair-weather days, ask for a spot on the deck, where you can watch pelicans fish in the bay. Open for dinner Tuesday–Friday; lunch and dinner Saturday–Sunday. $$–$$$.

Yaga's Cafe. 2314 Strand; (409) 762-6676; www.galveston.com/yaga. *Tropical* is the working adjective at this casual place, from decor to food to music. Try the spicy shrimp only if you have some very cool liquid to quench mouth fire. This is a good spot also for burgers and sandwiches, and it jumps with reggae at night. Open daily for lunch and dinner. $–$$.

wandering the back roads

Driving southwest on FM 3005 the length of the island brings you to great fishing at San Luis Pass. Go over the causeway, and it's another 38 miles to Surfside Beach and Freeport. For activities in that area, see Southwest Day Trip 2.

Heading east from Galveston along the coast is possible. Just take the free Bolivar ferry and continue on Highway 87 (see East Day Trip 4). In Galveston the Bolivar ferry slip is at the end of Second Street (turn north from Broadway), but don't plan to take it on a prime-time weekend unless you love waiting in long lines.

day trip 04

southeast

wine and dine:
alvin, santa fe,
hitchcock and la marque

alvin

Basically a farming community first settled in the 1840s, Alvin prospered with the coming of the railroad in the 1880s and remains a major agricultural center today. As a tourist destination its primary point of interest is the Nolan Ryan Exhibit Center at Alvin Community College, but you'll find several other things to do while you are in town.

Begin this day trip by taking Highway 288 south from Houston to its intersection with Highway 6, and then turning southeast (left) for 10 miles. En route, consider visiting the amazing Sri Meenakshi (Hindu) Temple on the outskirts of Pearland and buying some fresh fruits and veggies at Froberg Farms.

One of the nicest things about Alvin is the number of huge oaks that shade its older residential streets. A drive along either West Lang or Beauregard shows off a few century-old homes, as well. For more information contact the Alvin Convention and Visitors Bureau, 105 West Willis, Alvin, TX 77511; (281) 331-3944 or (800) 331-4063; www.alvintexas.org.

what to do

Alvin Opry. Eighth Street at Sealy Street; (281) 331-8181. Country and gospel music is the entertaining rule here on Friday and Saturday nights. Open year-round. Fee.

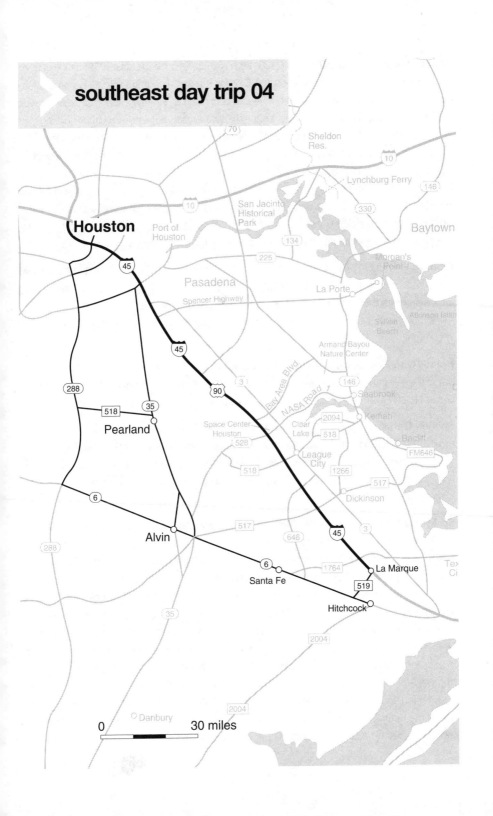

Bayou Wildlife Park. 5050 FM 517; (281) 337-6376. Take the Dickinson/FM 517 exit from Interstate 45, and then drive west on FM 517 for 6 miles. The entrance will be on the left. From antelopes to a zonky (a cross between a zebra and a donkey), more than 260 animals representing forty species roam this eighty-six-acre preserve. Many are either endangered or nearly extinct in their natural habitat. Visitors tour with a guide via an open-air tram, buckets of feed (fee) at the ready. This outstanding facility gives you a good look at major zoo-type animals roaming free in a natural environment. If you've never been nuzzled by a camel or scratched a giraffe's neck, this is the place. Also here: a children's barnyard (which includes pony rides in spring and summer), an alligator farm, a monkey island, and a feeding barn for young animals that need extra TLC. Although no human food is sold here, picnickers are most welcome. Open daily in summer; Tuesday–Sunday in winter. Fee.

Froberg Farms. 11875 Country Road 190 (off Highway 6, 3 miles northwest of downtown Alvin; watch for signs); (281) 585-3531. This rural fruit-and-veggie stand features locally grown produce that draws buyers from miles away. Their store also sells gift baskets, jams, jellies, pumpkins, beans, nuts, and homemade pies. Open Monday–Saturday in winter; daily in summer.

Nolan Ryan Exhibit Center. 2925 South Bypass 35; (281) 388-1134. This relatively small but extremely interesting museum chronicles the life of Alvin's celebrity native son, baseball player Nolan Ryan. Open Monday–Saturday until 4:00 p.m. Fee.

Shimek Gardens. On County Road 237 west of Alvin; (281) 331-4395. This must-stop for daylily lovers is a beautiful garden lush with 850 different types of daylilies and literally hundreds of roses. The owners are hybridizers who have two new types of lilies to their credit, with others in development. Open by appointment only year-round, but prime time to come is mid-May through July.

Sri Meenakshi Temple. 17130 McLean Road, Pearland; (281) 489-0358. From Highway 288 turn east on FM 518 toward Pearland and go 8 miles to a turn south on McLean Road. The temple is approximately 2 miles south. This honey-colored, highly ornate Hindu temple is a startling sight, tucked away amid assorted dwellings and small farms on a rural road southwest of downtown Pearland. The third traditional Hindu temple to be constructed in this country and the only one outside India that's devoted to a specific goddess (Shakti), this temple not only welcomes visitors but is a place of pilgrimage for Hindus from throughout North America. Although you are requested to take off your shoes before entering any of the interior worship areas, you are welcome to walk around the courtyard grounds and take photos. A free, well-written booklet available in the temple's administrative office explains all, and guided tours (donation) can be arranged by calling (713) 467-3022. Should you visit sometime between Friday evening and Sunday afternoon, you may find typical south Indian food being served at a very reasonable price, a real enhancement to this cultural experience.

The temple is open Monday–Thursday from 9:00 a.m. to noon and 5:00 to 8:00 p.m., Friday until 9:00 p.m., and all day on weekends and holidays.

where to eat

Joe's Barbeque Company. 1400 East Highway 6; (281) 331-9626. Even the parking lot smells good at this plates-to-steaks place. You order at the counter—beef brisket, steaks, sausage, ham, chicken, or ribs—plus there's an all-you-can-eat steam table and salad bar. Open daily for lunch and dinner. $–$$.

Santa Barbara Italian Cafe. 5012 Broadway Street, Pearland; (281) 485-5676. Croatia-native Jordana Putnik's reputation as one of the region's best cooks is luring Houstonians to Pearland for dinner alone. Her Italian- and Creole-inspired dishes include an authentic étouffée, chicken saltimbocca, veal Marsala, and fettuccine Alfredo. When Putnik is not behind the stove, she's checking on her loyal clientele, all of whom call her "Mama." Open for lunch and dinner Monday–Saturday. $$–$$$.

continuing on

Highway 6 more or less follows the original railroad right-of-way between Galveston and Richmond, connecting Alvin with Santa Fe, the next stop on this day trip.

santa fe

Haak's Vineyards & Winery. 6310 Avenue T; (409) 925-1401; www.haakwinery.com. From Highway 6 South turn right at Avenue T (the second signal) in Santa Fe and go 1.8 miles. The winery will be on your right. Established in 1980 by Raymond and Gladys Haak, this boutique vineyard (and our only stop in this very small town) has four acres planted with two varietals: Blanc du Bois (white) and Black Spanish/Lenoir (red). The results: an extremely fine port and a tasty white, both of which tend to be in short supply due to the limited production. If you want to taste totally Texan wines, your best bet is to come here in late August when each year's wines debut. The Haaks also buy grapes from other Texas vineyards and import grapes from California's upper San Joaquin Valley. The chardonnay is fermented in domestic oak barrels, and the port ages for two years in oak. Wine production here also includes a sauvignon blanc, cabernet sauvignon, and zinfandel, all of which can be sampled in the tasting room at no cost. Tours include the vineyard, the crushing area, a state-of-the-art winery, and an 1,800-square-foot cellar where the wines rest until they come of age. Buy picnic fixings and enjoy a snack on the winery's covered pavilion. Want to help with the picking? Give them a call. Grape vine cuttings are available free in February, until they are gone. Open daily.

hitchcock and la marque

Like Santa Fe, Hitchcock does not have a strong presence in and of itself. However, its lack of development is exactly why it's an ideal location for the following:

Gulf Breeze Downs. 7602 FM 2004, Hitchcock; (281) 337-8782. Take exit 15 from I-45 and turn west to FM 2004 South for 1.2 miles. When you see huge cement pillars on your left (the remains of an abandoned blimp base), look to the right for the entrance to this training track for Sam Houston Race Park. Visitors are welcome to tour the barns and watch the daily workouts, and there are match races here on some Sundays in nice-weather months. Call in advance to check if that's important to your visit. Also, there's an exotic-animal park in the making here. You can see zebras, elk, antelope, and other animals by driving to the fence at the end of the dirt driveway. Open daily, year-round, weather permitting. Free.

continuing on

The next stop on this day trip is La Marque. To get there, or to I-45 North and home, return to Highway 6 from Gulf Breeze Downs and continue southeast to a left turn on FM 519 to La Marque.

First stop here for shoppers is the Lone Star Factory Outlet complex on I-45 at Delany Road. However, the real reason for coming here is to go to the dog races, a day trip destination in itself.

Gulf Greyhound Park. P.O. Box 488, La Marque, TX 77568-0488 (30 miles south of Houston via exit 15 from I-45); (409) 986-9500 or (800) 275-2946; www.gulfgreyhound .com. This 110-acre, $50-million attraction is the world's largest greyhound racing facility— a Cadillac of racetracks—and when it opened in 1992, it offered the first legal pari-mutuel betting in the Houston area in more than fifty-five years. General admission is $2, parking is free, and the minimum bet is $2. If you want to go first class, choose valet parking ($3) and lounge/clubhouse admission ($3). Expect numerous well-designed lounge areas, closed-circuit color TV, and plenty of instruction on the various methods of betting. Post times on this 0.25-mile track are noon Wednesday, 7:00 p.m. Thursday and Friday, 1:30 and 7:00 p.m. Saturday, and 1:30 p.m. Sunday. Families are welcome.

celebrations and festivals

Check the calendar. While a trip to small-town Texas always has its rewards, if you time your visit to coincide with a festival or other special event, you'll find the welcome mat out and the locals looking their best—company's coming.

NOTE: Many of the telephone numbers given are answered on weekdays only. For specific dates consult www.traveltex.com, or request a free Texas Travel Information Packet by calling (800) 888-8TEX.

january

Festival Hill. Concerts followed by dinner and a classic film lure people to Round Top once a month from August through April—always enjoyable, but most welcoming during the quiet days of winter. The dinner includes wine, and overnight accommodations are available in attractive studio residences, as well as in the historic Menke House. Reservations required. Information: (979) 249-3129; www.festivalhill.org.

Gulf Coast Music Hall of Fame Show. Formerly known as the Janis Joplin Birthday Bash, this annual event pays tribute to Port Arthur's native daughter. Events culminate in a star-studded concert that also serves as induction ceremony for the Music Hall of Fame at the Museum of the Gulf Coast. Information: (800) 235-7822; www.portarthurtexas.com.

Spindletop—Gladys City Boomtown Days. The celebration held early in January commemorates the beginning of Texas great oil boom at Spindletop Oil Field outside of Beaumont. The Gladys City Boomtown Museum hit hard by Hurricane Rita reopened in January 2008. The event takes place annually at the wooden model of the original boomtown with shops, a post office, and blacksmith. During celebration there is a reenactment of the Spindletop gusher, which made news around the world and proved petroleum was a viable energy source. Information: (409) 835-0823.

february

Clear Lake Gem and Mineral Show. This show, on the fourth weekend of February, ranges from rocks and fossils to fantastic jewelry. It's held at the Pasadena Convention Center. Information: (281) 481-1591.

Galveston Mardi Gras. More than half a million visitors make the trip to the island for its largest, most colorful celebration. Events span two weekends and feature seaside parades, elaborate costume balls, concerts, and more beads than you can imagine. Information: (888) 425-4753; www.mardigrasgalveston.com.

Heritage Day at Jesse Jones Park & Nature Center. The reconstructed homestead in this Humble area park opens to the public in early February for tours. The day offers demonstrations of the homely arts that tamed the Texas frontier. Information: (281) 446-8588.

Mardi Gras of Southeast Texas. Port Arthur swings on a long February weekend with a Doo-Dah Parade, the Majestic Krewe of Aurora Grand Parade, fireworks, art and auto shows, a carnival, concerts, and children's activities. Information: (409) 985-7822; www.port arthurtexas.com.

Sacred Places Tours. Glimpse ten of the island's most historic churches and cemeteries on this special tour, sponsored by the Galveston Historical Society. Gems such as the 1860 St. Joseph Church, Texas's oldest German Catholic church, and Sacred Heart Catholic Church (1903), with its Gothic and Moorish design elements, are popular stops on the tour. Information: (409) 765-7834; http://galvestonhistory.com.

Yachty Gras Night Boat Parade. Boating enthusiasts in Kemah and Clear Lake join the Mardi Gras festivities with a light-festooned boat parade. Information: www.yachtygras.com.

march

Bellville Antiques Show. Bellville's fairgrounds are taken over by antiques dealers offering everything from furniture and pottery to jewelry and collectibles. There's also a farmers' market, plants, and prepared food. Information: (979) 865-3407; www.bellville.com.

Country Market Days. Charming Fayetteville hosts its market days—think homemade jams and jellies, crafts, and produce—the second Saturday of the month, March–December. Information: (979) 378-4021; www.fayettevilletx.com.

Fords of the 50s Old Car Show & Picnic. This longtime event draws hundreds of classic cars (none newer than 1980 models), their owners, and automobile buffs to the grounds of the San Jacinto Battleground State Historic Park midmonth. Information: (281) 252-3180; www.tpwd.state.tx.us.

General Sam Houston's Birthday. Celebrated on March 2, the general's birthday and, coincidentally, Texas Independence Day, this Huntsville event features a ceremony at the grave of the first president of the Republic of Texas, as well as birthday cake served at the 67-foot-tall sculpture of the general. Information: (936) 291-9726; www.huntsvilletexas.com.

Liberty Jubilee. Country-flavored festivities make this late-March event in downtown Liberty a favorite of families. Activities include three stages of live entertainment, a barbecue cook-off, a car show, parade, and street dance. Information: (409) 336-3684.

Montgomery County Fair & Rodeo. Everything from chicken flying to a barbecue cook-off keeps the fairgrounds hopping for ten days in March. Don't miss the children's pet parade. Information: (936) 760-3247; www.mcfa.org.

Nederland Heritage Festival. There's much to do in Nederland midmonth as the city celebrates its Danish and Acadian heritage. Among the festivities: a carnival, softball and golf tournaments, a chili cook-off, a crafts market, and an art and photography show. Information: (409) 722-0279; www.nederlandhf.org.

Round Top Herb Forum. Festival Hill in Round Top hosts a one-day celebration of herbs that includes lectures, a luncheon, and a plant sale. Information: (979) 249-3129; www.festivalhill.org.

San Felipe's Colonial Texas Heritage Festival. What was once one of the major colonial capitals of Texas celebrates its heritage in late March on the grounds of Stephen F. Austin State Park. Activities include Buffalo Soldier reenactments, arts and crafts booths, traders, exhibits, living-history demonstrations, guided tours of historic San Felipe, and a buffalo barbecue. Information: (979) 885-3222.

SpringFest. Old Town Spring's Wine and Art Festival celebrates Texas Wines and Texas artists in early March. Information: (281) 353-9310; www.oldtownspringtx.com.

Spring Fling Flower and Garden Show. Brenham's downtown square welcomes the entire family to a bloom-filled festival on the second Saturday of the month. Information: (979) 836-3695; www.brenhamtexas.com.

Texas Independence Day. Fireworks and a black-powder gun salute by the Texas Army are highlights of the Texas Independence Day festivities at Washington-on-the-Brazos State Historic Site in Washington. Also: Craft demonstrations, musical entertainment, and a re-creation of the signing of the Texas Declaration of Independence. Held the weekend closest to March 2. Information: (979) 936-2214; www.birthplaceoftexas.com.

Tomball German Heritage Festival. This late March event on the streets of a town built by German pioneers gives visitors a taste of the old days. Folk music and dancing highlight the fun and German food, arts and crafts, and antiques add to the celebration. Information: (281) 379-6844.

Tyler County Dogwood Festival. A weekend of events celebrating the beautiful white blooms of the wild dogwood culminates in the crowning of a Dogwood Queen. Festivities include a parade, trail rides, and more. Information: (409) 283-2632; www.tylercountydogwoodfestival.org.

Walker County Fair & Rodeo. Huntsville hosts rodeo events, livestock exhibits, a barbecue cook-off, a carnival, contests, dances, and more in late March. Information: (936) 291-8763; www.walkercountyfair.com.

april

Artisans in Nature. This event, a juried wildlife competition, is held at Matagorda County Birding Nature Center in Bay City. Festivities include boat tours and a birds-of-prey show. Information: (979) 245-3336; www.mcbnc.org.

Blessing of the Fleet. At this annual Freeport festival, a priest blesses both commercial boats and pleasure crafts as area captains parade through the marina. Information: (979) 265-2508.

Bluebonnet Festival. Texans pour into the eastern fringes of the Hill Country in April to enjoy the beautiful abundant blooms of the bluebonnet. Chappell Hill welcomes the crowds with this festival, which includes live entertainment, children's games, hayrides, and a handicrafts market. Information: (979) 337-9910; www.chappellhilltx.com.

Clear Lake Crawfish Festival. This early-April shindig at Clear Lake Park raises money for the community's Fourth of July celebration. In addition to heaping plates of freshly boiled crawfish, there's crawfish-eating contests, zydeco music, and carnival games. Information: (281) 488-7676.

Cotton Gin Festival. The tiny town of Burton's wonderful old gin hums with activity again in mid-April while locals give tours and explain how it works. Lots of food and entertainment as well as folk-life demonstrations. Information: (979) 289-3378; www.cottongin museum.org.

Depot Day. Proceeds from this mid-April event—which includes live entertainment, a Wild West shootout, and a car show—go to maintain Magnolia's historic rail depot. Sponsored by the Magnolia Historical Society. Information: (281) 356-8514; www.depotday.org.

Eeyore's Birthday Party. Costumes are a tradition for this annual Winedale event, which also includes music, games, maypoles, a lollipop tree, and birthday cake for everyone. This is an ideal outing for families with small children. And for the parents, there is a Shakespeare performance in the evening. Information: (512) 471-4993.

Good Oil Days Festival. Humble's Main Street fills with food, crafts, and entertainment on an early-April weekend. Information: (281) 466-2126.

Herb Festival and Children's Art Festival. Held on the grounds of Huntsville's city hall in late April, this kid-friendly event offers information and demonstrations on growing and cooking with herbs. Also: Live entertainment and hands-on children's activities. Information: (936) 295-7009; www.huntsvilletexas.com.

Heritage Days. Longhorn cattle are driven down Navasota's Main Street during this late-April/early-May event that also features a street dance, singing cowboys, and a car show. Information: (979) 777-0499; www.navasotaheritagedays.com.

Marburger Farm Antique Show. The week-long antique extravaganza spreads the wares of more than 350 vendors across 43 acres. Buyers and browsers have 27 acres of free parking. The show is held semi-annually the first Friday in April and October. Information: (800) 947-5799; www.roundtop-marburger.com.

Mercado Days Festival. Mid-April is time to break piñatas, enjoy carnival rides, and listen to live music in downtown Port Arthur. There are food booths, arts and crafts, and even clowns. Information: (409) 983-4006; www.sethcec.org.

Midnight Madness. All shops and vendors in Fayetteville stay open until midnight one of the first weekends in April. There's also an antiques show. Information: (888) 575-4553; www.fayettevilletx.com.

Migration Celebration. Bird-banding demonstrations, nature-photography tips, lessons in wildflower gardening, and tours of wildlife-filled preserves are part of this event, at the San Bernard National Wildlife Refuge near Lake Jackson. Information: (888) 477-2505; www.refugefriends.org.

Neches River Festival. Beaumont celebrates water for a week with historical pageants, shows, a lighted boat parade, a skydiving show, flower show and competition, a parade, and children's festivities. The April/May event culminates with the crowning of a Miss Neches. Information: (409) 835-2443; www.beaumontcvb.com.

New Ulm Arts Festival. Professional artists from all across Texas converge on the tiny hamlet of New Ulm in late April. Information: (979) 992-3337; www.newulm-tx.com.

Oleander Festival. Any bloomin' excuse for a party in fun-loving Galveston. Events from birding to garden techniques are spread across the island in mid-April. Information: (409) 683-4673, ext.4268; www.oleander.org.

Ole Tyme Days. Twenty blocks of Dayton are blocked off for an event that celebrates rural America. Festivities include a barbecue cook-off, a car show, street dance, and carnival. Information: (832) 229-0563; www.oletymedays.com.

San Jacinto Day Festival. A reenactment of the famous 1836 battle is the highlight of this festival, which is held the Saturday nearest to April 23, the day the Texas won its independence from Mexico. A living-history encampment on the grounds of San Jacinto Battleground State Historic Site gives visitors the chance to interact with reenactors in period costume. Information: (281) 479-2431; www.tpwd.state.tx.us.

San Jacinto Festival. East and West Columbia and Varner-Hogg State Park celebrate the early days of the republic in midmonth with entertainment, a barbecue cook-off, an arts and crafts show, a pentathlon, a baseball-card show, a petting zoo, street dances, and tours of a replica of the first state capitol. Information: (979) 345-3921; www.westcolumbia.org.

Spirit of Flight Air Show. Galveston's Lone Star Flight Museum hosts World War II–era air-craft in reenactments of explosive dogfights. Many of the old "birds" are open for tours. Information: (409) 740-7722; www.lsfm.org.

Sylvan Beach Festival. La Porte relives its heyday in late April with a parade, a chili cook-off, a carnival, a crawfish boil, and entertainment: Information: (281) 471-1123; www.laporte chamber.org.

Texas Barbecue Festival. The barbecue cook-off in Vidor combines country music with a Cajun flamboyance near the Louisiana border. Plus, it rounds up a carnival, vendors, and a classic car show for the Claiborne Park West event. Children are favored with games and a children's fun run. Information: (409) 769-6399.

Texas Crawfish Festival. Old Town Spring brews up pots and pots of those tasty little critters, along with all the multistage live entertainment you can handle, on two weekends in late April. Information: (281) 353-9310; www.oldtownspringtx.com.

Village Creek Festival. Lumberton rolls out the welcome mat for this three-day, midmonth affair that includes a 5K run, a carnival, craft and food booths, a car show, a pageant, and concerts. Information: (409) 755-0554; www.cityoflumberton.com.

Wine and Roses Festival. Messina Hof invites all for a grape-stomping good time at the winery in Bryan. Festivities include wine tastings and vineyard tours, art exhibits, equestrian shows, live music, and a cook-off. Information: (979) 778-9463; www.messinahof.com.

Winedale Spring Festival and Texas Craft Exhibition. Expect pioneer demonstrations of old-time skills, an outstanding juried craft show with working artists, live musical enter-tainment, barbecued chicken, and a barn dance at this early-April Winedale event. Information: (979) 278-3530.

may

Bay Day. Sponsored by the Galveston Bay Foundation mid-month, the one-day event on the Kemah Boardwalk offers fun activities for children and adults to emphasize the multiple uses of the Galveston Bay system. Information: (281) 332-3381, ext. 207; www.galvbay.org.

Blessing of the Fleet. Every year since 1968, Kemah has invoked heavenly blessings on the shrimp crop. Decorated shrimp cruise through Clear Creek Channel, where they receive a blessing. Catch the parade from the Kemah Boardwalk, where there also is musical enter-tainment. Information: (281) 334-9880; www.kemahboardwalk.com.

Columbus Live Oak Festival. Columbus rolls back time the third weekend in May with an opera house performance, a historic homes tour, canoe races, storytellers, and an antiques/crafts show. Information: (979) 732-8385; www.texasliveoakfestival.com.

General Sam Houston Folk Festival and Josey Park Craft Fair. The first festival weekend in Huntsville has expanded to include the Josey Park Craft Fair. Adding to the piney woods fun are the Airing of the Quilts, a Fireman's Fun Day, and a Classic Car Show. Information: (936) 294-7505.

Heritage Gathering. A longhorn cattle drive, chuck-wagon cooking demonstrations, a rodeo, and a fiddlers' contest are among the highlights of this early-May event in Bellville, which offers a glimpse into life in the late 1800s. Information: (877) 558-7245; www.bellville heritagegathering.com.

Historic Homes Tour. Sponsored by the Galveston Historical Foundation, one of the nation's oldest preservation societies, this home tour may be the best event of an event-filled spring. Held over two weekends in early May, the tour swings open the doors to private homes, many of which survived the infamous 1900 hurricane. In addition, the tour provides access to some of the city's most beautiful private gardens. Information: (409) 765-7834; http://galvestonhistory.com.

Ice Cream Festival. Brenham, hometown of Blue Bell, celebrates the coming of summer with this event on the first Saturday of May. Activities include an ice cream eating contest, arts and crafts, and entertainment on its charming town square. Information: (979) 836-3695; www.brenhamtexas.com.

Maifest. Learn to polka in Brenham as the city hosts one the oldest German festivals in the state in the heart of the wildflower season. Information: (888) 273-6426; www.brenham texas.com.

Pasadena Strawberry Festival. This third weekend in May event at the Pasadena Fair Grounds has continuous live entertainment, arts and crafts, many strawberry concoctions, specialty acts, and a carnival. The enormous variety of foods includes not only strawberries but a barbecue cook off and the "World's Largest Strawberry Shortcake." Information: (281) 991-9500; www.strawberryfest.org.

Pilgrimage & Maypole. Calvert, an old railroad town, opens the doors of its vintage homes. If you love Victoriana and antiques, don't miss this on the first weekend in May. Information: (979) 364-2582.

Texas Crab Festival. In early May, Crystal Beach pays tribute to the tasty crab and some of the best live music in Texas. Check out the crab races and crab cook-off, or take part in the talent show or golf tourney. Information: (409) 684-5940; www.bolivarchamber.org.

june

AIA Sandcastle Competition. Galveston's East Beach is the site of this tremendously fun early-June event that features elaborate and enormous sand sculptures. Information: (713) 520-0155; www.aiasandcastle.com.

Bomber Field Day War-Bird Fly-in. If you're into model aircraft, you won't want to miss this early-June event in Monaville, which spotlights large-scale radio-controlled aircraft as well as performances by replicas of World War II bombers. Information: (281) 471-6762; www.bomberfieldusa.com.

Festival Hill Concerts. Outstanding classical music by some of the world's best young professionals highlights weekends June through mid-July at the International Festival-Institute at Round Top. Information: (979) 249-3129; www.festivalhill.org.

Grimes County Fair. Head for the fairgrounds in Navasota for this early-June event. Festivities include a livestock show, calf scrambles, rodeo competition, junior barbecue cook-off, and more. Information: (936) 825-2066; www.grimescountyfair.com/.

Gulf Coast Jam. Port Arthur rocks in late June with headliner talent in Cajun, country and western, and rock. A good chance to see regional acts before they hit the big time. Information: (800) 235-7822; www.portarthurtexas.com.

Juneteenth. This celebration, which was first observed in Galveston and then spread across the nation, commemorates the date that Union soldiers brought news to Texas that the Civil War had ended and the slaves were free. The news came June 19, 1865, two and a half years after President Lincoln's Emancipation Proclamation. Several cities have major Juneteenth celebrations, including Galveston (409-763-6564; www.galveston.com), Port Arthur (800-235-7822; www.portarthurtexas.com), Huntsville (800-289-0389; www.huntsville texas.com), and Brenham (888-273-6426; www.brenhamtexas.com).

Kolache-Klobase Festival. East Bernard celebrates its Czech heritage in mid-June with a colorful costume parade, folk dancing, arts and crafts, and a cake walk. Information: (979) 335-4827.

Summertime Classic. This popular bike ride in early June explores the farm-to-market roads around Fayetteville, where the riders finish at its historic town square. Information: (888) 575-4553; www.fayettevilletx.com.

Texas Reds Steak and Grape Festival. Steak Cook-off teams and wineries square off in Bryan and compete in Texas red categories for this two-day event. It's live music day and night, with an entertaining Kidzone and many vendors. Information: (979) 209-5518.

Whispers in the Wind. Heritage Village in Woodville produces this historical program the third and fourth weekends in June. Locals perform the roles in a story about east Texas pioneers. Information: (409) 283-2272; www.heritage-village.org.

july

Fourth of July. Pick your direction for this weekend. There's not a self-respecting small town that doesn't muster some kind of Independence Day celebration, and many of them are charming old-fashioned affairs well worth the drive. Make overnight reservations so you can take in all the festivities. Our faves: the Fourth of July Parade in Chappell Hill (800-225-3695; www.chappellhilltx.com), with its Marching Kazoo Band and classic cars; and Texas' Oldest Independence Celebration, which is hosted by Columbus (979-732-8385; www.columbustexas.org).

Great Texas Mosquito Festival. Brazosport celebrates the area's bumper crop of buzzers on the last weekend of the month in Clute Municipal Park. Expect a Miss Mosquito Legs look-alike contest, a mosquito-calling contest, the Ms. Quito pageant, a "skeeter beater" baby crawling contest, musical entertainment, food, games, a barbecue cook-off, and bike and skate tours. Information: (800) 371-2971; www.mosquitofestival.com.

Hempstead Watermelon Festival. Here's your chance to test your seed-spitting skills for prizes. Other events include a parade, a street dance, and musical entertainment on the third Saturday of the month. Information: (979) 826-8217.

Legends of Western Swing. Some of the region's best swing bands gather in Navasota for this end of the month event, which began more than 25 years ago. Information: (936) 825-7338.

Lunar Rendezvous. The Clear Lake area celebrates its link to space exploration all month with art shows, festivals, tournaments, a boat parade, and more. Proceeds benefit the Bay Area Museum. Information: (281) 488-7676; www.lunarrendezvous.org.

august

Fireman's Fiesta. The Fireman's Training Center in Brenham comes alive in early August with dancing, water polo, pumper races, cook-offs, and horseshoe- and watcher-pitching competitions. Information: (979) 836-3695; www.brenhamtexas.com.

Hot Summer Nites Show & Beaumont Cruise. This mid-August event sees hundreds of classic cars, trucks, and motorcycles cruising the streets of Beaumont. Information: (409) 769-0877; www.11thstreetcruise.com.

Navasota Blues Festival. Top-flight Texas Blues performers gather at the Grimes County Fairgrounds the second weekend of the month for this two-day event. The program includes a Friday-night dance, activities for children, and more. Information: (936) 825-3222; www.navasotabluesfest.org.

Schulenburg Festival. This one-day annual event at Wolters Park has moved to early August, but it is still all about fun and family. Things to see and do include a Festival Parade, a Lions Club Carnival, and two Biergarten dances. Shoppers can browse arts, crafts, antiques, and collectibles. As always it has food booths galore. Information: (888) 515-1195; www .schulenburgfestival.org.

Shakespeare at Winedale. The historic old barn at this open-air historical museum rings with the immortal words of the Bard Thursday–Sunday evenings through midmonth, with weekend matinees. Information: (979) 278-3530; www.shakespeare-winedale.org.

Somerfest. This mid-August event on Lake Somerville features a Jet Ski tournament, a boat parade, a cake auction, and children's festivities. Information: (979) 272-1255.

september

Cat Springs Antiques Festival. This major event on an early September weekend draws primitive and country antiques dealers from around the country to this community's historic agricultural society hall. Information: (979) 865-5618.

Citywide Garage Sale. All of Needville turns out for this citywide event that is held the third weekend in September. Go to snap up some bargains or just chat up the locals. Information: (979) 793-7778.

Dick Dowling Days. Sabine Pass turns out on the first weekend of September at Sabine Pass Battleground State Historical Park. Special events honor Dowling, an Irish hero of the Confederacy. Information: (800) 235-7822.

Fiestas Patrias. This midmonth celebration of Mexico's independence from Spain is celebrated in Richmond with much fanfare and fun. Among the festivities: jalapeño- and watermelon-eating contests, mariachi performances, and a car show. Festivities are held on the grounds of the Fort Bend Museum. Information: (281) 342-6478; www.fortbendmuseum .org.

Longhorn Rod Run Days. Vintage cars line the streets of Old Town Spring and music fills the air on the last weekend of September. Information: (281) 353-9310; www.oldtownspring tx.com.

Rice Festival. The small town of Winnie (west of Beaumont on Interstate 10) pays tribute to its prime crop with a carnival, parades, art and antiques shows, rice-cooking contests, street dances, a horse show, a fiddling contest, and live entertainment. Information: (409) 296-4404; www.texasricefestival.org.

Stagecoach Days. On the second weekend of September, Fanthorpe Inn State Historical Park hosts cowboy music and stories, stagecoach rides, and stories of the historic inn. Information: (936) 873-2633; www.tpwd.state.tx.us.

Texas Gatorfest. The next chomp you hear is the sound of alligator season opening. The "Alligator Capital of Texas" celebrates this mid-September event with carnival rides, live entertainment on two stages, a 5K run, airboat rides, a street dance, and plenty of alligator on the grill. Information: (409) 267-4190; www.texasgatorfest.com.

Texas Pecan Festival. The last full weekend of September is just nuts in small Groves. This celebration of east Texas's favorite nut includes a pie-eating contest, a pecan toss, a car show, a carnival, golf tournament, and cooking demonstrations. It all culminates with the crowning of a pretty Pecan Queen. Information: (409) 962-3631; www.grovescofc.com.

Warrenton Antique Show. Antiques dealers and sellers of collectibles fill every free field, yard, and building in Warrenton (and for miles along Highway 237 surrounding town). Information: (979) 249-3141.

Washington County Fair. More than one hundred years old, this mid-September fair is held at the Washington County Fairgrounds in Brenham. Events include a rodeo, a carnival, livestock exhibits and auctions, and musical entertainment. Information: (979) 836-4112; www.washingtoncofair.com.

Wendish Fest in Serbin. The Texas Wendish Heritage Society celebrates the roots of this tiny community north of La Grange in late September. Events include costumed folk dancing, Wendish crafts (egg decorating, noodle making, sausage stuffing, quilting, and butter making), and a typical Wendish meal served on the Serbin picnic grounds. Information: (979) 366-2441.

october

Antique Extravaganza. The first weekend in October, Burton hosts a two-day antiques/ flea market orgy, complete with food and musical entertainment. If you can't find it here, it doesn't exist. Information: (979) 289-2485.

Ballunar Liftoff Festival. The Johnson Space Center in Nassau Bay opens its usually closed campus for this three-day, late-October event that includes more than one hundred hot-air balloons in competition flights, team sky diving, live entertainment, arts and crafts, and aviation exhibits. Information: (281) 488-7676, ext. 207; www.ballunarfestival .com.

Bellville Antiques Festival. Sponsored by the Bellville Historical Society, this traditionally is one of the most extensive shows in the state. Held on the fourth weekend in October in the city park, it features a farmers' market, folk-art show, and a quilting show. Information: (979) 865-9116.

Conroe Cajun Catfish Festival. This three-day, midmonth celebration is filled with music, food, arts and crafts, children's activities, a parade, and dancing in the streets. Information: (800) 324-2604; www.conroecajuncatfishfestival.com.

Czhilispiel Festival. Downtown Flatonia gets lively the last full weekend of October as the town welcomes guests for its heritage festival with the funny name. Activities include a chili cook-off, a car and truck show, and live music by some of the region's top musicians. Information: (361) 865-3920; www.flatoniachamber.com.

Fair on the Square. The first Saturday in October, Huntsville celebrates the harvest with fun and games, an arts and crafts show, and live entertainment on its historic downtown square. This is good family fun. Information: (800) 289-0389; www.chamber.huntsville.tx.us.

Haaktoberfest. The second weekend of October, Haak, the tiny little winery in Santa Fe, hoists a glass of wine to Texas's German heritage. Festivities include musical entertainment (German-flavored, of course) and free wine tastings and vineyard tours. Information: (409) 925-1401; www.haakwine.com.

Harvest Festival & East Texas Folklife Festival. In mid-October Woodville's Heritage Village literally comes to life with artists, musicians, and demonstrations of crafts such as soap making, blacksmithing, and basket weaving. Information: (800) 323-0389; www.heritage-village.org.

Houston International In-The-Water Boat Show. Ever dreamed of owning a yacht? Head to the Watergate Marina at Clear Lake Shores for this late September or early-October show to view sailboats, powerboats, and, yes, dream boats, as well nautical products and services. Information: (713) 526-6361.

Mushroom Festival. This high-falutin' but fun event held in Madisonville in mid-October boasts cooking demonstrations with the region's top chefs, wine tastings, a quilt show, arts and crafts exhibits, and a gala dinner. Information: (936) 349-0163; www.texasmushroomfestival.com.

Oktoberfest Round Top Antiques Fair. The first weekend in October draws antiques lovers to Round Top, where more than 450 high-end dealers show their wares in four locations. Information: www.roundtopantiquesfair.com.

Rice Harvest Festival. Katy's midmonth version of the harvest fest features live music, a parade, and arts and crafts exhibits. Information: (281) 391-5289; www.katychamber.com.

Richmond Pecan Festival. In mid-October Richmond cracks a few shells for an event that includes a barbecue cook-off, pecan bake-off, children's pecan derby, wagon tours of the city's historic district, and musical entertainment. Information: (281) 232-2155; www.historic richmond.org.

Scarecrow Festival. Chappell Hill's biggest event of the year includes arts and crafts booths, continuous entertainment, historic church and home tours, hayrides, a quilt raffle, and a scarecrow contest. Information: (888) 273-6426; www.chappellhilltx.com.

South Shore Dockside Food & Wine Festival. This midmonth, mouthwatering festival offers wine tastings, culinary demonstrations, a fashion show, and a yacht show. Festivities take place at South Shore Harbour Resort Marina in League City. Information: (281) 334-1000; www.southshorefestival.com.

South Texas State Fair. The Southeast Texas Entertainment Complex outside of Beaumont is the location of the second largest fair in Texas. It has a fifty-ride carnival midway and endless booths of fun and food. Live entertainment goes on throughout the ten-day event. Music includes Bluegrass, Blues, Children's, Christian, Country, Jazz, R&B, and Rock. The regional fair has livestock and poultry shows, arts and crafts, and an auto show. Information: (409) 832-9991.

Texas Maze. Beginning in early October and running through the end of November, Dewberry Farm near Brookshire becomes a farm of fun. There are twenty acres of cornfield mazes, a petting zoo, hayrides, and a pumpkin patch. Information: (281) 934-3276; www.dewberryfarm.com.

Texas Renaissance Festival. Sixteenth-century England is re-created every weekend in October and through mid-November in the woods between Magnolia and Plantersville. Amid parades, jousting, racing, and games of skill, you'll chat with Robin Hood, assorted wenches, minstrels, comics, jugglers, knights and their elegant ladies, and other anachronistic characters. Dress the theme and join the fun. Information: (800) 458-3435; www.texrenfest.com.

Victorian Street Fair. At the fair, Calvert visitors experience old-time street vendors and other yesteryear Main Street activities. Take a horse-drawn carriage to visit crafters, artists, and artisans, who enhance this nostalgic event. Wearing Victorian attire may make your day even more fun but it's not required. Fairgoers also may enjoy a Victorian tea in the afternoon and a gala at night. Information: (979) 364-2559.

november

Civil War Weekends at Liendo Plantation. Encampments and reenactors look right at home in this beautiful historic matrix. Held Friday, Saturday, and Sunday prior to Thanksgiving. Information: (979) 826-3126; www.liendo.org.

Fall Festival and Texas Heritage Days at Armand Bayou. All the old-time skills are demonstrated, including cane pressing and hay baling. Add a pie-eating contest, animal demonstrations, and horseshoes for family fun. Information: (281) 474-2551; www.abnc.org.

Fall Festival of Roses. Independence's Antique Rose Emporium hosts seminars, exhibits, demonstrations, and shopping the first weekend of the month. Information: (800) 441-0002; www.weareroses.com.

Fly Day at Lone Star Flight Museum. The state's largest collection of old warbirds, including B-25 bombers, takes to the skies. Displays, exhibits, and speakers explain it all at this Galveston complex. Information: (409) 740-7722; www.lsfm.org.

Home for the Holidays. Old Town Spring celebrates the holiday season each weekend until Christmas with special events, evening programs, and stunning decorations and lights. Information: (281) 353-9310; www.oldtownspringtx.com.

Poinsettia Celebration. Ellison's Greenhouses in Brenham brim with 80,000 blooming plants for the special benefit weekend just before Thanksgiving. Among the festivities are plant-care demonstrations, tips for holiday decorating, and entertainment. Information: (979) 836-0084; www.ellisonsgreenhouses.com.

Round Top Arts Festival. This juried art show on the first weekend of November spotlights paintings, sculpture, carvings, and ceramics. Information: (979) 249-3308.

Twilight Firelight at Fanthorp Inn. Celebrate the season with a journey back to the 1850s when Anderson's historic inn opens its doors for this event on the Saturday of Thanksgiving weekend. Visitors can board a replica stagecoach for a ride down Anderson's Main Street. At the inn, visitors are entertained by costumed actors with stories, poetry, music, wassail, and good cheer. On the grounds of the Fanthorp Inn State Historical Park. Information: (936) 873-2633; www.tpwd.state.tx.us.

december

Bellville's Small Town Christmas & Holiday Home Tour. This seasonal event also includes carolers and a show at the square on the first Friday of the month. Information: (979) 865-3407; www.bellville.com.

Bethlehem on the Boardwalk Las Posada. The Las Posada practiced by the Hispanic culture presents an ancient celebration of the hardships Mary and Joseph encountered searching for a place to stay in Bethlehem. The event takes place on the first or second Saturday in downtown Port Arthur at the city recreational boardwalk behind city hall. The event includes Christmas tree lighting and a lighted Christmas Parade. Information: (800) 235-7822.

Brookshire Christmas Festival. Santa, caroling, dancing, and a carnival welcome the season on the first full weekend in December. Information: (281) 375-8100; www.westi10 chamber.org.

Campfire Christmas. The George Ranch in Richmond lights up with campfires, a holiday feast, wagon rides, and more. Information: (281) 343-0218; www.georgeranch.org.

A Candlelight Christmas. Varner-Hogg State Park in West Columbia celebrates the holidays with interpretive tours of this Victorian and seasonally decorated plantation home. Information: (979) 345-4656; www.tpwd.state.tx.us.

Candlelight Christmas Tour: An 1845 Celebration. Two of Beaumont's historic jewels, the McFaddin-Ward House and the John Jay French Museum, glow with holiday decorations on the first Sunday of the month. You may get to help costumed French characters decorate an old-time tree. Information: (409) 880-3749; www.beaumontcvb.com.

Christmas at the Depot. Burton sponsors a holiday celebration at its restored train station. Information: (979) 289-2863.

Christmas Bird Count. Birders from all over Texas gather here between Christmas and New Year's for this annual event. Binoculars are essential, but birding experience is not. Each year, the Brazosport region ranks in the top three sites in North America for the number of species sighted. Information: www.audubon.org.

Christmas Boat Lane. Clear Lake, Seabrook, League City, and Kemah join floating forces on December's second weekend to celebrate the season in their own unique way. Clear Lake Park and the Kemah-Seabrook channel are the best public viewing sites. Go early, as this event pulls in such crowds that most people have staked out the prime viewing sites by early afternoon, hours before sunset and the parade's start. Information: (281) 488-7676; www.clearlakearea.com.

Christmas Fantasy of Lights in Sealy. The entire town turns out for a Christmas market and lighted parade on the first Saturday of the month. Information: (979) 885-3222.

Christmas in Calvert. Antiques sales and five or more old homes that are open for tours brighten the first weekend in December. Information: (979) 364-2559.

Christmas in Humble. Historic Main Street comes alive with carolers, choirs, and Santa Claus. Information: (281) 446-2128; www.humbleareachamber.org.

Christmas in Old Montgomery. Tour lovely old homes dressed for the season, as well as enjoy a cookie walk, an arts and crafts show, and a community dinner. Information: (936) 756-6644; www.conroe.org.

Christmas in Round Top. Wagon rides, caroling, shopping, and decorations liven up the town square early in the month. Information: (979) 249-4042.

Christmas on the Boardwalk. Kemah's waterfront glows with a tree-lighting spectacular. Information: (877) 285-3624; www.kemahboardwalk.com.

Christmas on the Colorado. Columbus puts on a three-day celebration in its historic downtown district early in the month. Expect guided walking tours, open houses in vintage homes, a market, *Messiah* in the old opera house, and cowboys serenading the crowds. Information: (877) 444-7339; www.columbustexas.org.

Christmas Open House at Winedale. All the old German Christmas traditions seem right at home for this one-day event early in the month. Information: (979) 278-3530; www .shakespeare-winedale.org.

Christmas Traditions in Orange. This town's magnificent W. H. Stark House wears its seasonal decorations. Information: (409) 883-0871; www.whstarkhouse.org.

Christmas trees. There are dozens of commercial Christmas-tree farms within the area covered by this book. Check out the Web site of the Texas Christmas Tree Growers Association at www.texaschristmastrees.com.

Clute's Christmas in the Park. Decorated trees, food, and crafts of the seasons, for four days early in the month. Information: (979) 265-8392.

Country Christmas in Chappell Hill. On the second Saturday, Santa arrives via fire engine, choirs sing and ring handbells, and children with teddy bears dressed for the occasion parade down Main Street. It's also open house at several historic homes. Information: (979) 836-3695; www.brenhamtexas.com.

Country Christmas in Fayetteville. Santa arrives on the square the first Saturday of the month, along with entertainers, crafters, wassail, home tours, and gingerbread. Free wagon rides pass by decorated homes. Information: (888) 575-4553; www.fayettevilletx.com.

Country Christmas on the Square. Coldspring gets into the holiday spirit on the second Saturday of December. Expect varied entertainments, a country market, a lighted Christmas parade, choirs, a fun run, and scads of food. Information: (936) 653-2184; www.coldspring texas.org.

Dickens-on-the-Strand. Galveston's famous Strand becomes a 4-block stage for Victorian Christmas past. Dress up in your best period duds and join the fun. There will be a mix of characters from Dickens: town criers, British bobbies, carolers, bell-ringing choirs, horse-drawn coaches, and more. Information: (409) 765-7834; www.galvestonhistory.org.

Holiday on the Brazos. Bryan–College Station welcomes December with a parade on the first Sunday, followed by light displays, church plays, and special arts and crafts events throughout the month. Information: (800) 777-8292; www.bryan-collegestation.org.

Light Up the First Capitol. West Columbia celebrates on December's first weekend with a night parade, caroling, story time with Mrs. Claus, and a holiday home tour. Information: (979) 345-3921; www.westcolumbia.org.

A Nineteenth-Century Christmas. Washington-on-the-Brazos State Historical Park demonstrates how the citizens of the Republic of Texas celebrated the holiday more than 150 years ago. Children get to make ornaments and rag dolls, and candlelight living-history tours light up Independence Hall and the Anson Jones Home. Information: (979) 936-2214; www.tpwd.state.tx.us.

Trail Lights in Huntsville. This town's historic central square glows with holiday lights throughout the month. Information: (936) 291-9726; www.huntsvilletexas.com.

Woodville's Christmas Extravaganza. A twilight tour of Heritage Villa, along with a crafts fair and bluegrass fiddling, highlight this event on the first Saturday of the month. Information: (800) 323-0389; www.heritage-village.org.

help us keep this guide up to date

Every effort has been made by the author and editor to make this guide as accurate and useful as possible. However, many things can occur after a guide is published—establishments close, phone numbers change, hiking trails are rerouted, facilities come under new management, and so on.

We would love to hear from you concerning your experiences with this guide and how you feel it could be improved and kept up to date. While we may not be able to respond to all comments and suggestions, we'll take them to heart, and we'll also make certain to share them with the author and the editor. Please send your comments and suggestions to the following address:

The Globe Pequot Press
Reader Response/Editorial Department
P.O. Box 480
Guilford, CT 06437

Or you may e-mail us at: editorial@GlobePequot.com

Thanks for your input, and happy travels!